The Government of
GREAT BRITAIN

The Government of GREAT BRITAIN

Graeme C. Moodie

UNIVERSITY OF GLASGOW

CROWELL COMPARATIVE GOVERNMENT SERIES

Thomas Y. Crowell Company

NEW YORK   ESTABLISHED 1834

Library of Congress Catalog Card Number: 61–15527

Series design by Joan Wall

Manufactured in the United States of America
by The Colonial Press Inc.

EDITOR'S FOREWORD

In our time the study of comparative government constitutes one of many fields or specialities in political science. But it is worth recalling that the most distinguished political scientists of the ancient world would have had difficulty recognizing the present-day distinction between the study of comparative government and study in other subject areas of the discipline. Think of Plato, for example, whose works abound in references to the political systems of his own and earlier days. Or consider Aristotle, whose *Politics* and related writings were based on an examination of more than one hundred constitutions. Twenty centuries after Aristotle the comparative emphasis continued strong in the work of Montesquieu and Rousseau, among others. In the nineteenth century the comparative tradition entered upon a period of decline, but there are signs that the merits of comparative political analysis are once more gaining recognition. At many colleges and universities, the introductory course in political science is no longer focused exclusively on American government. The comparative approach—in politics, in law, in administration—is becoming increasingly important in the political science curriculum.

This booklet, one of a series, is designed to reflect that approach, without, however, marking a sharp departure from the substance and method of most comparative government courses. With one exception (Arnold J. Heidenheimer, *The Government of Germany: West and East*), each booklet deals with one national government, but the booklets are distinctively comparative in at least two senses. Most of them include material descriptive of other political systems, especially that of the United States. In addition, the booklets follow a common outline, so far as possible, and are designed to promote comparative treatment. Of course, there is nothing to keep the instructor or student from treating a particular governmental system in isolation, if he chooses to do so. On the other hand, his approach to political institutions and functions can be as comparative as he wishes.

A further advantage of this series is that each booklet has been written by a distinguished scholar and authority in the field; each author is personally and professionally familiar with the political system he treats. Finally, the separate booklets make it possible for the instructor to design his course in accordance with his own interest or the interests of his students. One booklet may be substituted for another or any booklet put aside for one semester without affecting the others. The booklets, in short, unlike most one-volume textbooks, give the instructor maximum freedom in organizing his course. This freedom will be virtually unlimited as the forthcoming titles in this series complete a survey of representative governments of the world.

But to return to Aristotle once again, it remains true that the best judges of the feast are not the cooks but the guests. I have tried to indicate why, in my view, the recipe for the series is a good one. Let all those who teach comparative government, and all those who take courses in that field, proceed to judge the booklets for themselves.

ARNOLD A. ROGOW

INTRODUCTION

This book is not another conducted tour around the intricacies of British constitutional law nor another tourist's guide to the picturesque political legacies of a glorious past. It is, however, another introduction to British government and politics. Some explanation should therefore be offered of why it has been written and of the ways in which I hope it does more (or less) than merely duplicate the work of others.

It is, to begin with, written to form part of a series of booklets on different countries so organized as to lend themselves particularly to comparative study. But it is also meant to be a self-contained introduction to government and politics in Britain.

As such its guiding principle has been to try to put forward —so far as is possible in a restricted space—the information necessary to understand what British politics is about as well as how the system works. For this reason more attention has been given to the economic and social context than is customary in textbooks on the British constitution. This is not, therefore, merely an account of formal institutions and constitutional rules, but a book about the organization and functioning of government in British society.

Of necessity it includes an account of the structure of government, but it is an account which attempts to depict something of the dynamics of its construction as well as its form. In particular considerable attention is paid to the role of ordinary Members of Parliament, the nature of party discipline, and the actual operation of the rules about ministerial responsibility. In some respects, the treatment given to these topics also departs from the traditional story.

I hope that this book will be found useful in introductory courses of different kinds. It is, obviously, a configurative study, yet one intended to play a part in comparative government. Its framework is largely institutional, but I have tried not to neglect approaches centered on decision-taking or on theories of group interaction. It is, however, very definitely an *introduction* to its subject and is therefore not directly usable in purely functional comparative analyses (although I hope nothing here will have to be unlearned by anyone who might wish to proceed to this level of sophistication). For the same reason I have tried to give the maximum amount of information compatible with readability and, the final chapter excepted, to limit evaluation and the more speculative kind of interpretation to the minimum compatible with an understanding of the system.

A brief account must inevitably amount to a personal interpretation which reflects the opinions, the interests, and the prejudices of its author. The reader should therefore be given some advance indication of my preconceptions. Broadly speaking, they are radical and libertarian. I was a Labour candidate at the 1959 general election in what is still a fairly safe Conservative constituency.

For their help in eliminating at least some of the errors and obscurities of the original draft, I wish to thank Professor D. D. Raphael of Glasgow University and Dr. Geoffrey Marshall, Fellow of the Queen's College, Oxford, who read the entire manuscript, and Dr. Alfred Brown, Mr. Farquhar Gillanders, and Dr. Gustav Jahoda, all of Glasgow University, who read parts of it. For those shortcomings that remain, as well as for the general interpretation and approach, I must accept full responsibility. I wish also to thank the authors and publishers who permitted me to quote extensively from their works.

My principal debt of gratitude, however, is to my family, and especially to my wife. But for their affectionate encouragement and forbearance it is doubtful whether I could have found the time or the peace necessary to write this book. To them, therefore, I dedicate it.

G.C.M.

Glasgow, Scotland
June, 1961

CONTENTS

The Government of
GREAT BRITAIN

1 - Background

The continuity of its constitutional tradition is a distinctive feature of British political life.[1] English history over the past thousand years has often been bloody and violent, but it has been singularly lacking in drastic and lasting constitutional upheavals. England has not been successfully invaded and occupied by a foreign power since the Norman Conquest in 1066, nor has its form of government been changed by warlike means since the mid-seventeenth century. Moreover, these events introduced no lasting constitutional breaks and dramatic fresh beginnings comparable to those associated with the French, Russian, or even American revolutions. (The direct ancestry of today's monarchy, ministers, Houses of Parliament, and judicial system can therefore be traced back as far as medieval, if not (as was once taught) Anglo-Saxon, England.) Nevertheless, none of these institutions have become frozen in "Anglo-Saxon," or "stained-glass," attitudes. On the contrary: such continuity is possible only for a system which is consistently adaptable. Admittedly, much of Britain's constitutional law is antique, perhaps even antiquated, but the political and constitutional powers, status, and relationships of the major institutions of government have been and still are subject to continuous development and change.

One result of this process is that the task of describing the British system of government presents certain peculiar difficul-

[1] The tradition itself, however, is primarily English rather than British, as the Irish, Scottish, and Welsh components of the United Kingdom have contributed little, constitutionally speaking, to the present system of government. See Note at the end of the chapter.

ties. There is no one constitutional document, corresponding to the American Constitution, which can provide the student with a reliable outline in the form of a central corpus of constitutional rules. Acts of Parliament, of course, contain important constitutional rules in some areas. Judicial decisions help complete the picture, but to nothing like the extent that Supreme Court decisions do in the United States. Like a three-color reproduction from which one of the colors has been left out by the printer, any picture of British government remains grossly misleading if it does not include the nonlegal rules of the constitution. These binding "usages," as they are normally labeled in the United States, are referred to in Britain as the "conventions" of the constitution. There may be no simple or decisive way in which to determine the precise content of the conventions or how exactly they apply to particular situations. Yet they form a more extensive and fundamental part of the British constitution than, for example, the conventions of the American Constitution. This means that any description of the British political system, particularly a brief one, will inevitably be a personal interpretation in respect both to the choice of rules to be included and to the way in which they are stated.[2]

Another result of the process of change and continuity is that it is impossible to introduce British government without saying something about its history. It is equally impossible to survey the whole of that history here. Instead, it is proposed merely to pick out certain themes and events which seem particularly important for understanding the modern scene.

The death of Queen Elizabeth I in 1603 may arbitrarily be viewed as a watershed in British history. It marked the end of the so-called despotism of the Tudor dynasty, which began with the accession of Henry VII in 1485. The hundred-year rule of the Tudors comprised a high point of monarchical power. Before them, the principal theme of constitutional history is perhaps the development of the power of the central administration as represented by the monarch and his servants. The Tudors were followed immediately by almost a century of constitutional struggle and unrest. Thereafter, it may be said, the story is of the way in which the powers of the crown were brought increasingly under the control of other elements within the constitution.

---

[2] For a more comprehensive treatment of this and other difficulties involved in describing the British constitution, see G. Marshall and G. C. Moodie, *Some Problems of the Constitution* (London: Hutchinson, 1959), especially Chapters 1 and 2.

With Parliament and the courts acting as the spearheads in the struggle, the task was accomplished not so much by limiting or abolishing those powers as by transferring the right to exercise them from the person of the monarch to the collectivity of the cabinet. Today, indeed, "the crown" normally denotes the cabinet and other ministers drawn from the leaders of the political party or parties which possess a majority of seats in the popularly elected chamber of Parliament, the House of Commons. The cabinet itself, it might be added, is an entity almost entirely unknown to the law.

In the reigns of the Tudor monarchs, too, may be seen both the flowering of the medieval system of government and the secure foundations of much of the modern. The actual instruments of Tudor rule existed before them, if used less competently and under different circumstances. The distinguishing feature of their "despotism" lay rather in the energy and efficiency with which they pursued their aims than in any radical constitutional innovation. Yet changing conditions and the nature of their purposes helped create the bases for the successful resistance to and final defeat of greater (and less wise) royal pretensions under the Stuarts in the seventeenth century.

Government was financed basically from the revenues obtained from the extensive properties owned by the crown, from customs duties, and from judicial fines. The Tudors made sure that these sufficed for all normal purposes by good management of their own estates and of the nation's affairs. They ran both private and public affairs through their own servants and advisers, but the household and public servants came increasingly to be distinguished from each other. The latter, moreover, soon became simply the instruments of the Tudors' own executive will. The king's council, the principal center of royal decision-making in all fields of government, became less representative of the powerful landed nobility and instead consisted of men chosen for their ability and loyalty to the throne. In its nucleus, the holders of the great offices of state, may be seen the direct ancestors of modern ministers and cabinet.

Royal rule was maintained largely through the judges appointed by the crown to the central common-law courts and to the regional assize courts. One of their most important duties was to supervise the work of the unpaid justices of the peace, who were then, as they remained into the nineteenth century, the principal figures in local administration. The energetic and efficient use of these institutions made it clear that "government

is the king's business" and that no opposition would be allowed
to flourish, whether from peasants protesting violently against
economic conditions, aristocrats and pretenders plotting to seize
the throne, or from Catholics at home and abroad. The peasants
were in revolt against the impoverishment which resulted from
the private enclosure of common land, the beginnings of capital
accumulation required to finance expanding commerce, and
inflation. The aristocratic plots were largely the aftermath of a
century of conflict between contending magnates, centering on
the rival ambitions of the great houses of York and Lancaster.
This "War of the Roses" [3] had, however, weakened and dis-
credited the noble families concerned, allowing the Tudors
largely to confine their governmental role to membership of the
House of Lords (the Upper House of Parliament). The Tudors
thus finally established the supremacy of the crown over one of
its traditional rivals for power, the great aristocratic landowners.
The landed magnates continued, of course, to exert preponderant
influence upon government for another two centuries and more,
but no longer as king-makers, and they had increasingly to
share their influence with others.

The other great power of medieval times was the Church.
The Tudor breach with the Papacy, leading to the confiscation
of church property and the establishment, in place of the old
Catholic Church, of the reformed Church of England (of which
the monarch is still the temporal head), led to a continuous
threat of Catholic conspiracy and invasion. But it marked the
supremacy of the crown in ecclesiastical as well as lay matters.
These measures, the actions necessary to suppress the consequent
unrest, and the wide discretion exercised by the king's council
earned the Tudors the name of "despots."

Tudor power, great though it was or became, was yet bridled.
It was comparable neither with that of modern despotisms nor
even, at least in its aims and procedures, with that of other contemporary European monarchs. It is significant, for example, that
the same period saw the development of greater security of tenure
for the royal judges and the growing prestige and independence
of the legal profession as a whole, both of which were vitally
important in the later struggles against royal power. Nor was the
crown, even by itself, considered to be above and beyond the
law. The law was supreme. And within the legal system, supremacy lay with statute law, which was made by the king in Parlia-

[3] So called because of the white and red roses which were the emblems of
the two sides.

ment. Although the supremacy of statute law antedates the Tudors, the power of Parliament continued to grow during their "despotism."

Technically Parliament means the coming together of crown, lords (both lay and ecclesiastical), and Commons; any resulting legislation is enacted, in the words of the established formula, "by the King's most Excellent Majesty, by and with the advice and consent of the Lords Spiritual and Temporal, and Commons, in this present Parliament assembled, and by the authority of the same." More popularly, however, Parliament is taken to mean only the two Houses of Parliament. It is thus that the word is used when one talks of the increasing influence of Parliament under the Tudors. In particular, such references call attention to the increasing importance of the Commons, that is, of the local communities (commonalities), which were represented in Parliament by two knights elected from each shire and two burgesses elected from each borough. It must also be remembered that the landed magnates were forced increasingly to exercise their power through the Upper House rather than directly through the crown.

Parliaments were summoned and dismissed by the monarch only when he felt it desirable or necessary. Most commonly and most fundamentally it was the royal need for more money which prompted a summons. (Since the fourteenth century new financial burdens had come to be imposed upon the people only with the assent of their representatives in Parliament.) The attempts of the Commons to secure royal "redress of grievances" as a condition of its assent to new taxation constituted its earliest assertions of political influence. Given prudent management of the crown's independent sources of revenue, it was nevertheless only in times of war or other emergency that recourse to Parliament was necessary in order to obtain supply (i.e., agreement to supply the financial needs of the crown). By the time of the later Tudors, however, the Commons was acquiring another basis of influence, as the crown sought its support in struggles against rival social forces. Increasingly its members, or the communities which they represented, became a vital element in the national struggle for political power.

The Tudors recognized the potential strength available to them in the support of the landed gentry and urban merchants who, for religious and economic reasons, had become more politically conscious. These local community leaders were more and more drawn into central and local administration (in the council and as justices of the peace); and the Tudors were careful to obtain their assent, granted through their representatives in Parliament, to the statutes which authorized such major changes as those involved in the expropriation and reform of the Church. Indeed, the whole Tudor system may be said to have become increasingly dependent upon these ever more prosperous and influential sections of the nation. For although the crown continued to monopolize the initiative in government and to exercise extensive discretion and power, it could do so only in ways broadly acceptable to the Commons. The so-called Tudor despotism was in fact a balance of power, not a one-way system of command. It is memorable that the Tudors were among the most popular of British monarchs with the majority of their subjects, as they still are today in historical legend. In Britain the most popular monarchs and governments are almost always those which represent a comparable blend of strong and decisive leadership with concern for popular wishes; among these wishes, frequently, is one simply for a government which governs.[4]

This balance did not survive the Tudors. It was upset by a combination of factors, among them the increasing prosperity of the new landed and commercial interests, the religious attitudes of the Stuart monarchs and their claim to rule by divine right, and the personalities of the leading figures of the age. The result was the most turbulent period in British constitutional history. We are not here concerned with the details of the seventeenth-century disputes, in which one king was beheaded and another abdicated; in which there were experiments in royal rule without Parliament and parliamentary rule without a monarch; in which, for a time, England was subject first to civil war and then to military dictatorship. These controversies, however, slowly (after 1660) gave birth to a new constitutional settlement, the nature of which must be described.

The principal constitutional, as opposed to purely religious, developments were marked and consolidated by the Convention Parliament's invitation to William of Orange to succeed to the throne in 1689, the enactment of the Bill of Rights in the same year, and the Act of Settlement of 1701. With the addition of the Act of Union, 1707, whereby the union of the crowns of England and Scotland (1603) became a full political union with the creation of the new legal entity of Great Britain, the legal basis of the modern constitution is virtually complete. The Revolution Settlement, as it is usually called, is remarkable for its modera-

---

[4] Although never to the exclusion of other considerations.

tion and its concern with immediate practical problems rather than with declarations of resounding principle or doctrine. The English Bill of Rights, for example, is comparable, not to the first ten amendments to the American Constitution, but to the second and lesser known part of the Declaration of Independence, in which ringing statements about "inalienable rights" give way to a list of very concrete and specific grievances against the British crown. Like it, the English Bill of Rights talks in terms of the restoration of ancient rights rather than of legal innovations. In effect, it simply gave legal expression to one interpretation of past practice by prohibiting the crown's use of certain means whereby the Stuarts had attempted to evade the influence of Parliament and the courts. The crown was thus forbidden to maintain a standing army, to suspend the laws, or to levy money by prerogative rather than parliamentary grant (to name what are probably the most important provisions). In conjunction with the invitation to William III and the Act of Settlement, however, the Bill of Rights established the principle that monarchs rule in virtue of Acts of Parliament, and ensured that, in the last resort, they must bow to the will of Parliament. The Act of Settlement also provided that monarchs may not be or marry members of the Roman Catholic Church, that judges should not be subject to dismissal at the royal pleasure, and that holders of offices of profit under the crown may not sit in the House of Commons (a provision which was honored mainly in the breach, and which was modified by the Regency Act of 1705). In all other important respects the legal position of the crown remained and remains unchanged. The importance of the settlement lay more in what it made possible than in its immediate effects upon the working of the constitution.

Like the new American Constitution which it was to influence, the eighteenth-century system of government in Britain was characterized by a partial separation of powers modified by mutual checks and balances. The independence of the judiciary was by then firmly established. Parliament had successfully asserted its right to a share in governmental authority, and was not to be challenged again as the principal forum for public political criticism and debate or as the center of legislative activity. Within Parliament, the special authority of the House of Commons in the field of public finance was generally recognized. In other respects the two Houses were substantially equal: the same broad interests were represented in both, they were linked by personal ties of kinship and patronage, and not until these bonds were weakened in the early nineteenth century could the general issue of superiority be raised and decided.

Executive responsibility, moreover, still rested with the monarch, as did the power to withhold assent to bills passed by Parliament. In the discharge of his duties the king was, of course, dependent upon his advisers, his ministers, whom he appointed and dismissed. Just as American Presidents have varied in their relationships with their "cabinet," so did the kings take a greater or lesser degree of interest in the work of their ministers, depending both on the personality of the monarch and the ministerial talent available. That George III wielded a more constant and extensive power over policy than his two predecessors reflected differences in these respects rather than in constitutional doctrine. Monarchs had certainly to take account of political circumstances in their choice of advisers, as must all heads of government. In particular, because of the need for parliamentary co-operation in finance and legislation, they had to consider their ministers' ability to obtain that co-operation, which meant, increasingly, the ability of ministers to manage the House of Commons.

If the policies of a monarch and his ministers were broadly acceptable to the country, there were several ways in which they could assure themselves of the necessary parliamentary support. Firstly, but of limited efficacy, there was the appeal to party. The Tory and Whig parties, which had emerged from the constitutional and political struggles of the seventeenth century, still survived in a comparatively weak and loose form, probably divided by tradition and personality as much as by differences of policy and principle. From about 1714 onward, however, many, perhaps most, Members of Parliament owed uncertain allegiance to either party or none at all. At the turn of the century the party system (if such it can be called) was weak enough to encourage the formation of ministries drawn from both parties, but strong enough to prevent the experiment from being successful. Thus, although most governments were thereafter formed of men from only one party (insofar as they were party men at all), party loyalty was not sufficient to ensure the support of a parliamentary majority.

Recourse had therefore to be made, secondly, to crown patronage, normally administered by the First Lord of the Treasury. (When he was in the House of Lords, much of the patronage power had to be administered by the chief minister in the Commons.) Pensions, honors, and appointments to sinecure or working positions, granted either to Members of Parliament or to their friends, relatives, and dependents, played much the same part in British politics then as in American politics a century later, and for similar reasons. On the other hand, monarchs had more freedom politically than most American presidents, at the same time that they distributed their benefits over a narrower social stratum. However, among the recipients of offices who continued to sit in the House of Commons were men who, to all intents, must be regarded as civil servants rather than politicians, and who accordingly supported the king's governments because they felt this to be their duty rather than because they were bribed into agreement.

Thirdly, the king and his ministers had to obtain the support of various "independents" who were neither party nor place men, however much some might have relied upon local interests or the backing of private patrons. Their acceptance of any ministry tended to depend on the economy and efficiency of administration and, given these, they could normally be counted upon not to oppose the crown, with which governmental leadership undoubtedly still lay.

Should these methods fail to achieve the necessary co-operation, one final remedy lay in the hands of the monarch: the dissolution of the House of Commons in order to secure a fresh majority. The necessary votes were obtained by appealing directly to the country for the support required to maintan the king's government and by the exercise of crown "influence" (the contemporary euphemism for Treasury funds and patronage) in the constituencies amenable to it.

In all respects but the last (whose importance is easily exaggerated), and excepting the presence in Parliament of officeholders under the crown, the broad picture bears obvious and significant resemblances to the American Constitution. Had ministers been kept out of Parliament or had the United States persevered with the early experiment of having members of the President's "cabinet" appear before Congress, and had the monarch become elective or the President continued to be elected indirectly in fact as well as in law, the similarities between the two systems of government might still be as striking as their differences. (The federal nature of the American union, to mention but one additional factor, would have ensured that differences remained great, although possibly relating more to the atmosphere than to the formal structure of central government.)

In fact, however, the two constitutions have moved further apart. Not least among the reasons for this has been the influence of the hereditary nature of the monarchy and of the parliamentary membership of its ministers upon the later development of the British system.

What happened, briefly, is this. The failure of George III's American policy, his subsequent periods of insanity, and the various personal shortcomings of his two immediate successors lessened respect for (without yet discrediting) royal leadership. At the same time the rising costs of government, growing concern for administrative competence, and increasing attacks upon the extent of royal "influence" in Parliament (which were not confined entirely to those who had been excluded from its benefits) led to a more extensive and systematic supervision of public finance, a gradual paring of royal patronage (beginning in 1782), and the exclusion of new categories of officeholder from Parliament. Given these developments and the traditional legal immunity of sovereigns, who could not easily be removed or made politically accountable, it was natural that the personal authority of the crown should diminish. It was equally natural that the chief beneficiaries should be the king's ministers, whose position was simultaneously being strengthened by other political changes.

The accelerating industrial revolution, the increasing application of capital and knowledge to agriculture as well as industry, and the attendant social dislocations were diversifying the major interests within the nation. The groups deriving the most immediate economic benefits therefrom found that wealth did not automatically admit them to existing social and political privileges. The main legal barriers consisted of discriminations against Protestant as well as Catholic dissenters from the Established Church, and the traditional distribution of parliamentary constituencies which gave little or no weight to the new centers of industry and population.[5]

The interests of the new capitalists thus impelled them into political activity just as their wealth and economic influence provided them with the means to do so. Their grievances and attitudes were increasingly reflected by the Whigs, who were almost continuously out of office in the late eighteenth and early nineteenth centuries. Thus new life was injected into national politics and a corresponding intensification of the party political

---

[5] The new urban industrial centers had grown up largely outside the boundaries of the ancient boroughs, many of which, by this time, returned members to the House of Commons who represented few voters and, in effect, only the interests of some large landowner or of the most lavish spender. These were termed "rotten boroughs."

struggle. Inevitably, too, the growth of rationalism and radical social criticism, though never so great in Britain as in France, operated in the same direction. One of the principal constitutional effects of this was to forge new links between the various ministers. A common loyalty to their party tended to replace individual loyalties to the king. (It then became the custom to refer to the ministers collectively, or at least to the most important ones, as "the cabinet.") Similar links developed between the cabinet and at least a substantial body of their supporters in Parliament; in the relations of these two groups the older techniques of "management" were henceforth to play a much less conspicuous part.

The upshot of all these changes was, on the one hand, that it became more difficult to secure parliamentary co-operation with the executive by means of royal patronage and influence and, on the other, that it became less necessary to do so as the party came to provide an alternative source of political organization and initiative. In terms of the day-to-day working of the constitution, the most obvious change was that the king had less discretion in his choice of ministers because a Parliament organized on increasingly rigid party lines allowed him less room to maneuver. From this, in turn, resulted a diminution in royal influence over any particular set of ministers. If there is, or appears to be, but one group of ministers which can secure the support of Parliament, it is clearly in a strong position vis-à-vis any monarch who might be disposed to reject its advice.

Another part of the process was the development of a ministerial leader. The unofficial title and position of first, or prime, minister had been given to Robert Walpole in the first half of the eighteenth century. He had acquired them as a result of his own pre-eminence and the relative indifference to government of the first two Georges. By the end of the century both title and position became customary as a result of the changed relationships of monarch and party. It then required only an enlarged electorate, acknowledgment of the sovereign authority of the people represented in and by the House of Commons, and the development of the nationally organized two-party system for the monarch to become almost entirely nonpolitical through the transfer of his ruling power to the prime minister and cabinet. (Were the party system in the United States to permit Congress to assert and exercise continuing leadership as the embodiment of a majority electoral decision, then by the purposeful use of its powers of investigation, ratification, legislation, and finance, it could effect a similar transfer of executive power to a cabinet responsible to it and a similar political neutralizing of the President. Given such a change in the party system, the probability of which is not here being endorsed, the very few constitutional amendments which *might* be necessary would probably be secured with little difficulty.)

The developments of which we have been speaking were consummated during the nineteenth century, above all by the series of statutes which progressively extended the franchise to the majority of the adult population.[6] The first of them, the Reform Act of 1832, is now acknowledged to be one of the major landmarks of British history. Its most important provisions were to abolish most of the "rotten" boroughs, reduce the representation given to many areas whose size and significance no longer justified their traditional number of seats, and to redistribute the seats concerned to some of the new and populous areas, particularly London and the northern industrial cities. In addition, it modified the property qualification for voting. Probably the two most significant results were to enfranchise the middle classes in the boroughs and, in the counties, to give the vote to the rural tenant-at-will who paid a certain minimum rent, a group whose complete insecurity of tenure made them peculiarly susceptible to pressure from their landlords.[7] In all, the electorate was increased by about two hundred thousand, to a total of about six hundred thousand.

The significance of the Reform Act did not repose solely in its provisions, important though it was to have reduced the massive predominance of the landed interests. Its title, "an Act to amend the representation of the people," admitted a departure in principle from the old exclusive preoccupation with interests and communities, and thus anticipated the later and more radical adoption of number as the chief criterion for representation. The bill's passage resulted from and stimulated a further consolidation of the party system in the House of Commons, just as it recognized that House's superiority over the House of Lords. (The Lords' opposition to the Act had been overcome only when the king was persuaded to threaten the

---

[6] The process was not completed until much later. Women voted for the first time in 1918, but only if they were thirty years old or more. Not until the 1929 election could adult women vote on the same basis as men, and not until the election of 1950 was the system of "one man (or woman), one vote" and only one vote, fully adopted.

[7] The secret ballot was not introduced until 1872.

creation of sufficient new peers to provide a majority for the government.) Above all, perhaps, it and the circumstances in which it was passed intensified those forces which were limiting the monarch's discretion by strengthening the House of Commons and the ministers in which it placed its confidence. Conversely, after 1832 it was made clear that it was upon the confidence of the Commons and not of the monarch that the cabinet depended for its authority and its existence.

If the first and vital breach was made in 1832, the most extensive reforms were the product of later legislation. By the Reform Act of 1867 minor changes in the counties enlarged the rural electorate from over five hundred thousand to nearly eight hundred thousand, while the substantial enfranchisement of the workers in the boroughs resulted in an electorate there of nearly one and a quarter million—though the failure adequately to redistribute seats still gave a preponderant voice in Parliament to the representatives of the counties and small towns. Not until 1885 was this defect largely eliminated. The Redistribution of Seats Act of that year, combined with the extension of the vote to the rural worker in 1884, also served finally to reduce the share in government of the aristocratic landed interests to its proper size. These interests were also the chief sufferers from the introduction of secret voting in 1872, and from the succession of Acts which fixed upper limits to electoral expenditure in the constituencies and which declared many of the traditional ways of winning votes and influencing people to be corrupt.

With the Reform Acts, whose work was finally systematized and completed by the Representation of the People Acts of 1918, 1928, and 1948, it may be said that the modern constitution was born. It was through them that first the controllers and then the operators of Britain's modern industrial society were permitted a voice in the formal system of government. It was to organize this new mass electorate that, from 1867 onward, the political parties developed their extra-parliamentary structure. The impact of these new groups, demanding and then acquiring the right to vote and social emancipation, led to the transformation of the old Tory and Whig parties into the Conservative and Liberal ones, based more on principle than on mere personality and "influence," [8] and, in this century, to the rise of the Labour party. It was in answer to the demands of the new voters that the government was forced to intervene in ever wider areas of

---

[8] The names first appeared around 1830, but the transformation mentioned here was gradual and remained partial until the 1860's.

the national life—initially, perhaps, to remove "hindrances to the enjoyment of the good life" [9] represented by antiquated regulations and prohibitions (e.g., religious discriminations), and subsequently in more positive fashion. Finally, it was largely because of the strains imposed by these new activities that the apparatus of administration, both central and local, was reformed and the last vestiges of patronage removed from the permanent public service.

The British constitution is thus a continuously changing blend of the ancient and modern. One of its strengths has been that for the most part it has permitted governments to wield the power necessary to govern effectively without allowing them to rule for long in an arbitrary and irresponsible fashion, disregarding the wishes at least of the more powerful and articulate sections of the governed. Another source of strength has been that, on the one hand, no rigid constitutional or political orthodoxy has been able to ossify the institutions of government and, on the other hand, partly for this reason, it has not been necessary totally and swiftly to reorganize them at the cost of destroying established habits of thought, behavior, and sentiment. Although the British system of government is rarely free from criticism, and is on occasion the subject of acute controversy, yet its basic form today commands wide support.

Many labels may be attached to the system as it now is. No single one of the most common labels tells the whole story, but between them they provide a reasonably accurate short description, as follows:

1. CONSTITUTIONAL MONARCHY. The queen is still the head of state, and in law is the head of government as well. She plays an important role socially and symbolically, but for the most part the conventions of the constitution prescribe a purely formal part in the conduct of government. Much is still done in the queen's name, and many acts of government still require her participation, but with a few important exceptions she performs these functions only upon the advice (which she must follow) of Her Majesty's Government, which is to say, of the prime minister and his ministerial colleagues, and in accordance with the wishes of Parliament.

[9] The phrase is taken from T. H. Green, the late-nineteenth-century political theorist. See also A. V. Dicey, "The Debt of Collectivism to Benthamism," in his *Law and Opinion in England in the Nineteenth Century,* first published in 1905, Lecture IX.

2. CABINET GOVERNMENT. Broadly speaking, it is the cabinet, as the inheritor of the powers of the crown, which governs, in the sense that it directs the administration and determines national policy in the legislative as in all other fields. But it may be said to govern "by and with the advice and consent" of the Commons and, to a very minor extent, the Lords "in . . . Parliament assembled, and by the authority of the same." In the cabinet one finds the modern embodiment of a fusion of governmental powers which, more than the eighteenth-century separation, has generally characterized British government.

3. RESPONSIBLE GOVERNMENT. Cabinets are composed of the leaders of the party (usually) or parties which form a majority in the House of Commons as a result of the previous general election. Dependent for its existence upon the support of this majority, the cabinet is therefore responsible (accountable) to the electorate through the House of Commons, before whom it must be prepared to defend its actions and its record.

4. PARTY GOVERNMENT. Since 1945 there has existed, to all intents, a two-party system (Conservative and Labour). Both main parties are, compared to American ones, relatively cohesive and homogeneous in terms of policy and principle.[10] The parties organize the House of Commons, provide governments, act as the force which generally assures those governments of parliamentary support, and serve as indispensable links between the government and the governed.

5. PARLIAMENTARY GOVERNMENT. The supremacy of Parliament is frequently cited as one of the fundamental principles of the constitution.[11] It holds true today in the sense that an Act of Parliament is superior to all other forms of law and that there are no legal limits upon the legislative power of Parliament (meaning, in this context, the crown-in-Parliament) in constitutional as well as in "ordinary" matters. In practice perhaps the most important aspect is that no government with the support of Parliament behind it will find itself unable to carry through its policy simply because of *legal* obstacles. British government

[10] Although the Labour party, after 1951 and again since the election of October, 1959, has often appeared to be intent on falsifying this generalization.

[11] It receives its best known modern statement in A. V. Dicey, *Introduction to the Study of the Law of the Constitution* (London: Macmillan; 10th ed., E. C. S. Wade, ed., 1960), the first edition of which appeared in 1885. The principle is reiterated in most modern British texts and will be discussed more fully in Chapter 5 below.

is parliamentary also in the sense that Parliament, and principally the House of Commons, remains the foremost arena for political debate and for criticism of the government.

6. DEMOCRATIC GOVERNMENT. British government is democratic at least in the senses that the House of Commons is elected on a basis of universal adult suffrage, that the ultimate decision between alternative governments and policies lies with the electorate, and that the process of discussion and opinion formation is extensive and substantially free from political interference or censorship.

To analyze all the conditions necessary for the continuing and free working of the system would require a lengthy treatise. It is clear, however, that among them are the following: the evolution of the system along with the social forces which it must express and contain; its success in coping with the emergencies of war and economic crisis, as well as with what one continues to regard as normal conditions; a degree of social and political homogeneity in the country as a whole sufficient to encompass dispute without totally undermining toleration of dissent; and a general political temper that encourages forbearance (or possibly indolence) in the use of, and opposition to, power and privilege of all kinds.

Note: Scotland, Ireland, and Wales

Scotland was an independent kingdom until 1707. In 1603, however, there took place a union of crowns when James VI of Scotland succeeded to the English throne as James I of England. (He was the first of the Stuarts.) By the Act of Union of 1707 the two countries united to form the new country of *Great Britain*. By this Act Scotland retained its own established Presbyterian church and much of its own legal system, but gave up its own parliament and, instead, sent members to the one at Westminster. Today Scotland has its own minister, the Secretary of State for Scotland, who is always a member of the cabinet, assisted by a Minister of State and three Under-Secretaries. He is in charge of four departments located in Edinburgh and exclusively concerned with Scottish affairs. (They are the Home, Education, Health, and Agriculture departments.) This administrative devolution took place partly for reasons of convenience and partly in response to the ever-present national consciousness of the Scots.

The larger part of Ireland is completely independent, although its citizens enjoy full rights of British citizenship, including voting, when resident in the United Kingdom. The smaller part, Northern Ireland (sometimes referred to as Ulster), is subject to the British crown and government. With Britain it forms the *United Kingdom*. It sends representatives to Parliament in London, but also has its own cabinet and parliament in Stormont. Its constitution was designed as part of a federal Irish constitution enacted in 1920, but when that constitution was rejected in Southern Ireland, the Ulster government remained. Its constitutional relations with the United Kingdom government are not federal but devolutionary, since the United Kingdom Parliament possesses the right to pass any legislation it wishes for Northern Ireland, including an Act to abolish the Stormont government. In practice, however, this is unlikely to happen. The local political and party situation is quite unlike that prevailing in Britain, as it is centered upon Ulster's relations with the rest of Ireland, for which reason it is not discussed in this book.

Wales was conquered and constitutionally absorbed by England in the thirteenth century. In 1951 some 29 per cent of the population were Welsh-speaking, all but 1.7 per cent, however, speaking English as well. Despite the appointment of a Minister for Welsh Affairs in 1957, Wales must still be considered as an integral part of the English system of law and administration.

2 - Society and People

In this chapter an attempt is made to give a picture of British society today. The information set out is selected in the belief that it is particularly relevant to an understanding of the *political* life of the country. The portrayal is therefore very limited. It will necessarily both be incomplete and reflect to some extent the author's personal estimate of what is politically most significant.

Geography

That Britain is an island kingdom "anchored" off the coast of the European continent is perhaps the single most important, as it is the best-known, geographical factor. Even in World War II the surrounding waters served as a highly effective defense against invasion, if no longer against bombardment. The continuity of constitutional development which has already been noted clearly owes much to the immunity thus conferred. Significantly, it has also been possible to dispense with a large permanent garrison at home—large standing armies and free government being at best uneasy bedfellows. Probably the sea has helped to insulate Britain against the most disruptive effects of European political and ideological forces as well. Above all, the existence of such a clearly defined territorial boundary, combined with the absence of any corresponding barriers to internal communications, has facilitated the relatively early growth and development of national self-consciousness.

On the other hand, Britain is not so far removed from the European mainland (some twenty miles at the nearest point) as to be entirely isolated from it or able to ignore the possibility of invasion. Britain cannot, therefore, afford to stand aloof from European politics. And, in fact, it is impossible to divorce the study of British from European history. It is equally impossible, however, to study British history with reference only to domestic and European affairs. If the sea to some extent has separated the British from their nearest neighbors, it has played as great a part in their history by joining them to all parts of the world readily accessible to water-borne transport. From the sixteenth century on, therefore, the British have devoted many of their energies to overseas exploration, colonization, and trade. Britain's whole position as an influence in world politics, and indeed its existence as a relatively wealthy industrial community, has depended and still depends upon the maintenance (in some form) of its overseas connections.

The area of the United Kingdom is 93,053 square miles, but its population at the time of the 1951 census was just over fifty million. The density of population is thus among the highest in the world; excluding Northern Ireland, it is 580 people per square mile, and for England alone, it is 843 (in Japan it is 587; in the United States, 43).[1] On the other hand, the country

[1] Translating the British figures into American terms, it is as though (1950 census figures) one-third of the entire American population were to live in

possesses virtually no raw materials other than coal, and even in wartime could produce no more than about half the food it needed. Today domestic agriculture accounts for less than a quarter of the wheat, sugar, butter, and vegetable oil consumed, and for more than three-quarters only of milk, eggs, barley, and oats.

Population

The rate of increase in the population was at its greatest between about 1750 and 1900. The total was still in the region of seven million in 1750, but it quadrupled in the next hundred years, and reached forty million early in the twentieth century. Before then it was kept low by a high death rate, which was reduced rapidly as the industrial revolution and the increase in knowledge proceeded, and since then it has been slowed down by a rapidly falling birth rate, which has shown signs of recovery only during and since World War II.

The estimated population in 1957 was about 51,500,000, with the following age distribution:

Age group	Number (millions)
0–14	11.96
15–29	9.82
30–44	10.79
45–59	10.37
60–69	4.72
70 and over	3.79

At present, therefore, there is a "bulge" at and below school age, but otherwise Britain has an aging population. At the beginning of the century less than one in fifteen had reached retirement age (sixty-five); by 1957 just under one in eight had, and by 1980, it has been estimated, the figure will approach one in six. Estimates of the future total population vary widely according to the assumptions upon which they are made, and there is no sure way of deciding between them. The projected figures for the end of the century, for example, range from about twenty-five million to over twice that amount, the higher figure being the most recent authoritative one.[2] Apart possibly from

the state of Oregon, or if eight times the population of Texas were to live in one-third of its area. Even so, large areas of Britain are still very sparsely populated, particularly in Scotland.

[2] *Report* of the Committee on the Economic and Financial Problems of the Provision for Old Age (London: H. M. S. O. Cmd. 9333 of 1954).

the efforts of both major political parties to demonstrate their interest in the financial position of old-age pensioners (and for this there may well be reasons other than mere vote-catching), the size and age-distribution of the population have not yet had any noticeable impact upon politics. Some political interest has been taken, however, in other aspects of Britain's population.

Religious divisions have played an important part in British history, and to this day continue as a permanent undercurrent. Membership of the principal denominations (in so far as it can be ascertained) is as follows:

Established Church of England (Episcopalian)	2,923,000
Other Episcopalian	250,000
Established Church of Scotland (Presbyterian)	1,300,000
Other Presbyterian	250,000
Methodist	1,000,000
Baptist Unions	320,000
Congregationalist	250,000
Roman Catholic	4,100,000
TOTAL	10,393,000

Such sample surveys as have been carried out suggest that attendance figures are appreciably smaller, and average about 10 per cent of the total population on ordinary Sundays, while something between 25 per cent and 40 per cent of the adult population attend, if at all, only for weddings and funerals. On certain issues the churches appear to have considerable political influence, among them education, marriage and the family, the public behavior of the royal family, and other "moral" questions. Primarily this influence takes the form of indirect pressure politics rather than direct intervention in elections, although few politicians would care knowingly to offend the religious susceptibilities of any denomination with a significant membership in their constituencies.

The Roman Catholic Church, however, has publicly urged its members not to vote for Communists, and is commonly believed to exercise a wider influence upon the votes of its members. Particularly in those urban areas where there is a sizable Catholic population, many active politicians believe the Church to be an important factor even within the political party (or parties) to which, largely for other reasons, its members belong. These beliefs have not been publicly substantiated—nor need they be; the beliefs themselves may suffice to influence political behavior.

In any case, it is certain that in parts of cities like Glasgow and Liverpool it may be a political advantage to possess an Irish name or be a known Catholic, just as in other areas it is, or has been, advantageous to take a prominent part in the affairs of another denomination. But, in general, public religious observance, except possibly in predominantly Catholic areas and parts of Scotland or Wales, no longer seems essential to a political career, nor do the relations between the various religious groups constitute a major political issue.

Ethnically the British population is relatively homogeneous —at least for most political purposes. This does not mean that it is, by any standard, racially or ethnically "pure." The Norman Conquest served only to add one more strain to an already mixed heritage of Celts, Angles, Saxons, Jutes, and the rest. Even to call this mixture "Anglo-Saxon" is to endorse a serious misconception. Since the time of the Normans there have been many additions, particularly from Europe. On the other hand, there have been no minorities sufficiently distinctive, physically or culturally, and sufficiently numerous to give rise to serious social or political problems on more than a local scale. In recent times, too, the net effect of migrations has been a loss of people, particularly to other parts of the Commonwealth and to the United States. In the postwar period the story is the same: from 1946 through 1955 the net loss was over 750,000 people, five-sixths of them to the Commonwealth, and most of the others (about 180,-000 of them) to the United States. The loss of these people, most of them fairly young and skilled, has recently begun to cause worry, but can hardly be called a political issue except possibly in Scotland, where the drain (much of it to England) has been particularly severe.

These are net figures, however, and should not be allowed to conceal the existence of the opposite flow. From 1921 to 1955 almost 100,000 immigrants became naturalized British subjects, over 70,000 after 1941. In addition, in December, 1957, there were 384,214 registered aliens (people sixteen or over who are resident for over three months, not including members of the diplomatic and consular corps). Of these, about 100,000 were Polish; 53,000, Italian; 38,000, German; and 25,000, from the United States. People from Commonwealth countries do not have to register; they automatically have full rights of citizenship. Unlike aliens, they require no special permits for residence or employment. In 1957 there were 51,300 new arrivals from the Commonwealth.

In general there have been no major problems of assimilation, although there have been cases of usually local resistance by certain trade unions to the employment of aliens, the musicians and miners providing the best-known examples. The one, and recent, exception is the reception given to "colored" immigrants.[3] It has been estimated that there are now about 190,-000 colored people in Britain, of whom some 50,000 come from India and Pakistan, and 100,000 from the West Indies. At least nine-tenths of the latter have arrived in the country since 1953, and about 70 per cent of them have settled in London and the cities of the English midlands. Concentrated and overcrowded into a few predominantly cheap housing areas, their presence has given rise to the very occasional riot (most notoriously in the Notting Hill area of London in 1958) and widespread reports of violent and nonviolent discrimination. Most serious of all, the prejudice against them is being stimulated and capitalized by a revived fascist party in one or two areas, just as anti-Semitism was used for its own purposes in the 1930's.[4]

Even there, however, racial politics do not yet provide the central issues of the party struggle, nor are they expected to do so unless the social and economic circumstances of the majority of the population deteriorate rapidly. In the country at large racial prejudice is not a major factor in the political life of the community; nevertheless, a colored man is unlikely to attain the highest posts in government.

Essentially, established opinion is opposed to prejudice, and few people publicly admit that they discriminate. In personal relations, however, there appear to be no well-established norms; actual behavior ranges from complete acceptance to total rejection. Much the same may be said of employment practices.

---

[3] The vocabulary of skin color is most unsatisfactory. "White," a color, is an inaccurate label for people of predominantly European extraction whose color is white only when they are very ill or dead, at other times "pink," "pale," or at best "off-white" are the more correct epithets. However, to talk of "colored" and "white" people is now standard, and since adequate substitutes do not exist, we have to make use of these terms here for the sake of intelligibility.

[4] Especially in the East End of London, where there was a fairly large Jewish population. There are now estimated to be 400,000 Jews in Britain. But see the report on the former fascist leader's unsuccessful candidature in the Notting Hill area in D. E. Butler and R. Rose, *The British General Election of 1959* (London: Macmillan, 1960), pp. 173–85.

There are also indications of a general tendency to regard colored people as belonging to a lower social class—probably because of cultural rather than "racial" differences.[5]

By and large, it may safely be concluded, the divisions within the British population which matter politically are based on occupation and class rather than race or religion. They will be discussed in the next two sections.

The Economy

Throughout the greater part of the nineteenth century Britain justifiably could claim to be "the workshop of the world." Its early start in the industrial race, abundant domestic supplies of cheap fuel (coal), and its many established trading links throughout the world enabled it to become, and for many years remain, the leading manufacturing nation. It is still one of the wealthiest, measured by income per head of population.[6] In terms of absolute wealth, of course, it cannot be compared with, for example, either the United States or the Soviet Union.[7] The economy's rate of growth has slackened considerably since the end of the nineteenth century. One reason is that the country's surplus was increasingly invested overseas rather than in boosting home capacity. The resulting income did much, in the inter-war years, to conceal the relative decline in productive power. But this cushion is no longer available because, in order to pay for World War II, about half these foreign assets were sold (out of a total of £4,000,000,000 in 1939 [8]). Overseas investment continues, particularly in some of the Commonwealth countries, but recent production figures suggest that this is not the basic cause of slackening industrial expansion. Between 1951 and 1957 industrial production in the United Kingdom increased by 18 per cent as against, for example, 73 per cent in Western Germany, 48 per cent in France, and 19 per cent in the United States. At the same time only 15 per cent of the national product

[5] On the whole subject of "race" in Britain, see Institute of Race Relations, *Coloured Immigrants in Britain*, 1960.

[6] Estimated in 1958 to be $778, as against $1,870 in the United States, $739 in France, and $510 in West Germany.

[7] For example, whereas Britain produced (1957) 22,000,000 tons of crude steel, 224,000,000 tons of coal, and a negligible quantity of crude petroleum, the corresponding figures for the United States were 100,000,000, 460,000,000, and 353,000,000 tons, and for the U.S.S.R., 50,000,000, 456,000,000, and 98,000,000.

[8] The equivalent of $16,000,000,000 at the then prevailing rate of exchange.

was devoted to capital investment, as against 23 per cent in
W. Germany and 17 per cent in France and the United States.
The decline in Britain's relative position is therefore likely to
continue unless there is a dramatic change in economic policy
designed to increase British productivity. In the 1930's, Mr.
Rostas has estimated,[9] factory productivity in Germany was 11
per cent greater, and in the United States, 125 per cent greater
than in Britain. A later estimate, in 1949, was that the output
of the average British worker was only 40 per cent of his American counterpart's, reflecting the fact that he had less than half
the horsepower to help him in his work.[10] It seems likely that the
greater natural resources of the United States provide only a
partial explanation for this state of affairs.

International trade is the basis for Britain's industrial production and its standard of living alike. In 1957 the main constituents of that trade were as follows:

	Imports	Exports
Class A: Food, drink, tobacco	£1,496,441,000	£ 206,196,000
Class B: Basic materials	1,169,361,000	122,986,000
Class C: Mineral fuels and lubricants	466,302,000	152,704,000
Class D: Manufactured goods	928,315,000	2,754,375,000
Class E: Postal packages, etc.	15,169,000	88,719,000
TOTAL	4,075,588,000	3,324,981,000
	Re-exports	133,000,000
	TOTAL	£3,457,981,000

(Shipping, interest on investments, insurance and banking earnings, and the tourist trade are normally counted upon to bridge
the gap between imports and exports—though grants and loans
from Canada and the United States have also played a vital
part at different periods.) In 1954, Britain received over 54 per
cent of its imports from, and sent 53 per cent of its exports to,
other members of the Commonwealth or Ireland. Outside the
Commonwealth, the principal trading partners were America,
Scandinavia, the rest of Western Europe, and the Middle Eastern
oil states. Trade with the Commonwealth is fostered by the
system of tariff concessions ("imperial preferences") introduced
in 1932. In recent years, however, Commonwealth trade has declined slightly, and since the formation of the six-country European Economic Community in 1959, Britain has been forced to

[9] *Economic Journal* (April, 1943).
[10] Paul Hoffman in a press statement, August 29, 1949.

devote increasing efforts to the problem of expanding, or even maintaining, its trade with Western Europe.

The importance of manufacturing in the economy is also demonstrated by the occupational distribution of the population. In 1954 the total labor force was about 22,800,000 (an increase of nearly a million compared with 1948). The following table gives the main occupational divisions and the change in numbers compared with 1948 in order to indicate the trends. Note that manufacturing, distribution, and services account for the vast majority of people, with less than 5 per cent engaged in agriculture and forestry.

Principal occupations of the British people

	Numbers	Change
Agriculture, forestry, fishing	1,022,000	− 156,000
Mining and quarrying	876,000	− 1,200
Manufacturing industries	8,137,000	+1,034,000
engineering, shipbuilding and		
electrical goods	2,020,000	+244,000
vehicles	1,176,000	+242,000
Building and contracting	1,438,000	− 12,000
Gas, electricity, and water	376,000	+ 55,000
Transport and communication	1,692,000	− 95,000
Distributive trades	2,802,000	+ 318,000
Professional, financial, and		
miscellaneous services	4,037,000	+ 83,000
Central government service	583,000	− 99,000
Local government service	728,000	+ 28,000
Unemployed	280,000	− 2,000
Armed forces (including women)	830,000	− 16,000

SOURCE: The figures are from G. D. H. Cole, *The Post-War Condition of Britain* (London: Routledge and Kegan Paul, 1956), p. 47.

British politics are therefore those of an advanced industrial society vitally affected by its relations with other countries. They are also primarily the politics of an urban society. In 1954, 79 per cent of the population could be classified as urban, and only 21 per cent as rural. Furthermore, over 39 per cent of the population lived in seven major population centers, one of which, Greater London, contained about 17 per cent of the total population of Britain. This is not to say that farmers and the agricultural community generally are neglected by governments, nor that they have no political voice of importance. In fact, the interplay of the large number of constituencies which contain *some* agricultural electors, the need to obtain the farmers' co-operation in increasing agricultural production since 1939, and the effectiveness of the National Farmers' Union in presenting its case to successive governments has ensured that the interests of farmers have been well taken care of. But the principal political issues and the fundamental cleavage between the parties rest upon the divisions felt most acutely among the urban and industrial population. Fundamentally, the contest between the two major parties in large measure reflects the conflict of interest between organized capital (property) and organized labor. It is now necessary, therefore, to look at the industrial organization of the society.

There has been bitter controversy about the publicly owned industries, but they have not yet had much effect upon the general character either of the economy or the political structure of the country. The "nationalized" sector includes the Bank of England (the central bank for the financial system), railways, coal production, the production and distribution of gas and electricity, the principal airlines, the British Broadcasting Corporation, the Atomic Energy Authority, sections of long-distance road haulage, and (as part of the National Health Service) hospitals. In addition, it has not proved possible to return to private owners all those sections of the iron and steel industry taken over in 1950 and "denationalized" shortly afterward. Between them, however, the nationalized industries provided employment (1956) for only 11 per cent of the total number of people in civil employment, as against 77 per cent working in the privately owned section of the economy (the remainder worked in central or local government). The nationalized industries thus work in an economic context of predominantly private ownership and control, and their board membership is largely composed of private directors and managers who have grown up in private industry. Britain may have a "mixed" economy, but the public sector does not yet provide a basis for any political group or attitudes distinguishable from those found in private industry.[11]

The anatomy of industry in Britain has been studied far less intensively than in the United States, but there appear to exist the same broad characteristics of concentration in the hands of large units, divorce between ownership and control, and the development of links (through interlocking directorates, mem-

[11] The nature and extent of public control over the nationalized industries will be discussed below, in Chapter 5.

bership of trade associations and the like) between the large units. Measuring concentration by the proportion of employment provided within an industry by the three largest units, a survey by H. Leak and A. Maizels demonstrated that, in 1935, there was over 40 per cent concentration in chemicals, public utilities, and engineering and vehicles. Within certain subsections of these wide industrial groups the degree of concentration was, of course, very much higher. It reached, for example, 90 per cent in manufactured fuels, over 80 per cent in petroleum and explosives, and over 70 per cent in the sugar trades and in the production of wrought iron and steel tubes. Moreover, several units were among the three largest in several trades, for example, the Cooperative Wholesale Society, in twelve trades; Imperial Chemical Industries and Lever Brothers, in seven; and the General Electric Company, in five. In all, there were thirty-three trades or subdivisions in which the degree of concentration was above 70 per cent. At the time these were *minimum* figures, given the strict definitions adopted, and there is no doubt that the process of growth and merger has proceeded much further since then.[12]

Some indication of the present position is given by the National Institute of Social and Economic Research, which recently studied company accounts issued in 1953–54. Out of a quarter of a million companies, the 50 largest took 19 per cent of all the profits; the 100 largest, 25 per cent; and the 512 largest, nearly 40 per cent. Among the 512 largest companies, the top three in each industry surveyed held, on an average, 50 per cent of the total quoted company assets, and the largest 100 units, in whatever industry they operated, held about 65 per cent of the assets. Even these figures probably understate the degree of concentration in the 1960's: the intervening years have been filled with reports of fresh mergers and "take-over bids" in such widely separated industries as banking, brewing, automobiles, newspaper and periodical publishing, real estate, and retail distribution—to name only those which have attracted the widest publicity.

No statistics about ownership of assets, numbers employed, proportion of output, or any other comparable measure of productive concentration gives a complete picture of the structure of industry. The relations between the legally separate and formally autonomous units must also be taken into account. In

---

[12] See H. Leak and A. Maizels, "The Structure of British Industry," *Journal of the Royal Statistical Society,* CVIII (1945), 142–207.

Britain the most significant aspects of these relations are the extensive network of interlocking directorates between the major industrial, banking, and insurance companies on the one hand and, on the other, the proliferation of trade associations which, in their turn, are interlinked through membership of other associations for such purposes as relations with the public and, above all, with government.

Politically, the most important of these "peak" associations appears to be the Federation of British Industries (F.B.I.). Its members, consisting both of individual firms and of trade associations, cover at least 75 per cent of the productive capacity of the country, and its direction is drawn largely from the bigger industrial, banking, and insurance companies. On all major questions of economic and social policy the F.B.I. may expect to be consulted by the government directly or through the many advisory committees on which it has permanent representation. On questions primarily affecting but one industry, the appropriate trade association rather than, or as well as, the F.B.I. will normally be the official spokesman.

World War II and the attempts of the immediately postwar Labour government to plan the economy stimulated both the formation and the enlargement of these associations—for administrators it is much easier to deal with one body than with all the members of a trade or industry separately—with the result that there are now few (if any) important sections of the economy not covered by a trade association. Much of the work of the associations is concerned with technical problems of common interest, collective bargaining with trade unions, and public relations, as well as dealing with the government. But one cannot ignore their effect upon prices and output. It is clear that many of them either formulate and embody agreements of a monopolistic, or cartel-like, nature or pave the way for them. The controllers of the private sector of the economy are also linked through such bodies as the British Employers' Confederation, the British Institute of Management, and the Institute of Directors, all of which are directly connected with each other and the F.B.I. It is thus impossible to form any impression of the British economy other than that it is directly controlled by an oligarchy.[13] The same people are also to be found on the boards of the nationalized industries.

[13] It has been suggested that the key members could all meet together in a fairly small motion-picture theater. It is not being asserted that they act on all political issues as a homogeneous group, nor even that in any way they

It is becoming fashionable, particularly in official Labour party publications, to emphasize also the fact that the control of large modern companies is increasingly being divorced from ownership. Against this it is sometimes pointed out that, in fact, substantial shareholdings still exist. Professor Sargant Florence found, for example, that in eighty-five large firms with over £3,000,000 paid-up capital, the typical one had between ten and twenty thousand shareholders, but that about twenty of them (individuals and/or other companies) owned nearly a third of the voting shares. He also concluded that it is possible for such a small group, with as little as 20 per cent of the voting shares, to establish "oligarchic minority owners' control." [14] However, it is not very important to determine whether control rests with a majority or minority of owners, or even with nonshareholding directors—at least, not for our present purposes. The essential point is that those who control the private economy are directly accountable at best to a small number of people whose outlook on broad policy questions is likely to be akin to their own,[15] and at worst, only to themselves. It does not follow, of course, that they need pay no attention at all to the interests or opinions of anyone else. Most obviously, they cannot afford to ignore the social and political context (including the possibility of direct governmental action) in which they must survive and carry on their business, but over which they themselves exercise some influence, partly (but by no means solely) through the Conservative party.

The principal countervailing force is probably the trade-union movement. In 1955 the Ministry of Labour recorded a total trade-union membership of almost 9,500,000, but this figure includes several bodies not normally considered to be trade unions. In 1958 the Trades Union Congress (T.U.C.) represented affiliated unions with a membership of 8,300,000. The correct figure probably lies somewhere between these two totals. It represents about 40 per cent of the total number of employees in the country, many of whom no union could ever expect to enroll. In 1955 union membership in various industries ranged

form a single organized or self-conscious group. See the further discussion in Chapter 11 below.

[14] P. Sargant Florence, *The Logic of British and American Industry* (London: Routledge and Kegan Paul, 1953).

[15] The total number of adult shareholders appears not to exceed 2,000,000, 90 per cent of whom have very small holdings indeed and play no part whatsoever in the management of their property.

from over 75 per cent in coal-mining and transport to under 25 per cent in, for example, banking and the distributive trades. In manufacturing generally membership is high and most basic wage-rates are determined by nation-wide collective bargaining conducted by the unions. In the same year there were over 650 unions, 45 per cent of which had fewer than 500 members and covered 0.6 per cent of all members, and 2.5 per cent of which (17 unions) had 100,000 members or more and accounted for 67.2 per cent of the total. All but two of the last, representing local government officials and schoolteachers, were affiliated with the T.U.C. Among the unions may be found examples of craft, industrial, and general unions as well as federations of many separate ones. But organization by trade, skill, or type of work is more typical than organization by industry, which may account for some of the thorniest problems in industrial relations.

It is not possible precisely to measure the power and status of unions, although they are now firmly established features of British society. Like their counterparts among associations of employers, they, either individually or through the T.U.C., are represented on numerous government advisory committees, and will be consulted on many major issues of social and economic policy. However, trade-union representatives have rarely been found on government-sponsored committees fulfilling a direct controlling or administrative function affecting prices, output, or investment in an industry. Trade unionists are found on the boards of nationalized industries, but in 1957 there were only 47 of them (both full time and part time), as compared with 106 company directors and 71 managers. One reason for this has, of course, been the reluctance of the unions to become too closely associated with the management of these industries, lest it interfere with their freedom to negotiate on wages and conditions of work. On the other hand, through their intimate connection with the Labour party, they are able to supplement their direct economic influence with some measure of political power.

As a natural corollary of the organization of the economy, there exists a considerable inequality of income and wealth, although the impact of the former is appreciably modified by taxation. The figures can best be left to speak for themselves. In 1957 the distribution of incomes before and after income taxes had been paid was roughly as follows, counting the incomes of man and wife as one, and of juveniles separately:

Distribution of income before and after income taxes

Range	Before taxation		After taxation	
	Nos.	Total income	Nos.	Total income
£50–£499	12,600,000	£3,690,000,000	13,700,000	£4,091,000,000
£500–£999	11,190,000	7,890,000,000	10,760,000	7,425,000,000
£1,000–£2,000	1,702,000	2,180,000,000	1,250,000	1,583,000,000
£2,000 and over	378,000	1,490,000,000*	190,000	535,900,000*

* Before taxation there were 15,000 incomes over £10,000, totaling £245,000,000; after taxation there were 900 incomes over £6,000, totaling almost £7,000,000.

The redistributive effect of the principal means of direct taxation are obvious. Comparisons with the prewar situation are complicated by changes in the value of money, but it is clear that incomes are less unequal now than they were in 1938, both before and after tax. Thus it has been estimated that in 1938 some 88 per cent of incomes were below £250, as against 65 to 70 per cent under the equivalent income of £660 in 1956. At the upper end of the scale, the 2,000 highest incomes in 1938 averaged £43,500, of which a third was retained after taxes, and in 1956 they averaged £35,000, of which little over a sixth was retained (no allowance being made here for changes in the value of money).

Comparing personal incomes before tax in 1938 and in 1955, it has been shown that the share of total income accruing to the first hundred thousand dropped from 11.7 per cent to 5.3 per cent; to the first half-million dropped from 21.5 per cent to 12.3 per cent; to the first million dropped from 27.8 per cent to 17.4 per cent; and to the first five million from 51.6 per cent to 42.6 per cent. Taking account of the price level, it appears that the top groups also had appreciable drops in real income (by about a half in the case of the first hundred thousand) while every group from the second million downward has secured a rise in real income before tax. Another index of change is provided by the share of personal incomes accounted for by different types of income. Between 1938 and 1956 the share of personal incomes paid out in the form of wages and salaries rose from 56 per cent to 65 per cent, for example, while rent, dividends, and interest fell from 22 per cent to 11 per cent.

Despite the redistribution of incomes which has taken place

—as a result of taxation and inflation principally—inequality is still obvious and extensive. It should be emphasized, however, that inequality in spending power (standard of living) is only roughly measured by income figures alone. They take no account of "income" derived from capital gains, expense allowances to business executives and others (for automobiles, meals, and in some cases houses and education), or the spending of capital, which play an increasing and (in London's West End, for example) very noticeable part in modern Britain. Nor do they take account of the different kind of addition represented by expenditure on consumers' durable goods under installment-plan schemes, the total indebtedness for which was $1,033,000,-000 (£369,000,000) in mid-1957 and rose to over $2,500,000,000 (£900,000,000) three years later.

Fewer figures are available for the distribution of property, and they are less precise, but it is possible to indicate the general pattern. Using the published figures about estates on which death duty was payable, it has been calculated that in 1946–50 the poorest 89 per cent of the population owned under 15 per cent of all private property, while the richest 1 per cent owned nearly 21 per cent (the wealthiest 19,000 people owning almost exactly the same proportion as the poorest 89 per cent). In 1936–38 the poorest 93 per cent had owned about 17 per cent as against the 56 per cent owned by the richest 1 per cent. More recently a survey carried out by the Oxford Institute of Statistics suggested that the top 5 per cent of income units accounted for some 59 per cent of total net worth, while about one-third of income units had no net worth or had liabilities greater than their assets. To judge by the estates worth £2,000 or over in 1954–55, the type of property varies considerably according to wealth. Industrial shares, for example, are relatively unimportant for estates worth less than £20,000, but form over 40 per cent of all estates worth £30,000 or more, while land is significant only in estates valued at £100,000 and more. Insofar as it can be established, wealth and high incomes are not exactly correlated. An estimate for the year 1948–49 suggests that those with gross incomes above £10,000 held 8 per cent of private capital, while about 60 per cent of the total wealth belonged to people with incomes of £1,000 or less.

To the extent that money brings political power and social prestige, then power and prestige are very unequally distributed. Fortunately for the survival of democratic government in Britain the power of the purse is not unlimited either socially or politically.

Social Structure

Occupation and social class

It is a matter of common experience among visitors and residents that the British people are divided by a complex system of social stratification of which they are highly conscious. In addition to the separation imposed by differences of occupation and income common to most societies, they are further kept apart by differences in accent, appearance, and manner to an extent rarely found in, say, the United States.[16] The system, moreover, is national in the sense that there is, broadly, one system rather than a series of local or regional ones; indeed, to possess a "regional" accent may suffice to bar an individual from full acceptance at the hightest level and, generally speaking, the thicker any such accent is, the lower in the scale will a person be placed. The result is that, for many people, an awareness of their status colors their whole approach to life—though by no means necessarily committing them actively to waging a political class war. On the other hand, the enforced mixing and sharing imposed by national participation in World War II led to a temporary breakdown in class feeling which, when it received comment at all, was welcomed by almost everyone known to the author.

Giving an objective picture of the class structure is not made any easier by the prevalence of class consciousness. Different people attach different meanings to the concept of "class," and different pictures emerge according to the criteria of "class-membership" adopted. The official 1951 census, for example, groups the population into five social classes and thirteen socio-economic groups, but G. D. H. Cole and others have criticized the bases on which these classifications rest. The British Market Research Bureau, on behalf of the Hulton Readership Survey, has produced a fivefold classification based on the appearance, speech, occupation, type of house, and residential district of the subjects interviewed. The resulting categories are named the well-to-do, middle class, lower middle class, working class (some 60 per cent of the total), and poor. Yet again, a detailed investi-

[16] At certain periods it is probable that in Boston, Massachusetts, and the Deep South comparable social conditions prevailed.

gation being carried out by the London School of Economics has found a substantial agreement among its subjects about the status ranking of occupations and a general belief that the population should be divided simply into upper, middle, and working classes, although agreement did not extend to the precise boundaries and nature of each class. The first reported conclusions of this study perhaps provide the most useful and concrete introduction to class in Britain.[17]

The London study is primarily concerned with occupational mobility as at least one dimension of social mobility. For this purpose occupations have been grouped, by the investigators and after confirmation by a survey, into seven categories, as follows:

Category	Percentage of employed men in Britain (approx.)
1. Professional and higher administrative	3%
2. Managerial and executive	4½%
3. Upper inspectorial, supervisory, and other non-manual workers	10%
4. Lower inspectorial, supervisory, and other non-manual workers	12½%
5. Skilled manual workers and routine nonmanual	41%
6. Semiskilled manual workers	16½%
7. Unskilled	12½%

The confirmatory survey revealed remarkable agreement upon the status ranking of particular occupations and upon the general reliability of this sevenfold classification, although the gaps in status between the categories are nowhere very large.

On the basis of a sample of almost ten thousand adults throughout Britain, a measure of mobility between the generations was then obtained. In crude figures, it was found that the proportion of adults who, in 1949, had reached the same occupational status as that last possessed by their fathers averaged 35.1 per cent, but that the proportions varied among the categories. Thus it ranged from 47.3 per cent for category No. 5 and 38.8 per cent for No. 1, to 21.2 per cent for No. 4 and 18.8 per cent for No. 3. This is somewhat misleading in that it takes no account of changes in population and the number of available positions in each category. Accordingly, Professor David Glass and his associates compiled indices of association which take

[17] See D. V. Glass, ed., *Social Mobility in Britain* (London: Routledge and Kegan Paul, 1954).

these into account and measure the departure from a purely random association between the status of father and son; the higher the figure, the greater the degree of intergeneration stability (with unity representing "perfect mobility"). It was then found that categories No. 1 and No. 2 showed a high degree of stability, with indices of 13.158 and 5.865 respectively, while category No. 5 was in fact highly mobile, with an index of 1.157. On the other hand, in all categories, and whether movement was up or down, a person's status rarely moved far from his father's.

A more restricted survey disclosed that the vast majority in all categories felt that opportunities for social advancement were much wider for their children than themselves, primarily because of improved educational opportunities—although in the main survey there was no significant change in the indices of association for different age groups, a discrepancy which might be explained by the fact that the younger men are still moving upward. Most important for social stability, the smaller survey also showed that, for the most part, parents had ambitions for their children which were in line with the general pattern of mobility, the upper categories having a professional career as the target and the lowest ones, a category No. 5 career. Not measured by the London study, but overwhelmingly borne out by personal testimony, is the fact that the gap between the highest and lowest categories has narrowed appreciably in the past sixty years, however wide it still may be in terms of living standards, sickness and death rate, consumption patterns, or leisure interests, to mention some of the main criteria.

Occupational categories are not, however, identical with class at all points. The smaller survey carried out by Glass and his associates, for example, showed that members of categories No. 1 and 2 saw themselves as middle class, as did categories No. 3 and 4, while categories No. 5, 6, and 7 saw themselves as working class; but one-third of categories No. 3 and 4 (plus routine nonmanual workers) labeled themselves working class, while about a quarter of No. 5, 6, and 7 placed themselves in the middle class. The deviant groups were concentrated, so to speak, at the margin: among routine white-collar workers and skilled manual workers. Women as a group tend to upgrade themselves, while the sons of manual workers tend to see themselves as working class, whatever their occupations. (It appears that the reasons for these "deviations" did not consist of snobbery, inverted or otherwise, but of images of the classes concerned, which were in some ways unique: the "deviants" would have placed other members of their occupational category in the same class as themselves to a very large extent.) Moreover, the same survey indicated considerable divergencies in the definitions of the various classes put forward by different groups and individuals: for example, categories No. 1 and 2 tended to define "upper class" in terms of family or "breeding" (a metaphor commonly used in discussions of the aristocracy or upper class, and apparently drawn from the royal sport of horse racing, but rarely pursued further), a definition applicable to a minute section of the population, whereas the lower categories tended to define it in terms of income, to equate it roughly with "the rich," and thus to include within its boundaries most, but not all, members of categories No. 1 and 2.

Occupational ranking is not identical, either, with income or wealth, since it apparently takes account of the type of income (salary, fees, commission, or wages, for example), the source of income (government service or shopkeeping, for example), and education as well as monetary reward.[18] The last of these, education, should really be thought of as a distinct criterion of social status, along with money and occupation. Not only do many consider it an essential part of a class image, but it is clearly an important determinant, and result, of income and occupation.

Education and social class

Although many well-known schools were founded in the sixteenth century and before, it was not until the nineteenth century that even a rudimentary primary education was available for any substantial portion of the population (the first government grants to private, mainly church-run, schools being made in 1833), and not until 1870 that legislation was passed compelling school attendance (up to the age of twelve).[19] Acts of Parliament in 1902 and 1918 placed state education under the control of the larger local government authorities and extended its scope into the field of secondary education, while compelling school attendance or other full-time instruction be-

[18] Even this is not intended to be a comprehensive list of the criteria whereby people evaluate the status of various occupations.

[19] These statements, and most of this section, apply only to England and Wales. Scotland's system and history differ in some important respects. However, because less than 10 per cent of the British people live in Scotland, and therefore it is the English system which is most important politically, it will be safe and convenient largely to ignore the Scottish one. Since 1870, moreover, the differences have tended to lessen.

tween the ages of five and fourteen. No other major change took place before World War II.

In order to appreciate the educational background of the present adult population, it is necessary to say something about the general shape of the prewar system. In 1931 some 80 per cent of the population between the ages of eleven and fourteen attended state elementary schools, some of which provided, in their senior classes, more advanced education of an academic or scientific nature. The number of these classes, and of separate state secondary schools, increased during the thirties while, in the more senior schools, some provision was being made for children staying on after the school-leaving age of fourteen. But it cannot be said that any adequate system of secondary education existed for most of the school population. Quite outside the state system there existed, and continue to exist, the private (sometimes called "independent") schools. These included some pioneering progressive schools and many schools possibly better classified as money-making rather than educational establishments, but the most important were the grammar schools and the "public schools" in the field of secondary education, and those primary ones, known as preparatory schools, designed to prepare pupils for entry to the public schools at the age of twelve or thirteen.

The grammar schools generally provide a high standard of education up to the age of about eighteen, mainly but not exclusively in general arts subjects. (Their name derives from the fact that the earliest ones taught Latin grammar.) Most of them draw their pupils, who attend during the day only, from their own local area, and support themselves from the fees paid by their pupils and from endowments. Today the name is applied to many other schools—under local authority as well as private management—which provide an academic education. The public schools are mainly boarding schools, draw their pupils from a regional or national area, and also support themselves from endowments and fees (which must be high to pay for board as well as tuition). They are thus exclusive as well as private. The name "public school" is a nineteenth-century creation. It refers to the fact that, unlike many of the private schools which then existed, they are run by a board of governors who have no personal financial stake in the schools but who serve as trustees, while the schools themselves are designed to be no more than self-supporting financially. They have tended to be distinguished by their emphasis on sport, "character-building," and the development of "leadership qualities," although the degree of success varies widely. The best of them, however, are also, even primarily, noted for the high quality of the education they provide. By encouraging at least the best of their pupils to accept responsibility, they have performed a very useful social function in providing administrators for government, business, and the colonies, particularly as the need for them expanded rapidly in the late nineteenth century. They have also been most valuable in helping to fuse the old upper class with the children of the newer professional and business classes.

Not everyone would agree that the type of character and social outlook encouraged in public-school children is ideal either for society or for the individuals concerned. There can be no argument, however, about the place of the public schools and, to a lesser degree, the grammar schools in the social structure. Briefly it can be said that the higher the status of the father, the greater the child's chance of attending a grammar or public school, and that to have attended one or the other is an invaluable passport to high occupational status, directly or by means of further study at a university. Two examples of the influence of schooling upon career will have to suffice. J. F. S. Ross has estimated that in the interwar years, the House of Commons on average obtained 56 per cent of its members from public schools, $21\frac{1}{2}$ per cent from other independent secondary schools, and $22\frac{1}{2}$ per cent from the state elementary schools, and that one member in five had been at one or other of two public schools, Eton and Harrow, with annual outputs of about 250 and 120 boys respectively.[20] Of the top five levels in the civil service, those normally carrying a significant degree of authority, over one-third in 1939 had been to a boarding school, under a fifth to a state secondary school, and the others to various other kinds of fee-paying secondary school.[21] To buy education at a public or other independent school has thus been an important means of transmitting high social status to one's children. Conversely, gaining entrance into a grammar school or public school, where scholarships, savings, or luck permitted, was and is an almost certain way of moving up in the status

[20] In his *Parliamentary Representation,* 2d ed. (London: Eyre and Spottiswoode, 1948), pp. 41–52. The definition of a public school is vague, and the one adopted by Ross may be too wide; but it would apply to schools attended by less than 3 per cent of the population.

[21] R. K. Kelsall, Higher *Civil Servants in Britain* (London: Routledge and Kegan Paul, 1955), pp. 118–34.

scale. At best, however, "education as such appears to modify, but not to destroy, the characteristic association between the social status of father and son." [22]

The Education Act of 1944, passed by the wartime coalition government, was designed to equalize educational opportunity. It remains the legislative basis for today's educational system, the salient features of which may now be described. About 15 per cent of the schools in England and Wales, with 8 per cent of all schoolchildren, and including the vast majority of public schools, remain totally independent of the national system, although local authorities may (and very occasionally do) pay fees for a boy or girl in their area to attend such a school. Within the state system there are the so-called county schools wholly maintained by the local authority; the voluntary schools provided by some other body (mainly churches) but wholly or partly maintained by the local authority; and the direct-grant schools, which receive a grant from the Ministry of Education and are subject to inspection, but which are outside the control of the local authority. The last category, mainly consisting of secondary schools, must provide up to 50 per cent of their places to the local authority, but in total cater to less than 2 per cent of all schoolchildren, as opposed to 75 per cent in the county schools.

One of the main principles of the 1944 Act was to introduce a sharp break between primary and secondary education at the age of eleven and over. On the basis of intelligence and aptitude tests, often supplemented by reports from primary-school teachers, children are allocated to one of three types of secondary school some time between their eleventh and twelfth birthdays. The three types are the grammar schools, providing a more or less academic education designed to equip children for further education or the higher white-collar occupations; the secondary modern schools, which form the bulk of all secondary schools, and whose "main role . . . is to staff the lower echelons of Britain's vast industrial machine—particularly with unskilled and semi-skilled workers";[23] and the secondary technical schools (the smallest category) providing training in various industrial, agricultural, and commercial subjects.[24] Only in the grammar

[22] D. V. Glass, *op. cit.*, p. 307.
[23] To quote a special article in the Manchester *Guardian,* July 28, 1959.
[24] There are, in addition, various special schools for children with various kinds of mental or physical handicap, both at the primary and secondary level.

schools are the pupils normally encouraged to stay on after reaching the minimum school-leaving age of fifteen, but a very small (if increasing) number of pupils at secondary modern schools are also staying on until sixteen or later. The grammar school, however, is the highroad to subsequent prestige and material reward. Only there, for example, will the majority of pupils take the examinations for the General Certificate of Education (G.C.E.). These are conducted under the auspices of the Ministry of Education, but administered by examination boards consisting largely of university teachers. G.C.E. results serve increasingly as the basis for admission to a university and the award of grants for further education, as well as for acceptance in numerous skilled and white-collar occupations.

This system of segregation in secondary education is a continuing subject of dispute, both on educational and social grounds. Its defenders claim that it provides a varied system of education suited to the widely different capacities and aptitudes of the children, giving them the sort of training suited to the occupational opportunities accessible to them. In particular, it is asserted that only a relatively small porportion of the population are capable of attaining a high level of performance in intellectual studies. It is therefore felt to be desirable, in the national interest as well as that of the individuals concerned, that they be given a more intensely intellectual and specialized education in schools designed solely for this purpose, always provided that entry to such schools is available to all children with the requisite ability. (At present about 20 per cent of all children between the ages of twelve and fifteen attend grammar schools.)

Against this the critics maintain that the selection process itself is not sufficiently accurate, while the arrangements for later transfers from one type of school to another are inadequate, and, most fundamentally, that the whole principle is wrong. They assert that comprehensive schools, like American high schools, can make equally good provision for variety in subject and standard without introducing a rigid educational class system which cannot but consolidate wider social-class divisions. Furthermore, it is alleged, the distinction between modern and grammar school is already widely regarded as a prestige differential, and this reacts adversely upon the morale of both pupils and teachers in the modern school. London and a few other cities are therefore experimenting with comprehensive schools, and the Labour party is pledged to abolish the principle of segregation at the age of eleven and over.

It is too early to estimate the precise effects of the 1944 Act upon social mobility. It is clear, however, that equality of educational opportunity has not yet been achieved. The independent fee-paying schools remain largely unaffected and, indeed, are reported to have longer waiting lists for entry than ever before. Within the state system itself, moreover, the children of parents from the higher occupational levels not only appear to stand a better chance of attending a grammar school, but, once admitted, fare better and stay on past the minimum leaving age longer than do children of (say) manual workers.[25]

However, there are signs that the difference is now lessening. In any event, the extent to which the remedy for the differences *within* the state system lies in further educational reform is probably slight. Insofar as one is here presented with non-hereditary factors, like the incentive to study or the facilities to do so at home, the remedy must consist of more radical and more generalized types of social action which deal directly with the bases of social stratification. The degree of inequality is well summarized in the table on page 42.

To complete the picture it may be noted that, of United Kingdom entrants to all British universities in 1955–56, only 28 per cent were the children of manual workers, and that 23 per cent came from independent or direct-grant schools, 67 per cent from local-authority grammar schools, and 8 per cent from all other schools, with the proportion of grammar-school pupils and children of manual workers at Oxford and Cambridge being appreciably lower than the national average.[26] On the whole, university education appears to be less important for social mobility than school education, although it may be decisive for some individuals (for example, the very few university entrants from a secondary modern school).[27] The numbers involved may be comparatively small.

[25] Thus, according to investigation of a 10 per cent sample, 35 per cent of those entering grammar schools in 1946, and over 50 per cent of those staying on after fifteen were children of people in census classes I and II, as opposed to about 21 per cent and 15 per cent from classes IV and V (Central Advisory Council for Education *Report on Early Leaving*, 1954). Of those who left school in 1953–54, about 95 per cent of pupils at secondary modern ones left at fifteen or under, as against some 16 per cent from the grammar schools, while less than 2 per cent of leavers from the former, and about 25 per cent from the latter, went on to some other educational institution, including universities and teachers' training colleges. See also D. V. Glass, *op. cit.,* pp. 291–307.

[26] Kelsall, *op. cit.,* pp. 32–34 and 37. The figures include children educated in Scotland, grouped in the rough equivalent categories of school.

[27] D. V. Glass, *op. cit.,* pp. 291–307.

Children's school records classified by father's occupation

	Nonmanual		All manual		Skilled manual only	
	Male	*Female*	*Male*	*Female*	*Male*	*Female*
Grade I in selection test for secondary school	33.5%	36.1%	66.5%	63.9%	45.3%	43.9%
Category A in maintained grammar school record	52.6%	62.1%	47.5%	37.9%	38.8%	32.8%
Admitted* to British universities from maintained grammar schools, 1955–56	63.5%	74.5%	36.5%	25.5%	30.3%	21.9%
Admitted* to British universities from all secondary schools, 1955–56	74.0%	81.4%	26.0%	18.6%	21.7%	16.1%

* United Kingdom students with permanent addresses in England.

SOURCE: Adapted, by permission, from R. K. Kelsall, *Report on an Inquiry into Applications for Admission to Universities* (London: Association of Universities of the British Commonwealth, for the Committee of Vice-Chancellors and Principals of the Universities of the United Kingdom, 1957), p. 10.

University education nevertheless does provide a possible means of promotion into the professional middle class or beyond, even for children from much lower in the social scale: for those affected, it may have dramatic results.

There are twenty-two universities in Britain (not including one in Northern Ireland), all but six of them (Oxford, Cambridge, and the four Scottish universities) being nineteenth- or twentieth-century creations. They are all self-governing, coeducational, and private in the sense that they are neither owned nor managed by the state, although on the average they are dependent upon government grants to the extent of over 70 per cent of their revenue. In 1958–59 almost one hundred and ten thousand students were enrolled, three-quarters of whom received financial assistance from central or local government, in many cases amounting to the full cost of their fees and maintenance, and, in others, having a university or other award supplemented by the public. Subject to comparatively few exceptions, all who are accepted for entrance by a university can normally count upon receiving at least the minimum essential financial aid from government or other sources. Of those students enrolled for a first degree, all but 10 to 15 per cent may be expected to graduate after (in most cases) three or four years. Some thirteen thousand of them were engaged in full-time postgraduate study for a teaching or other diploma, or for an advanced degree.

There is thus one student to roughly every four hundred and fifty-four inhabitants, as opposed to a ratio of one to seventy in the United States, despite the fact that the number of students has more than doubled since 1938 and is still increasing. This bald comparison is misleading, however. The proportion of students who graduate is much higher in Britain (about 85 per cent as against 50 per cent), the general standard is higher,[28] and many people who, in America, would go to a college or university, in Britain continue their education by other means. Thus, in 1954, over 2,250,000 people were obtaining some form of further education—full time, part time, or in the evenings—from establishments enjoying financial aid from the government. Of these, 74,000 were full-time students seeking qualifications as teachers, scientists, technologists or technicians, and artists, or were obtaining further training in commercial, artistic, and general subjects. Nevertheless, it is widely felt that a pressing need exists to expand the facilities for post-school education, at universities and elsewhere, particularly in the scientific and technical fields.

Graduation from a university is obviously an important determinant of occupational status, although, as we have seen, admission is itself greatly influenced by a person's secondary education. Among the universities, moreover, Oxford and Cambridge have a special pre-eminence. Having for centuries been the only universities in England and Wales, and possessing further advantages in their residential and collegiate nature, they attract a large number of the ablest members of each generation. This is both a cause and a result of their reputation for providing the best available university education (the extent to which the reputation is justified is irrelevant here) and is also closely related, again both as cause and effect, to the disproportionate number of Oxford and Cambridge graduates in the higher levels of business, government, and the civil service, as well as university teaching, to name only the most important examples. Thus, to amplify this statement in the political sphere, on the average from 1918 through 1951, 32 per cent of Members of

[28] This is not to be taken as an assertion of superiority, and applies only to the standard of the first degree. The educational systems in the two countries have different aims and are geared to very different social circumstances. The standard of learning achieved at a particular stage is thus not the only criterion of judgment.

Parliament had been to either Oxford or Cambridge (56½ per
cent had not attended any university); of the 306 persons who
had been cabinet ministers from 1801 to 1924, 118 had been at
Oxford, while, in the 1955 Government, 47 out of the 70 members had been to Oxford or Cambridge; and, in 1950, some 60
per cent of the most senior members of the civil service were
Oxford or Cambridge graduates (the proportion rising to over
70 per cent in some departments), although there has been a
significant drop among postwar recruits.[29]

In the universities, as in the schools, there has been an appreciable widening of opportunities since 1938, although once
again it is impossible yet to measure the effect of this upon social
mobility or the class structure as a whole. It is clear, however,
that the educational system still reflects and helps to maintain
the unequal distribution of status, prestige, and, as a necessary
accompaniment, political power and influence in British society.
But at the same time education as such does something to modify
the influence of mere wealth upon social stratification.

Politics and the social structure

Education, occupation, and income thus appear to be the
primary determinants of social status. Particularly at the peak of
the social scale, however, an individual is liable to classification
in terms of his ancestry and not only on the strength of his
achievements. The existence and prestige of the monarchy probably provides a partial explanation for the continuing vitality of
this older idea of a hereditary aristocracy whose claim to social
pre-eminence does not rest upon, although it is closely associated
with, the monetary and occupational badges distinctive to modern
industrial societies. This small "upper class" is not an exclusive
caste. Intermarriage and other ties link it closely with other
highly placed groups. It is not by any means to be identified with
the possessors of titles, not even with the peerage: many lords,
as well as knights, must be classified as middle class and, in a
few cases, working class, while many acknowledged members of
the upper class do not themselves bear any title.

It is easy, perhaps, to criticize the notion that heredity confers social status directly. On the other hand, no account of the

---

[29] Figures from J. F. S. Ross, *Elections and Electors* (London: Eyre and
Spottiswoode, 1955), p. 419; Mary Stewart, "A Family Affair," *New Statesman
and Nation,* July 16, 1955; and R. K. Kelsall, *Higher Civil Servants in Britain*
(London: Routledge and Kegan Paul, 1955), pp. 134–45. See also the tables
printed in Chapter 5 below.

rise of socialism in Britain can ignore the role of the aristocracy as the concrete embodiment of a classification system alternative to that of purely economic and financial success. Socialist criticism of social differences must surely have been facilitated by aristocratic resistance to the social ambitions of industrial and commercial leaders as well as by the challenge the latter presented to the older system. British society has not yet been permeated by the capitalist or industrial ethos to the same extent as American. Today it is the coming together of the aristocracies of birth and wealth at the top levels, rather than the distinctions between them, which is most apparent to the outside observer. The educational system, the incursions of the aristocracy into business (necessitated by taxation and the declining profitability of landowning), and external pressure from political radicalism have probably been the most important factors making for upperclass "togetherness." Throughout history, however, the British aristocracy has shown itself, when compared with many of its continental European counterparts, to be remarkably adaptable and receptive to new blood.

Given the significant degree of occupational immobility and its relation to the educational system and the distribution of income, and given also the degree of class consciousness present in British society, it is inevitable that class and status should be essential elements in the political life of the country. In the next chapter we shall see the close connection which exists between class and allegiance to the Conservative and Labour parties. Equally important, however, is the influence of class upon the relations between some of the principal wielders of power and influence within the community.

One effect of the social structure we have described is to create a wide network of personal links among many of the top decision-makers in government, the civil service, the armed forces, the Established Church of England, and certain sections of the economy. Inevitably, something of the sort is to be found in any society. People of wealth and influence naturally come together socially as well as in the course of business. But in Britain, not only do the "top people" acquire social ties through membership of the same clubs or patronage of the same hotels and resorts; many of them already share a common background of public school, Oxford or Cambridge college, or even of ancestry.

The associations with government (i.e., with ministers and Members of Parliament) are particularly notable under Conservative party rule, when kinship, business, and educational back-

ground combine to produce an extensive and intricate web of relationships throughout the political, financial, and social worlds.[30]
The importance of this web, it may be suggested, lies in its nature
as an informal system of access to some of the key decision-making
areas, and the encouragement it gives to an equally informal
system of decision-making and mutual consultation "between
friends," sometimes referred to as the "old boy network." [31] From
it the Labour party is largely excluded.

Undeniably, informal discussions and negotiations are indispensable adjuncts to any system of government. It is also undeniable, however, that relying upon them very extensively may
raise grave difficulties for all concerned when a non-Conservative
government is in office, and at any time may lead to irresponsibility, excessive secrecy, a failure to consider relevant information
or opinion, and the frustration of the democratic process. On
the other hand, it may also lead to flexibility, speedy decisions,
and, for those involved, a high degree of confidence in the
decision-making process.

The foregoing picture of a ruling elite, or interconnected
set of elites, lacks sufficient perspective and may be misleading if
it isn't qualified. The immobility at the top levels is by no means
total: people from a wide range of social origins are to be found
in all the key groups mentioned. The educational reforms of 1944
may, and probably will, in time lead to greater mobility into the
top positions. These points affect only the personal composition
of the ruling groups, however; they do not affect the groups'
position in society, and may not radically affect the behavior of
the groups. More important is the fact that the top decision-
makers are by no means united on all issues. Clearly the interests
of key people in such occupations as the civil service, banking,
and insurance will frequently be in sharp conflict with each
other.[32]

Nevertheless, it is probably safe to assume substantial

[30] For a study of some aspects thereof see the study by T. Lupton and
C. Shirley Wilson, the results of which were published in the *Manchester
School,* January, 1959, extracts of which were printed in the Manchester
Guardian, January 20, 1959.

[31] The *Report of the Tribunal appointed to Inquire into Allegations of
Improper Disclosure of Information relating to the Raising of the Bank
Rate* (London: H.M.S.O., Cmnd. 350 of January, 1958), and its *Proceedings
and Evidence,* provide a revealing and unique account of its operation.

[32] Lupton and Wilson, *loc. cit.,* "suggest that 'top decision-makers' as well
as being linked by kinship, business interests, and similar background, are
also divided by competing, even conflicting, interests. Indeed kinship itself,
in certain circumstances, may act as a divisive as well as a uniting force."

agreement upon the desirability of maintaining the conditions—
social, political, and economic—which permit these people to
exercise their influence and pursue their interests in the accustomed fashion. (Disagreement exists about the precise nature
of these conditions, and about the way in which the "top people"
can best ensure the continuance of their power in the face of
uncontrollable changes in circumstances. Such disagreements
should not be confused, although they often are, with arguments
about *whether* the present ruling groups are entitled to their
positions of special power. It is equally important not to con-
fuse arguments about the personal composition of ruling groups
with ones about the desirability or otherwise of fostering any
small ruling groups at all. The "progressive" character of the
Conservative party since its defeat at the 1945 general election,
in the author's judgment, relates only to the personal composition
of the ruling groups and to the methods of maintaining their
position; on the more fundamental questions the Conservative
outlook is little different from what it has been in earlier years.)

The most important and obvious qualification which must
be made to an "elitist" picture of British society is provided by
the representative system and the existence of political parties
which provide a direct challenge to the power of the established
decision-makers in society. The Liberal party, until World War
I, and thereafter the Labour party, have not only been channels
whereby excluded groups have achieved a share in government
and an acknowledgment of their right to do so, but, by their
very existence and programs, they have made it necessary for all
parties and groups to exercise their power in ways more acceptable to the people as a whole.

The distribution of power in society has placed severe limitations upon what any reform government can achieve by democratic methods, and at no time in this century can it be said that
either the Liberal or Labour parties have successfully sustained
a direct radical attack upon the power of the ruling groups. On
the other hand, they have made it possible for manual workers
to attain government offices which would have seemed unthink-
able fifty years ago, and they have been influential in bringing
about at least the sense of wider opportunity to which we have
already referred, as well as a wide extension of the material
badges of status and recognized worth. It is the impact of political democracy and liberal ideals upon an oligarchical society,
and vice versa, which give much of the tone and style to British
politics.

A Postscript on "the Establishment"

In the last few years references to "the Establishment" have become increasingly common. By this term is usually meant people in established positions of power and prestige. It may thus be roughly equivalent to the "old boy network" we have discussed. However, the word usually carries with it connotations of "respectability," orthodoxy, and even "stuffiness." It therefore refers to a state of mind as much as to a specific group of people. One badge of membership in "the Establishment" thus seems to be a firm belief that those who at present wield the greatest degree of power and influence are the right people to do so, and that the believer is (or soon will be) one of them. This belief is commonly held by the type of person who is "in the know" and also is convinced that he knows what is good for other people to know. The term is perhaps best left to refer, pejoratively, to all such believers (other than oneself), in whatever group, organization, or society they are to be found.[33]

3 - The Political Public

The election of a new House of Commons must by law be held no later than five years after the previous one. It may, however, be postponed with the consent of the House of Lords. This provision has only been invoked during the two world wars. On the other hand, there is no need for a government to wait five years before advising the monarch to dissolve Parliament and order the election of a new one, and it rarely does. There were, for example, eleven elections in the thirty years following the 1918 one—and this includes ten years, 1935–45, in which no election was held.[1]

There is only one election, of members of the House of Com-

[33] See the discussion of Oligarchy in Britain, Chapter 11 below.
[1] See the further discussion about the power to dissolve the House of Commons in the next chapter.

mons, but the choice of prime minister and the cabinet is immediately dependent upon its outcome, as the government consists of the leaders of the party winning a majority of seats in the House.

The Electoral System

For electoral purposes Britain is divided into six hundred and eighteen constituencies,[2] each returning one member to the House of Commons. The average size is about fifty-seven thousand electors. As a concession to nationalist feelings, it is smaller in Scotland and Wales. It also tends to be smaller in the more rural constituencies than in urban ones, not in order to give a greater voice to the country voter, but to prevent areas from becoming unmanageable. Since 1944 the task of defining the constituencies has been entrusted to permanent boundary commissions, which apply certain general rules agreed upon by the major parties and embodied in Acts of Parliament, and which are appointed by the government, although they are independent of political control in their operations. By an Act of 1958 the commissions must review constituency boundaries every ten to fifteen years. Their recommendations are generally, if not necessarily, accepted by the cabinet and Parliament.[3]

Universal adult suffrage is the rule, each qualified person having one vote in the area in which he or she resides. The local registration officer, a senior local-government official, is responsible in each area for compiling the annual register of voters. Those who move their place of residence between registers, if they give sufficient notice and satisfy certain other very minor conditions, may vote by post in their former constituency (as may invalids and others prevented by the nature of their employment from polling in person). Only a person whose name is on the register may vote, and it is an offense to vote in more than one constituency.[4] A few people may be disfranchised through omis-

[2] There are twelve more in Northern Ireland, with an electorate in 1959 of 874,000.

[3] However, the recommendations have not always been accepted cheerfully. See P. G. Richards, *Honourable Members* (London: Faber, 1959), pp. 44–49; and G. Marshall and G. C. Moodie, *Some Problems of the Constitution* (London: Hutchinson, 1959), pp. 96–101.

[4] As recently as the 1945 election it was possible to cast more than one vote if a person resided in a two-member constituency, or qualified to vote

sions when the register was compiled or through failing to apply
for a postal vote, and in some constituencies where there have
been large movements of people, this may be important. But the
great majority of the adult population find themselves automatically entitled to vote near their homes at each election. Voting machines are not used, votes being cast by marking the official
ballot papers with pen or pencil. The papers are numbered, so
that allegations of fraud or irregularity may be checked if necessary. Only under those circumstances would the secrecy of the
vote be in any way violated, and even then the way in which
individual legitimate votes were cast would not be made public.
The counting of the votes is carried out manually by the returning officer and his assistants (also normally local-government
officials) in the presence of the candidates and their representatives. The candidate who secures the largest number of votes is
elected, regardless of whether or not it amounts to an absolute
majority of all the votes cast. Where there are three or more
candidates standing in a constituency, it is thus possible to be
returned to Parliament with well under 50 per cent of the votes.

One result of this "first past the post" system, taken in conjunction with the different sizes of constituency, is that the
number of seats won by a party in the House of Commons is
never in exact proportion to the number of votes won in the
country. If one takes the eight elections fought since women
secured the vote on the same conditions as men, namely those
from 1929 to 1959 inclusive, we find the following notable "injustices" (as critics of the system would put it): only in 1931 and
1935 did the government with a parliamentary majority also win
50 per cent or more of the total number of popular votes. In
1929 and 1951 the party with the largest number of popular
votes did not even win the most parliamentary seats (the sufferers
being, respectively, Conservative and Labour) but, on the other
hand, only in 1929 did no party secure an absolute majority of
seats in the House of Commons. The Liberal party, in this period,
has been consistently underrepresented—for example, in 1929 it
gained over one-fifth of the votes but less than one-tenth of the
seats, and in 1950, almost one-tenth of the votes but only about
one-seventieth of the seats. The experience of the Labour party
might also suggest a need to reform the system: it won about one-
twelfth of the seats with nearly one-third of the votes in 1931;
almost two-thirds of the seats with 48 per cent of the votes in

for a university member, or had a "business vote," i.e., had business premises
above a certain value in another constituency.

1945, and then, in 1951, a hundred fewer seats with a slightly increased share of the vote.

In fact, however, neither the Conservative nor Labour party favors electoral reform today, and the consensus of academic opinion supports them in this.[5] The system is not purely capricious. Its main effect is to exaggerate majorities rather than create them, ensuring that a parliamentary majority sufficient for purposes of government be given to that one party which gains the largest share of the votes or, as in 1929 and 1951, to that one of the two biggest parties whose popularity is on the increase; for any given swing in votes it is possible to predict, within reasonable limits, the resulting change in parliamentary strength. It is thus substantially fair as between the two major parties. The winning party, moreover, can normally be counted upon to pay as much attention, in the conduct of government, to its popular as to its parliamentary support.

It is the lesser parties which suffer most, but not necessarily mortally. If the support for a minor party is geographically concentrated, as was the case with the Irish Nationalists before World War I, rather than diffused thinly and evenly over the whole country, as has been the case with the Liberals more recently, a party will probably win *at least* its fair share of seats. But even in the case of the Liberals, it is difficult to believe that the electoral system has done more than hasten a decline brought about by internal disunity and the party's failure to retain or capture the support of any major socioeconomic interest. The supplanting of the Liberals by Labour as the other main party itself demonstrates that the system puts no insuperable barrier in the way of a newer party, provided only that its potential appeal is strong enough and wide enough.

For these reasons, reinforced by the traditional preference for strong governments (which calls for governments with cohesive majorities behind them in the House of Commons), the electoral system is generally acceptable to the British people. It is supported largely because it works reasonably well in terms of a two-party system, and may even help to maintain a two-party system—just as, in turn, it is maintained by the two major parties and criticized only (since they became a minor party) by the Liberals.

[5] See, in particular, D. E. Butler, *The Electoral System in Britain 1918–51* (London: Oxford, 1953); the case for reform is well argued in J. F. S. Ross, *Elections and Electors* (London: Eyre and Spottiswoode, 1955), and E. Lakeman and J. S. Lambert, *Voting in Democracies,* 2d ed. (London: Faber, 1955).

The Party System

It is not literally true to say that Britain has a two-party system. Besides the two major parties, Conservative and Labour, the Liberals have never contested fewer than a hundred seats in any postwar election, and seats have also been fought by Communists, Welsh and Scottish Nationalists, members of even smaller groups, and a handful of people independent of any party. Moreover, splits in existing parties (such as those affecting the Liberals in 1886 and 1932), or the rise of new organizations (like the Irish Nationalists in the nineteenth century and the Labour party in the twentieth), may at any time add to the number of parties.

It is substantially correct, nevertheless, to talk of a two-party system in the sense that this appears to be the parliamentary norm and that, whenever it is departed from, it tends to re-establish itself. Historically it was in the interests of the crown and its chief advisers to try to unify their supporters, which encouraged a similar unification among their parliamentary opponents if they were to be successful. Once established, such polarizing tendencies are in some degree self-perpetuating. The desire to defeat its former comrades may impel a break-away group to adhere closely to the other major party, from which, in time, it becomes barely distinguishable. Thus the Liberal Unionists and later the Liberal Nationalists have been absorbed by the Conservative party in all but name.[6]

The desire to remain one of the two chief contenders for office makes the established parties anxious to prove third parties unnecessary by embracing their policies so far as their own principles and supporters will allow. A third party will probably have difficulty in maintaining a "balance of power" role in Parliament. It is liable to find that only one of the major parties is sympathetic to its aims, in which case it becomes increasingly dependent upon that party, or else is forced into unconstitutional action, as happened eventually to the Irish Nationalists. Alternatively, if it is in a position to determine which of the two other parties shall form a government, it is not only subjected to internal division about which party to support, but it is also liable

---

[6] In Scotland the Conservatives, who had little support there before being joined by the Liberal Unionists, are called Unionists officially, as are their allies from Northern Ireland (Ulster Unionists). The Liberal Nationals maintain a degree of organizational independence in Parliament and elsewhere— but to the outsider this is their only distinctive feature.

to become increasingly unpopular with the electors for confusing the issue, blurring the lines of responsibility, or for making the "wrong" choice of government. The Liberal party almost certainly suffered in this way after it had first supported, and then later withdrawn its support from, the minority Labour governments of 1924 and 1929–31. On top of all this, the ascendancy of the two major parties is ensured by the electoral system and, since the end of the war, by the electorate's manifest dislike for any diversion from what it apparently regards as the main issue, namely the decision as to whether there should be a Conservative or Labour government in the succeeding Parliament.[7] We may therefore concentrate upon these two parties in discussing party organization.

The leaders of the Conservative and Labour parties in the House of Commons are either past, present, or potential prime ministers. The other leading figures in each party will be past, present, or potential members of a government. Whether in office or in opposition, therefore, the parliamentary party leadership is normally the most powerful single group within each party. Its position is bolstered, too, by the tradition of "collective responsibility" when in office,[8] according to which all the members of a government must be prepared publicly to defend the whole record of the government or resign. That is, they must present a united front to the public. To lend conviction to its claim to be the alternative government, the opposition party must show that it, too, is capable of promoting a correspondingly cohesive team. Politically, unity almost always brings strength. But the strength of this leadership is not unlimited, nor its power unrestrained. They can be maintained only by constant effort, for they derive not from blind followers but from critical supporters whose allegiance is never unconditional.

The leader of each party is selected by his colleagues in Parliament. In the Labour party the Members of Parliament

[7] No independent members were returned from 1945 through 1955, and during the same period the proportion of the total poll won by the two main parties steadily increased. In the House of Commons elected in 1955, only the six Liberals were independent of the two major parties. The 1959 election added one Independent Conservative, and produced a slightly larger vote for some Liberals, which may indicate the beginnings of a new party alignment. Whether it develops depends, however, upon the success of the Labour party in its attempts to acquire a more potent electoral "image." (For a fuller discussion of the prospect before the Labour and Liberal parties, see Chapter 11 below.)

[8] See Chapter 4 below.

choose their leader by ballot (repeated annually when in opposition); but after his initial election a leader has only once been opposed, in 1960. The deputy leader and the other members of the parliamentary committee are also chosen by annual ballot when in opposition, although it is becoming clear that a Labour prime minister would not feel bound to appoint every member of the committee to an important ministerial post, despite the practice of referring to them collectively as the "shadow cabinet."

In the Conservative party the election is carried out by a larger body, including peers and prospective candidates for Parliament as well as Members of Parliament themselves, and it is not finally ratified until and unless the leader is appointed prime minister by the monarch. (When the party is in power and it is a change in prime minister which is in question, the "election" takes place only *after* the monarch's choice has been announced.) As the procedure when in power suggests, the election appears to be a mere formality. The real decision seems to be taken by the elder statesmen of the party in consultation with the party whips, one of whose primary functions is to interpret the will of the party, and particularly of its members in the House of Commons.[9] It is then up to the leader to appoint the other members of a Conservative cabinet or "shadow cabinet." Not even the latter is elected, but a Conservative leader nevertheless always heeds the wishes of his parliamentary supporters. Substantially, despite these procedural differences, it may be said that in both parties the leader leads by courtesy of the parliamentary party.

There is a similar difference in the formal relations between the leadership and the annual party conference, reflecting the different origins of the extra-parliamentary party organizations. The Conservative party in Parliament antedates its national organization, and any attempts to give the latter a greater than ancillary status have failed. The Labour party, on the other hand, was established in 1900[10] jointly by trade unions and Socialist organizations as their parliamentary spokesman. The constitution of the party still embodies this conception to the extent, for example, that the annual conference is stated to be the supreme policy-making body, whose decisions must be implemented by the other party organs, including, it might be thought, a Labour

---

[9] For more about the whips, see Chapter 4 below.

[10] As the Labour Representation Committee. It did not adopt the name of the Labour party until 1906.

cabinet. The practical need for day-to-day policy decisions in Parliament and the centripetal influence of the cabinet system have undermined this original intention, but have not been able to free Labour leaders from a heavier and more difficult task of "managing" their conference than faces the Conservatives. By and large they have succeeded: but only so long as the leadership is fairly united and can maintain sufficient support among the largest trade unions.

In Labour conferences all organizations represented wield a block vote—i.e., they cast, in one block, as many votes as they have members affiliated with the Labour party, without regard to the divisions of opinion within the organization.[11] The decisive voting power then rests with the unions, which accounted in 1958 for over 5,500,000 out of a total of 6,500,000 party members, and particularly with the seven largest unions, which, when they are all in agreement, command a majority.

Through the National Executive Committee, which is elected by the conference and normally includes important parliamentary and union leaders, and by more informal means, the party leaders try to ensure that they and the unions remain more or less in step. In this way the conference is usually induced to endorse all major policy decisions, although not without an occasional debate of great dramatic interest, and often at the cost both of frustrating the constituency organizations through which the individual members make their views known and of creating an unattractive, if somewhat distorted, public image of ruthless, even irresponsible, trade-union power. The party has prided itself, however, on the public way in which its major decisions are reached, and its equally public acknowledgment of its political and financial dependence upon the trade-union movement.[12] Conversely, it attacks the Conservative party for its failure to disclose the sources of its income, or to acknowledge its widely believed dependence upon the business world in respect to both policy and finance.

In both parties, then, the leaders emerge from the parlia-

[11] Cf. the system of block voting by states in an American presidential election.

[12] In the year ended December 31, 1958, the unions contributed over five-sevenths of the total income accruing to Labour's general fund and almost all of its General Election Fund. This does not include contributions to the local party organizations in each constituency. Martin Harrison's *Trade Unions and the Labour Party since 1945* (London: Allen and Unwin, 1960) is now the indispensable work on this subject.

mentary conflict, and are immediately (but not wholly) dependent for their position upon their parliamentary colleagues. They
must also be acceptable to the business and trade-union sources
of finance. And by no means least, they must be acceptable to the
party militants, i.e., the actual rank-and-file members. Their support is necessary not only because of their participation in the
conferences, for all that it may be secured or alienated there
(in which fact, perhaps, lies the main significance of conference).
It is necessary rather because of the other bases of rank-and-file
influence: they constitute the indispensable, and almost entirely
voluntary, helpers who do the actual work of the parties in the
constituencies; and they select the party candidates for all elections. These local party workers are enticed into the party to some
extent by its policies and personnel. Once in, however, their
attitudes and their morale will influence both—primarily through
their contacts with and importance to the successful party candidates. And once in, they are subject to little control from the
central party organization and leaders. In effect, central control
consists only of the power to refuse to recognize a candidate or
constituency organization as authorized users of the party label,
and to expel, or refuse to sanction the local expulsion of, individual party members. The power rarely needs to be used, and
then mainly in the Labour party (subject to ratification by its
conference), but it is an indispensable weapon in the hands of
any party jealous for its reputation and anxious to maintain a
noticeable degree of political homogeneity.

Both parties thus contain hard cores, in terms of interests
and members, from whom they draw their finances and their
workers, and who limit as well as inspire party policy. It is one of
the tasks of their leaders to reconcile the inevitable conflicts
within the party cores, and then to reconcile the interests and
attitudes of the cores with those of the electorate at large. Success
in this task is neither easy nor inevitable. But it is recognized to
be the duty primarily of the parliamentary leaders to accomplish
it, and in both parties the basic difficulties are similar. The important differences between the parties lie more in the tone and
atmosphere of the intraparty struggle than in the constitutional
provisions.[13] The Conservatives are apparently prepared to allow
more discretion to the leader, while being no less prepared to
change him; and Labour members appear to demand more con-

[13] See R. T. McKenzie, *British Political Parties* (London: Heinemann,
1955).

sideration from their leader, while being no more prepared to change him.[14]

The most important feature of the party system is, of course, that it provides and supports governments. It is this, as has been suggested, that largely determines the location of power and initiative within the parties. It is also, with their work in organizing, mobilizing, and educating the voters, the parties' great justification. This aspect of the parties' role is most evident in the House of Commons, where they provide the leaders from whom governments are formed, and then, in the case of the majority party, vote loyally and regularly in support of government policy. Most distinctively and effectively, however, it is the very fact of there being only two major parties which, in conjunction with the electoral system, normally assures a government of a fairly stable and coherent majority, large enough to facilitate the conduct of business and to free the cabinet from continuous preoccupation with the purely tactical problems of maintaining that majority.

The two-party system ensures, also, that at any given moment there exists both a government and a clear alternative government.[15] The government is thus constantly reminded of its mortality and the need to justify its actions; the opposing party is thus constrained, not only to criticize and oppose in the hope of supplanting the government, but to do so in a responsible manner fitting to a party which may itself have to contend, as the next government, with the same problems; and the electorate is thus presented continuously with a concrete choice—the government or the alternative government—which encourages their sense of responsibility, as well as giving them the final power of decision. The party system, in other words, normally ensures both organized support for and organized opposition to the government of the day. The importance of this confrontation and interplay receives formal recognition in the official title of Her Majesty's Opposition for the alternative party, and a state salary for its leader.

[14] Since Labour's defeat in the 1959 election many members of the party have urged some constitutional revision intended, among other things, to increase the powers of the parliamentary party, including the leader, and to lessen the impact of the unions' block vote.

[15] That is, it ensures this result to the extent that any institution can do so. No machinery can ensure that an opposition party will in fact appear to the electors as sufficiently united, responsible, wise, and different to justify serious consideration as an alternative government.

The parties are able to sustain this organized confrontation only to the extent that they are united in the support of their leaders and policies and so, at least on all major questions, can rely upon their members to vote solidly together. The requisite degree of party voting in the House of Commons is not simply a product of central "discipline," but rather of party loyalty, of the constitutional relations between the cabinet and its majority, and of a significant degree of agreement upon the distinctive principles for which each party stands.[16]

There is, as there must be in any viable democratic system, considerable common ground between the programs of the two parties, and a near-identity of approach among the most moderate members of each. Nevertheless, the parties are divided by conflicts of doctrine. The Conservative party is imbued with the principles of respect for (existing) authority and tradition, Burkean reform, and, partly consequentially, private ownership of productive wealth. The Labour party, on the other hand, stands for a greater degree of equality, social reform, and public control or ownership of productive wealth as a means to the construction of a (variously defined) democratic socialist society. These principles in part provide criteria for party membership, and in part reflect the aims and desires of the party members and the interests which form the party cores. In neither party are the principles kept entirely pure and unsullied by electoral or other practical considerations—although the Conservatives have the advantage that their principles lend some endorsement to such empirical adjustments, whereas Labour's principles are less readily accommodating. But it is impossible to understand either party without appreciating the importance of its doctrinal tensions and commitments, which may exacerbate as well as assuage the other conflicts within its ranks.

Voting Behavior

The British elector votes for the party rather than the man. Indeed, it is often asserted that the personality of the candidate is not likely to attract, or repel, more than five hundred votes. This is probably too small a figure in some cases, but at best the candidate's individual qualifications are much less influential than his party label.

The reason for this does not lie primarily, if at all, in the slavish partisanship of the voter. It is the natural result of the

[16] See the further discussion below, Chapter 4.

fact that the basic electoral issue is the party composition of the government during the succeeding parliament. Since the House of Commons may be referred to as the "electoral college" for the prime minister, the voter will necessarily be vitally interested in the parliamentary voting intentions of each candidate. Since the prime minister is normally a party leader, chosen because of his party support, this means that the voter must pay great attention to party labels. More than that: any nonparty or minor party candidate is at a considerable electoral disadvantage simply by virtue of the fact that his intentions are unclear (or unreliable) or that he will not be in a position to influence the choice of prime minister.[17] Of course, unlike the members of the Electoral College for an American President, M.P.'s are not only electors. They are also the continuing members of a representative assembly with other important duties. For this reason the qualifications of each candidate are given some attention by a portion of the electorate and, in part consequentially, by the party which nominates him.

Candidates, being primarily party standard-bearers, are all expected to give public support to their parties' policies. This means that the same basic issues and arguments, by and large, are presented in each constituency. Since, as we have seen, Britain is a fairly homogeneous society, with centralized governmental and economic systems, it is not surprising that remarkably uniform swings of opinion throughout the country have been distinctive features of recent elections. General elections are thus truly national events—with a national decision reached on national issues.[18] Only when the fate of a government is not involved, that is to say, at isolated by-elections, do the voters appear ready to give support to minor parties or to pay much heed to purely local and personal matters. Not even at by-elections, however, does one encounter radical departures from national voting habits.

The basic appeal of the two major parties is, apparently, to socioeconomic class.[19] It is true that women, people over fifty,

[17] If he were, he would be a member of a majority group (actually or potentially), and voted for on that ground.

[18] Another aspect of the national character of elections is the absence of any "locality rule" about the residence of candidates. Most M.P.'s will have stood for more than one constituency in the course of a long career, and rarely will an established parliamentary figure be allowed to remain for long out of the Commons, should he be defeated, before being returned from a safer constituency or, as a last resort, being given a peerage.

[19] See such electoral studies as: John Bonham, *The Middle Class Vote* (London: Faber, 1954); R. S. Milne and H. C. Mackenzie, *Straight Fight*

and non-trade unionists, for example, are slightly more likely than others to vote Conservative, but none of these factors is nearly so closely correlated with party support as class. Benney's study of Greenwich voters in 1950 found this typical relationship between voting and occupation (as classified in Glass's studies of social mobility)[20]:

Voting patterns of occupational classes

	Occupational categories			
	1–3	*4*	*5*	*6–7*
Conservative	66%*	80%*	28%	17%
Labour	23%	16%	66%	80%
Liberal	4%	4%	6%	3%

* The difference in the percentages voting Conservative in the first two columns may be due to a sampling error.

If account is taken also of the class in which the individual rates himself, whether middle or working class, the correlation becomes yet more striking:[21]

Voting patterns according to subjective class ratings

	Occupational categories					
	1–4		*5*		*6–7*	
	Subjective rating					
	M.	*W.*	*M.*	*W.*	*M.*	*W.*
Conservative	74%	67%	59%	15%	37%	13%
Labour	15%	27%	31%	82%	52%	85%
Liberal	11%	6%	10%	3%	11%	2%
NOS. (= 100%)	(85)	(18)	(71)	(74)	(27)	(201)

M. = middle class.   *W.* = working class.

(London: Hansard Society, 1955), and *Marginal Seat* (London: Hansard Society, 1958); Mark Benney and others, *How People Vote* (London: Routledge and Kegan Paul, 1956); A. H. Birch, *Small Town Politics* (London: Oxford, 1959); and the series of articles by Mark Abrams, "Why Labour Has Lost Elections," *Socialist Commentary*, 1960.

[20] *Op. cit.*, p. 103.
[21] *Ibid.*, p. 118.

All the published studies of British voting behavior support the same general conclusion: that the way a British elector votes is closely related to his social and occupational status and, more particularly, to the way in which he sees his own status. Moreover, this conclusion is not simply a "discovery" made by political analysts. The electors themselves tend to characterize the Conservative party as predominantly representing the middle or upper classes, and Labour, the working classes. Highly significant were the suggestions that, in category No. 5, party allegiance influenced the way in which people rated their own social status as well as vice versa.

Birch[22] has suggested that the key factor in any explanation of this correlation between class and party is the degree of economic security attaching to each type of occupation. A top manager, paid a yearly salary, with ample provision for holidays, pension, and sick pay, and with reasonable (from his point of view) security of tenure, would be more likely to support Conservative "free-enterprise" policies; and an unskilled laborer, paid by the hour and employed by the day or week, with no job-provided "fringe" benefits, would be more susceptible to Labour's emphasis on welfare and full employment.

Whether or not this is the proper explanation, it is undeniable that despite much class-war rhetoric (in public and private among many Labour supporters, and usually only in private among Conservatives) we are not confronted here with a militant "Marxist" class war. For one thing, all parties draw their support from all classes and occupations: in particular, much of the Labour leadership is middle class, and the Conservative party could not win any election without substantial voting support among manual workers and even among trade-union members. There is every indication, too, that movements of support from one party to another occur in all classes together. In this sense, too, opinion swings are national. The differences between the voting preferences of different classes are important, but they are still differences of degree only. The great majority of voters appear also to believe that the party of their choice, whichever it is, is best not only for their own class and supporters, but also for other classes and their political opponents.[23] This is hardly compatible with a belief in an inevitable conflict of class interests. It also emphasizes the parties' need to rationalize sectional inter-

[22] *Op. cit.*, pp. 104–5.
[23] See Benney, *op. cit.*, pp. 120–23.

ests in terms of national policy or, less cynically, the fact that major parties must be concerned to shape their policies at least as much to national problems as to meeting the wishes of their core organizations—if it is possible clearly to distinguish between them.

It is the general impression or "image" presented by the parties, not a detailed assessment of their approach to each issue, which seems to be most influential in winning or keeping votes. Particular issues may, of course, determine the choice of some electors. For most voters, however, it seems that particular issues are important mainly insofar as they symbolize the distinctive approach of a party, or to the extent that they are "annexed" [24] by one party and thus incorporated in its image. Thus the Conservatives managed to annex the theme of "prosperity" in 1959, while Labour suffered electorally from its identification with nationalization, as it had previously benefited by annexing the issue of full employment.

The period since 1945 has been marked by small voting "swings" between the parties from one election to the next, and by a relatively even division of support between the two major parties. Even after the 1959 election the Labour party required a national swing of only 4 per cent in order to regain office. But a small change in total vote may conceal an appreciably larger number of individual shifts, some (even most) of which may be canceled by shifts in the opposite direction. Nevertheless, the number of voters prepared to alter its party allegiance seems to have been comparatively small. In one Bristol constituency only 19 per cent of those interviewed confessed to having voted for more than one party over the three elections 1945, 1950, and 1951; and in Greenwich (1950) only 8 per cent of those interviewed switched parties in the three months before polling day.[25]

It is easy to overrate the political stability of the British electorate. As well as the 8 per cent who switched parties in Greenwich, about 15 per cent of those interviewed either crystallized their attitudes or decided to abstain from voting in the three-month period surveyed. Bonham, moreover, basing his calculations upon Gallup Poll surveys for the period 1945 through 1951, depicts a more fluid situation, with large shifts between the two major parties on the one hand, and, on the other, either abstention or voting for a minor party. The elec-

---

[24] The term comes from Milne and Mackenzie, *Straight Fight*, pp. 136–38.
[25] See Milne and Mackenzie, *op. cit.*, and Benney, *op. cit.*, respectively.

tion results between the wars suggest that, under sufficiently dramatic circumstances, the British electorate may be more volatile. The deaths of old voters and the coming of age of new ones introduces another element of political flexibility. The British electorate may not be prone to sudden and unpredictable changes of allegiance. But it is clear that a significant shift of opinion has taken place over the whole period 1945–59, and that the situation in the 1960's is far from frozen.

The Campaign

These electoral studies have rightly deflated earlier notions about the nature, purpose, and importance of the election campaign. This is salutary if, by so doing, it is intended only to emphasize that the electorate does not wait, open-minded (and empty-minded), for the campaign before coolly and rationally assessing the comparative merits of competing party platforms. Elections are not isolated and enclosed events impinging upon people who, at other times, have no ideas or emotions about political happenings, nor are they a kind of "open season" for political conversions. It is therefore well to remember that perhaps only 5 to 10 per cent of the electorate go to political meetings and that they are mainly already committed, although rather more read some propaganda, while still more are reached by radio or TV. It is also of importance that those who change sides at election time tend to be less rather than more interested or learned in political affairs. It would nevertheless be unwise dogmatically to assume that an election campaign is a sheer waste of money and effort.

The modern campaign is directed largely to "getting out the vote" and, in particular, to doing so in the "marginal" constituencies whose small majorities (two or three thousand or less) invite strong attack by the prospect of relatively easy victories, the prize for which may well be a majority in the House of Commons. (In the era of small swings, only the "marginals" have seemed to offer the possibility of change.)

The campaign may be divided into two parts—the national and the local. The former consists partly of speeches by the leading party figures, delivered at strategic points throughout the country, chosen with a special eye on the marginal constituencies whose candidate may be helped by such visits, and partly by use of the press, radio, and TV, in which the target is the electorate as a whole. The newspapers vary in the extent and fairness of their coverage, as well as in editorial advice, although the greater part of the press is Conservative in approach.[26] The radio and television authorities, on the other hand, must, by statute, give fair and equal opportunities to all parties. In practice this means that equal time is given to the Conservative and Labour parties, and considerably less time to the others, depending upon the number of seats they are contesting. The details are arranged beforehand by the broadcasting authorities and the parties. Radio and TV time, although rationed, is free, apart from any incidental expenditure on films or other "visual aids." All broadcasts had been nationally organized and presented up to the 1959 election. Then, in addition, many candidates appeared in discussions on regional TV programs. (The year 1959 also marked the first time in which radio and TV gave news coverage to particular constituency campaigns as well as to the activities of the national party leaders.) For many, radio and TV provide the principal, and in some cases only, direct contact with the campaign. Their precise impact is not known, but they appear to have considerable influence upon the degree of political awareness, if not so noticeably upon the way in which people vote.[27]

The national campaign interacts continuously with the local one, although the methods differ. Locally, the parties make use of three principal weapons. The political meeting, particularly in large rural constituencies, is still a mainstay, although open-air loud-speaker meetings, and speeches in factories and institutions, are being used increasingly, to some extent at the expense of formal meetings in local halls and schoolrooms. The essential feature of these meetings is a speech by the candidate, followed by a period for questions from members of the audience —with the majority of questions usually coming from opponents[28] or, less frequently, the genuine doubter. Despite small attendances, the meeting still provides the main opportunity for a candidate to make some impression upon a constituency and, if successful, to get people talking.

The printed word is the second local weapon. Posters, pamphlets, and leaflets (most of them obtained from party headquarters, but some calling upon the elector to "vote for Smith")

[26] See the section on the press later in this chapter.

[27] See the discussion in D. Butler and R. Rose, *The British General Election of 1959* (London: Macmillan, 1960), pp. 75–97, and in J. Trenaman and D. McQuail, *Television and the Popular Image* (London: Methuen, 1961).

[28] It is not unknown for as many as nine-tenths of the questions asked to emanate from a handful of opponents present only for this purpose.

are spread as widely as time, labor, and money permit. In addition, each voter receives a letter or message from each candidate. In this Election Address, a more or less formal or personal appeal or sometimes a mere recital of party policy is briefly set out, along with a photograph of the candidate, some biographical information, and possibly notice of meetings to be held. The Election Addresses are delivered free by the post office (if of the correct size and weight), but their printing may be the largest single item of electoral expenditure. They also seem to be the most widely read items of election literature.

Finally, the local campaign includes door-to-door canvassing. The purpose is sometimes to introduce the candidate. Basically, however, the aim is simply to discover where supporters live, so that on polling day they may be encouraged to visit the polling stations—if need be, in party cars. Time and labor being always short, little or no attempt is made to persuade people on the doorstep, but only to discover their voting intentions, and each party tends to concentrate on the type of housing in which they expect to find the greatest numbers of their own supporters. Thus middle-class Labourites or Conservatives living in municipal housing estates may receive no visit from their own party's representatives.

Both nationally and locally the campaign can be directed to any or all of the following ends: encouraging party workers and supporters, strengthening doubters, crystallizing the attitudes of waverers, laying the basis for future conversions by intensive persuasion and propaganda, and organizing the electorate to ensure the maximum turnout on polling day. Only to a limited extent will the means used to further each end be similar. Recently, as we have said, all parties have tended to emphasize the need to get out the vote and rally the faithful during the campaign, and, before it begins, to frame their policies in such a way as to win the "floating voter" in the marginal seats. In both respects the Conservatives have tended to be more proficient than Labour —and inevitably so: a reform party can only win if it also raises issues with a view to conversion and crystallization.[29] While it may be true that, at any given election, organization wins more votes than argument, it is not and cannot be true in the long run.

[29] At least since the turn of the century, furthermore, there has seemed to be a permanent Conservative majority in England which is only exceptionally overcome, and which radical strength in Scotland and Wales does not entirely balance.

Two other factors have important effects upon the character of the campaign. The first is that no mention of party is to be found on the ballot paper or within the polling station. One of the major purposes of every local party must therefore be simply to make known the name of its candidate. The political parties as such are not known to or regulated by the law. Only the candidate, the election agent, and their helpers and voters have a definite legal status in an election. The legal limits upon the candidates' activities and, particularly, their expenditure constitute the second factor. The maximum permissible expenditure on the campaign is £450 plus 1½d. per elector in urban and 2d. per elector in rural constituencies[30]—which means, in effect, a maximum of about £1,000 to £1,500 ($2,800 to $4,200) per candidate. In fact, the maxima have rarely been spent, and their importance lies more in the corresponding limits upon type of expenditure (nothing which would smell of bribery being permitted) and upon the provision that this should include all expenditure *on behalf of* the candidate, and not only expenditure incurred or authorized *by* him or his agent. The advantage accruing to wealth is thus limited. But political expenditure *between* elections and even expenditure during a campaign which is not linked to a particular area or candidate so far have been excluded by the courts from comparable legal regulation. During the 1959 election this was the subject of intense criticism by the Labour party, which declared its intention of amending the law if returned to office. It is, in any case, arguable how important different levels of party expenditure have been, given the restrictions on the type of political spending which is permitted and, in particular, the prohibition upon the use of paid canvassers during the campaign. The importance may increase, however, after the Conservatives' apparently successful use of advertising in the months preceding the 1959 election.[31]

Whatever may be accomplished by the parties during an election, it will probably be less important than what happens between elections. However much, or little, the campaign can educate or galvanize the electorate, the effectiveness of each party's efforts will ultimately be determined by the voters' own experience of the record of each party and of life under the exist-

---

[30] Plus £100 ($280) for the candidate's personal expenses.

[31] For detailed discussions of the finances of the pre-election campaign of 1957–59 and of electoral law as it bears on this and other points, see Appendices III and V to Butler and Rose, *op. cit.*, pp. 241–55 and 280–81.

ing government.[32] By "experience" here is meant, of course, the personal experience of each voter and that of his relatives, friends, and acquaintances (most "conversions" being the result of the influence of such persons), plus such awareness of other events as may be obtained through the press and over the air.

Media of Communication

More books per head of population are published each year in Britain than in any other country in the world. In 1957 over 20,000 titles were published, 14,000 of them new, by some 2,000 publishers. More daily newspapers are sold per head of population than in any other country—over 600 for every 1,000 inhabitants, according to a UNESCO survey published in 1953, against less than 400 in the United States, although the United States consumed more than twice as much newsprint. By 1958, 56 households in every 100 owned television sets and over 90 had radio receivers. Despite this massive exposure to the means of acquiring information, the ignorance of parts of the public survives unscathed. In Greenwich in 1951, for example, of some 900 people interviewed, a third did not know the party of their M.P. (only a quarter knew his name); of the members of a girls' club interviewed on TV in 1957 not one could offer any clue as to the identity of Mr. Nehru, and only one knew who Mr. Eisenhower was; and, in 1954, of 1,000 people asked to identify five names then prominent in the news, few could place Senator McCarthy accurately, and the man known to most (to 820 out of 1,000) was famed only because of his conviction for murder.[33] On the other hand, any candidate at a parliamentary election who expects to survive question time at his meetings by trusting to that ignorance will certainly be stopped short by encounters with a surprising amount of knowledge in unexpected quarters.

The press

The press probably remains the most extensive and important medium of mass communication. There are about one hundred daily and Sunday papers, of which a fifth are published

[32] "*Existing* government" because a dissolution of Parliament is not accompanied by the government's resignation. The government which advises the holding of the election continues in office at least until the results are known.

[33] See, respectively, Benney and others, *op. cit.*, p. 129; *The Spectator,* November 1, 1957, p. 579; and *The Economist,* April 17, 1954.

in London, and over a thousand weekly or biweekly local or provincial papers. Of the total, eight daily (all morning papers) and eight Sunday papers have national circulations. The smallness of the country and the existence of well-developed transport services from London and Manchester (the principal printing centers), make it possible for a morning paper to be distributed on a national scale, and there is now only a minority of households not reached by at least one national paper, each with an average readership of three people or more per copy.

Only two national papers have direct and explicit connections with a political party, apart from the small-circulation Communist *Daily Worker*. The *Daily Herald*, although published and controlled by a large private firm prominent mainly in the field of nonpolitical periodicals (Odham's Press), is part-owned by, and gives general support to, the Labour party. In 1960, however, the party surrendered all rights of editorial supervision. *Reynold's News*, a Sunday newspaper, is owned and published by the Cooperative Movement, and also supports the Labour party. Neither paper has a large mass circulation, however, nor are they politically distinguishable, in most of their material, from the rest of the popular press.[34] For the most part, the press is independently managed and predominantly conservative in tone, but with the *Guardian* and Sunday *Observer* putting forward consistently liberal opinions.[35]

From the table on the opposite page it will be seen that the dailies are independent of each other, although six of them are linked with six Sunday ones. It will also be seen that only two of the "quality" papers (the name generally used for the *Times*, *Guardian*, *Daily Telegraph*, *Observer*, and *Sunday Times*) are so linked, but traditionally even the *Sunday Times* (which is not connected with the daily *Times*), has kept its proper distance from its less august stablemates.

In the words of the *Report* of the Royal Commission on the Press, issued in 1949, "the gap between the best of the quality papers and the general run of the popular Press is too wide, and the number of papers of an intermediate type is too small." [36]

Since this report the circulation of the quality papers and of the two most popular (*Express* and *Mirror*) has risen, and that

---

[34] *Reynold's News*, however, devotes a greater proportion of its space to serious political news and comment than the *Daily Herald* or other papers aimed at a popular readership.

[35] Although not necessarily supporting the Liberal party.

[36] Cmd. 7700 of 1949, §678.

of the more serious popular papers has dropped; meanwhile the minimum circulation needed to cover increasing production costs continues to rise. Except at the top level, bigger headlines, less overseas news, more gossip and crime stories and less adequate coverage of genuine domestic, social, political, or economic issues, biased selection of fact and its blending with opinion, more features and less strict reporting seem to be the recipe for success. These emphases are even more apparent in the Sunday than the daily papers—sex, crime, and sensation being the staple week-end diet of some two-thirds of the over eighty million readership.[37]

National newspapers in June, 1960 [1]

DAILIES	Politics[2]	Proprietor	Circulation 1947	1958
The Times	Ind.	Col. Astor	268,769	248,248
The (Manchester) Guardian	Ind. Lib.	Scott Trust	over 100,000	178,692
Daily Telegraph	Cons.	Berry family	1,015,514	1,133,585
Daily Herald	Labour	Odham's Press[3]	2,134,566	1,523,334
Daily Mail	Cons.	Northcliffe group (Lord Rothermere)	2,076,915	2,105,988
Daily Express	Cons.	Lord Beaverbrook	3,855,776	4,040,572
Daily Mirror *	Labour[4]	Public company[5] (Sunday Pictorial)	3,702,332	4,526,453
Daily Sketch *	Cons.	Mr. Roy Thompson[6]	772,380	1,223,948
[News Chronicle][7]	Liberal	Daily News Trust	1,623,158	1,267,341
SUNDAY				
Observer	Ind. Lib.	Trust	384,001	638,074
Sunday Times	Ind. Cons.	Roy Thompson[6]	568,346	795,192
[Empire News][8]	Cons.	" "	N.A.	2,161,230
News of the World	Ind.	Public company[5]	7,890,461	6,767,348
The People	Ind.	Odham's Press	4,670,746	4,899,748
Reynold's News	Co-op. and Lab.	Co-op. Press, Ltd.	720,440	367,574
[Sunday Dispatch][9]	Cons.	Northcliffe group	2,061,315	1,834,857
Sunday Express	Cons.	Beaverbrook	2,577,752	3,397,913
[Sunday Graphic *][10]	Cons.	Roy Thompson[6]	952,781	1,185,787
Sunday Pictorial *	Labour[4]	Public company[5] (Daily Mirror)	4,006,241	5,378,242
[Sunday Telegraph][11]	Cons.	Berry family	——	——

[1] Asterisk indicates tabloid newspapers.   [2] Author's labels, not necessarily the same as the newspapers'.   [3] Early in 1961 Odham's was taken over by the Daily Mirror group, which thereby acquired a virtual monopoly of the popular periodical press.   [4] Until 1959 election at least. Since then it prefers the label of "radical."   [5] A public company with no single personal controlling interest, and not connected with other national dailies. However, the Daily Mirror and Sunday Pictorial, each owning at least 20 per cent of each other's ordinary shares, are each other's largest shareholders, and are members of a group which is also the largest publisher of periodicals in Britain.   [6] Taken over from Kemsley Newspapers in 1959. Also Scotsman.   [7] The News Chronicle was sold to and absorbed by the Daily Mail under disquieting circumstances in October, 1960.   [8] The Empire News was sold to and merged with the News of the World. October, 1960.   [9] The Sunday Dispatch was sold to and merged with the Sunday Express in June, 1961.   [10] The Sunday Graphic ceased publication in December, 1960, on the ground that it did not pay its way.   [11] The Sunday Telegraph only began publication early in 1961.

SOURCE: The Royal Commission on the Press, Report, for 1947 circulation figures; and the Newspaper Press Directory, 1959.

[37] See Appendix VII to the Report for a detailed analysis of newspaper content.

In part this dualism must be seen as a result of the develop-ment of a national press. The quality newspapers write for an audience who demand reliable and full information, combined with intelligent comment, on a wide range of serious topics. It is limited in number, but over the nation as a whole it is large enough to sustain several first-rate papers. The rest cater to a mass audience whose range of interests seems to be fundamentally limited to essentially local, personal, or domestic matters within their own experience, or to other matters treated in analogous terms. The "human-interest" story, the deflation of political dis-putes into purely personal rivalries, the "features," are perhaps the inevitable result of writing nationally for a market more attuned to local gossip, yet deprived thereof by modern im-personal urban life, and hungry for some human link with, some interpreter of, the wider and more potent social context. The survival of the local press, albeit under increasing economic dif-ficulties, attests to the impossibility of catering to all genuine local interests on a national scale, just as the apparent need for stories of sex and sensation may attest to the shallow and un-satisfying quality of synthetic "human interest." [38] The national character of the market is thus partly responsible for the exist-ence both of some of the best and some of the worst newspapers in the Western world.

Some of the gaps in public knowledge thus become easier to understand. Nor does the periodical press close them. The three most influential political weeklies—the *New Statesman, Specta-tor*, and *Economist*—between them had (in 1958) a circulation of under 200,000, while no others had a circulation of even 50,000, except for the *Listener* (in which are printed the more serious radio talks on all subjects), with over 100,000. These should be compared with the 9,000,000 copies of the four most popular woman's weeklies, and over 300,000 for a popular movie journal —from none of which can any information or mental stimulus be obtained on serious political questions.[39]

The royal commission could find no evidence of outside pressure from any source or of a deliberate policy of distortion, but only of a willingness (or need) to "give the public what the public will buy," and a failure sufficiently to resist the temptation

[38] On the whole question of modern trends in "popular" culture, see Richard Hoggart, *The Uses of Literacy* (London: Chatto and Windus, 1957), where the point is made that those who claim to cater to popular taste may in fact be seriously underrating (and corrupting) their readers.

[39] The Greenwich survey found that less than one-third of lower-status women were even moderately interested in politics. Benney, *op. cit.,* p. 127.

to lower standards in the interests of commercial success. It proposed the establishment of a General Council of the Press, composed mainly of newspaper people but with some lay members and a paid lay chairman, "to safeguard the freedom of the press" and "to encourage the growth of the sense of public responsibility and public service amongst all engaged in the profession of journalism." [40] In fact, the council has not needed to review the best papers, and has seemed reluctant to censure the others. It has not therefore noticeably advanced its second objective—possibly because the newspaper proprietors vetoed the suggestion to appoint any lay members or a full-time chairman. Nor has it been able to deal with the one major potential threat to the freedom of the press, the renewed movement toward concentration of ownership.[41]

The commission did not feel it necessary to recommend any change in the pattern of ownership and control, nor was it unduly worried about the political color of the press. Neither issue, certainly, is urgent so long as other media of communication exist, so long as the general political climate continues to encourage or permit free criticism and discussion, and so long as one assumes that the primary duty of a newspaper is to give the public what it is most willing to buy. Moreover, it is clear that owning or running a newspaper confers less political influence than once was thought. Politically, too, the conservative bias of most newspapers is probably less influential than the triviality and half-knowledge characteristic of the popular ones. And this seems to be a product of the battle for circulation, not of any deliberate manipulative intention. On the whole, however, and whatever the reason, the press tends to uphold the existing distribution of power, and to hinder rather than help any program of wide-scale social change.

Radio and television

From its inception sound broadcasting has been subject to social regulation. Since 1926 it has been the monopoly of the state-owned, but not government-run, British Broadcasting Corporation, and been financed entirely out of the sale of licenses for receiving sets (in effect a form of earmarked tax).[42] Until 1954 TV was also exclusively its preserve. The administrative control

[40] *Report,* 676–84.
[41] In 1961 a new Royal Commission on the Press was set up to examine this and other problems.
[42] The overseas services of the B.B.C. are, however, financed out of general taxation. As a result they operate under government supervision.

of the B.B.C. lies with a director-general, appointed by and responsible to a board of governors. The governors are appointed and paid by the government for limited terms of office, but once appointed, are independent of the government in almost all respects. They are drawn from people who have reached some distinction in public life other than, and usually exclusive of, party politics. Broadcasting was placed under the control of a public corporation to prevent its misuse by private interests and not to confer additional persuasive power upon the government of the day. Its political independence has, indeed, been a matter of constant public concern and, at least in peacetime, rarely if ever encroached upon. On the other hand it has been criticized frequently for being too afraid of controversy, too lacking in imagination, and, more as a result of these things than of conscious decision, too little inclined to challenge established beliefs and institutions.

It was at least partly because of the B.B.C.'s alleged "stuffiness" that an energetic lobby succeeded in ending the television monopoly and in having commercial TV introduced in 1954.[43] To appease the opposition, however, control of this second network was vested in another public corporation, the Independent Television Authority. The I.T.A. owns the transmitting stations, being financed by payments from the companies which contract to provide programs in the different regions. The I.T.A. is also charged, by law, with ensuring the observance of certain standards of performance. For the most part the companies have been formed by people already established in the popular entertainment and newspaper worlds. They seem to have carried the same basic approach to life into this newer medium, in that a desire to provide mere entertainment takes precedence over their concern to educate or develop the tastes of their consumers. They are financed by the sale of time to advertisers who do not, however, thereby acquire any *direct* control over the programs. The companies' choice of programs must nevertheless be influenced by the need to attract the widest viewing public with which to entice the advertisers into the maximum expenditure.

The result is that the peak viewing hours tend to be filled with films and features and parlor games of little intellectual or cultural content, while the more serious programs (the best of which are popular, enlightening, and stimulating) are allocated to other times. The presentation of the more formal news bulletins on the whole is both interesting and fair—possibly because

[43] See H. H. Wilson, *Pressure Group: Commercial Television* (London: Secker and Warburg, 1961).

they are the responsibility of a division of the I.T.A. itself and not of the program companies. In the new network's favor is the fact that they have undoubtedly succeeded in making the tone of many programs, the B.B.C.'s as well as their own, more lively and, at times, controversial.

The program companies' financial success is now undoubted. The proprietor of one company has described his contract as "a license to print your own money." Not surprisingly, therefore, pressure is now being exerted upon the government to permit commercial radio, too, and to allot the third TV channel (at present the B.B.C. and the I.T.A. have one each) also to the commercial interests. Other suggestions being mooted for the third channel include a "pay-as-you-view" system and the establishment of a second noncommercial public corporation. Those less favorably impressed by commercial TV also maintain that the powers of the I.T.A. should be extended and that it be made to use its present ones more noticeably, to ensure that TV is used to educate as well as merely to entertain, or even to entertain rather than stultify the minds of its viewers.[44]

At present all broadcasting, whether of vision or of sound alone, must by law maintain strict impartiality between the main political parties, both between and during elections. The only criticisms which can be made here are that at times impartiality is interpreted so narrowly as to lead to a failure to educate or inform, and that an avoidance of controversy too easily becomes an implicitly partisan defense of the *status quo*. Nevertheless, there is no doubt that it is possible to obtain a great deal of information and mental stimulus as well as some excellent entertainment from the better programs of both networks. It has even been suggested, not implausibly, that the sober and informed interest of many electors in 1959 owes more to the "telly" than to any other medium of communication.

Despite the many criticisms which have filled the last few pages, it must be remembered that it is possible to find newspapers, periodicals, books, and, to a lesser extent, radio and TV programs to cater to any level of almost any interest, and, in the larger centers particularly, to supplement them by attendance at meetings, lectures, and courses of all kinds. But none of these exist solely to give information to the public and to influence or mold public thought. They also serve the vital functions of expressing public opinion and of articulating public discontent. The press in particular performs an indispensable

[44] See C. Mayhew's pamphlet: *Commercial Television—What Is to Be Done?* (London: Fabian Society, 1959).

service in these respects, with newspapers representing as well as catering to the interests and attitudes of their readers. Thus, at opposite poles, the *Daily Mirror* has for years been anxiously and avidly read by politicians who believe that it speaks for the under-thirty age group, and the *Times* continues to provide, in its correspondence column, something of a national forum for discussing everything from national policy to bird behavior: and, if the *Times* does not now have the pre-eminence and the semi-official status it had, for example, in the nineteen thirties, it is still the first outlet for those at all within the social pale who wish to call attention to some national "scandal" or "disgrace," or to comment upon some event of national interest. All the quality national papers now perform a comparable service, as do the leading political periodicals. It is probably safe to say that no strong current of opinion or discontent can long exist without reflection in the press or on the air—although the more far-reaching or unorthodox criticisms of society are, the longer they will probably have to wait and the more support they will have to receive before they will be given adequate attention.[45]

In favor of the existing media is the fact that the best of them at least operate to keep the prevailing climate of opinion generally friendly to the expert and the learned. It is not sensible to expect nor, possibly, to desire that everyone be expert, least of all in political affairs. Social health demands only that there exist some people knowledgeable and interested enough effectively to stimulate and criticize the government and those in positions of power generally, and that these people be cut off neither from the rest of society nor from the information they require. It cannot be said that, by these criteria, British society is sick. It remains to be seen whether, in the future, the expansion in secondary and university education will be of the right kind and affect enough people to counterbalance the trivializing influence exerted by the less worthy kinds of journalism and mere entertainment. This, however, is by no means an exclusively British problem.[46]

[45] For example, the initial meetings of the Campaign for Nuclear Disarmament were scarcely mentioned in the *Times*.

[46] The theater and cinema have not been discussed here because of a shortage of space and also because, in the author's opinion, neither has as great an influence upon the political and social climate as do the media we have considered. The theater is too highly centralized in London to be widely influential, while the cinema is regarded, and perhaps regards itself, as too much concerned with entertainment. However, the cinema's position

4 - Cabinet Government

The essential features of the modern British system of cabinet government may be stated briefly. The monarch selects as prime minister a man who can command the support of a majority of members of the House of Commons. Normally only one man can do so—the leader of the party which has won the greatest number of seats at the previous general election. The prime minister then appoints (more technically, advises the monarch to appoint) his colleagues to the cabinet and other ministerial positions. He and his colleagues together constitute Her Majesty's Government and on most occasions wield Her Majesty's governmental powers. As such their powers may be summarized as comprising:

a) the final determination of policy to be submitted to Parliament;

b) the supreme control of the national executive in accordance with the policy *endorsed* by Parliament; and

c) the continuous coordination and delimitation of the activities of the several Departments of State.[1]

On coming to office the prime minister has about seventy ministerial positions to fill from the ranks of his supporters in both Houses of Parliament. The majority of those appointed will be members of the Commons, but some must be members of the Lords, and all must be or become members of one or the other.[2] Up to forty of them will be ministers. Thirty will be heads of the various administrative departments and offices. The rest will be either nondepartmental ministers, such as the Lord Privy Seal, or Ministers of State. Neither of these are in charge of departments, but the latter are attached to large and im-

---

may rather be the result of its own censorship: see D. Hill, "Censorship and Dirty Minds," *Encounter* (July, 1960).

[1] The *Report* of the (Haldane) Committee on the Machinery of Government, 1919. In the original the word italicized above was "prescribed."

[2] Either by winning a by-election or being made a peer. During World War II a few men became ministers without any previous parliamentary experience, the most notable being Ernest Bevin, but this is rare.

portant ones and are usually given some special responsibility; one of the Ministers of State in the Foreign Office is specially concerned with the work of the United Nations. In addition, all the main departments will have one or more parliamentary secretaries or undersecretaries[3] to assist the ministers in, particularly, the parliamentary aspects of their duties. The most important members of the administration, however, are those senior ministers who are included in the cabinet, the inner group of fifteen to twenty people, meeting regularly under the chairmanship of the prime minister to discuss and decide the major questions of policy over the entire field of government. The heads of the most important departments are always included, but the precise boundary of cabinet membership is a matter entirely for the discretion of each individual prime minister.[4]

Whenever people talk of "the government" in Britain, they are referring primarily to the prime minister and his colleagues in the cabinet. This has been the practice only since the mid-nineteenth century. Before that "the government" meant " 'Government' by King, Lords and Commons." [5] In law, government is still carried on by these three ancient institutions, assisted, of course, by various servants of the crown, ministers among them. The existence of the prime minister and of cabinet ministers is legally acknowledged, in statutes standardizing their salaries and providing the prime minister with an official country residence, and in letters patent placing him ninth in the official order of precedence. But neither from statute nor from common law can one obtain any idea of the vast powers of the cabinet and its head. It is by convention only that the cabinet has come to occupy its central position in the constitution, as it is also by convention that the doctrine of ministerial responsibility has come to determine its constitutional status and behavior. To this doctrine there are three main aspects. The first is the

[3] The difference in nomenclature is of historic importance only. The older ministerial positions have descended from, and retain the title of, the Secretaries of State who were among the earliest full-time political servants of the crown. The later departments have almost all been placed under a minister, and their juniors are simply termed parliamentary secretaries, the "parliamentary" distinguishing them from the permanent civil-service ones.

[4] What is said here refers to normal peacetime practice. In both world wars, under Lloyd George and Mr. Churchill respectively, special war cabinets were set up along somewhat different lines.

[5] Edward Freeman, *The Growth of the English Constitution from the Earliest Times,* 3d ed. 1876, p. 124.

principle that the cabinet collectively, or some minister individually, shall be responsible for the great majority of the political or governmental acts of the monarch.

The Monarch and Cabinet Government

Under English law the monarch can do no legal wrong (the principle that *rex non potest peccare*). It has, however, been possible to bring certain actions against the monarch's servants, including ministers and their antecedents, for acts in fact done by or at the request of the monarch. Ministerial responsibility, indeed, originally meant little if any more than the ministers were the people to be held legally responsible, if anyone could be, for the political decisions of the crown. One effect was to safeguard the monarchy, at least to some extent, from direct involvement in controversy and thus to protect its superior position. The principle was not, and could not have been, an effective defense against unconstitutional or nonconstitutional action. The turbulent events of the seventeenth century dramatically emphasized this inadequacy. Thereafter the rise of liberal and, later, democratic ideas, the increased power of Parliament, and the accompanying need to devise peaceful constitutional means of changing government policy and personnel made it possible to preserve the monarchy only by steadily restricting its actual powers to govern. This has been achieved, in effect, by extending the doctrine of ministerial responsibility to mean that, in most areas of government, the monarch should exercise his or her powers only upon the advice of ministers supported by the House of Commons.

In the eighteenth century the monarch still exercised a considerable influence upon the selection of the advisers upon whom he had to depend: he could, in effect, pursue any policy for which he could find ministers prepared to accept responsibility, and by changing his ministers he could often secure a change in policy. To this end it was in order for the king to appoint ministers, dismiss them, dissolve or refuse to dissolve Parliament, and attempt to influence the outcome of the resulting elections so as to obtain a majority for *his* government. Even Queen Victoria (1837–1901) regarded it as an "affront" when Lord Melbourne's government was defeated at the polls in 1841. Today monarchs are not personally involved in elections—the choice nowadays being between the government and the *loyal* opposition—nor in any other aspect of the party struggle. The power to govern rests squarely with ministers, whose advice the monarch must normally accept, and who derive their authority to govern from election and not hereditary right.

Today more than ever, perhaps, "ministerial responsibility is the safe-guard of the monarchy. Without it the throne could not stand for long, amid the gusts of political conflict and the storm of political passion." [6] Yet is is argued by some that the queen may still, under certain circumstances, decide which advisers she shall heed. Undoubtedly the formal language of government implies this—but that language frequently misleads.

The doctrine of ministerial responsibility clearly does not and cannot apply to the selection of a prime minister, although it is sometimes imagined that the retiring prime minister gives binding advice about his successor. In fact, he need not even be consulted, nor need his advice be taken. Simply because he is retiring, there is less security against mischievous advice, while there no longer exist any political penalties which can be inflicted upon him. This is, of course, particularly but not exclusively so if his successor must come from another party. To appoint a prime minister is therefore regarded as a personal prerogative (power) of the queen, for all that circumstances very rarely permit the use of any personal discretion. The queen must select someone who will be supported by a majority in the House of Commons, and normally there is but one man in a position to do so: the leader of the party with a majority of seats. Only when there is no such party (or when a coalition government must be formed for some other reason) or when the majority party has no chosen leader is there ever room for royal discretion —and not always then. In fact, only in 1931, when the National Government was formed under MacDonald, and in 1923 and 1957, when a Conservative government had to obtain a new prime minister before its own choice of successor had been made,[7] has the monarch apparently made a real choice. Even in these cases, however, the monarch's choice in effect lay only between two men, and it appears, although not all observers agree on this point, that the monarch in fact did no more than ratify the decisions or preferences of the various party leaders concerned. Should similar situations arise in the future, moreover, there is

[6] From a Memorandum to George V written by his private secretary, Lord Esher, in 1913. Quoted in Sir Ivor Jennings, *Cabinet Government*, 3d ed. (Cambridge: University Press, 1959), p. 338.

[7] Following upon the personal resignations of Bonar Law and Sir Anthony Eden respectively.

ground for arguing that the monarch would more clearly leave the decision to the parties themselves. Some twenty times has a prime minister been selected in the first sixty years of this century; on all occasions except those mentioned the monarch's "choice" has been clearly dictated by the parties and their leaders.

The monarch must avoid the suspicion of partisanship, lest the powers or even the existence of the monarchy become a political issue. So long as the present two-party system lasts, this is best ensured by allowing each party to choose its leader in its own way, and then automatically selecting the leader of the majority party as prime minister. Should a more fluid party system develop, then, like the president in the Third and Fourth French Republics, the monarch would have a more active part to play, although one still limited by the need to remain impartial.

The powers to dismiss a government and to force or refuse a dissolution of Parliament against the advice of an existing government are also sometimes listed among the monarch's personal prerogatives. Even prime ministers, for example, are careful to talk of "advising" or "requesting" a dissolution. However, it is difficult to see how these powers could be exercised in a two-party system without appearing obviously to favor one party as against the other. They cannot, therefore, seriously be considered as attributes of monarchy under normal circumstances. One exception must be noted, however. Should a prime minister who has been honestly and decisively defeated at an election request another immediate election or attempt to govern in the face of a majority in the House of Commons, then the monarch may well refuse the dissolution or dismiss the government. Only thus might it be possible once more to obtain a government backed by the authority of the electorate. It is also probable that, *with a multi-party system,* the monarch would on occasion be entitled to refuse a dissolution to a defeated government when another strong government could be formed without the need for a fresh election. Under such circumstances great care would still have to be taken to prevent an appearance of partiality, but it is only under a two-party system that to deny something to one party must inevitably appear to favor another. Furthermore, if there were a change in the number of parties, it is likely that there would also be a change in the behavior expected of and permitted to the monarch by politicians and the general public.[8]

[8] The precise powers even of constitutional monarchs depend closely upon political circumstances and national custom. Thus, despite the existence of

If it be granted that, as it is often put, the British monarch reigns but does not rule, and that the general principle governing the queen's political role is that of public impartiality and private discretion, then it may be asked: What useful functions does the queen perform? Does she have any important powers at all?

She may attempt personally to influence the advice given to her, upon the basis of the information about the government's deeds and intentions which she receives by right.[9] There is no evidence to suggest that her advice is now a major determinant of government policy. An able monarch who has reigned for many years could, however, acquire a more intimate and extensive knowledge of recent political history than any political figure, and might thus be in a position to give very valuable advice to any government. On occasion the monarch may usefully try to mediate between the parties, as George V tried to bring the Conservative and Liberal parties together over the Irish question on the eve of World War I. He failed, the bases for agreement being too weak. These, like the numerous formal functions (signatures, inspections, receiving ambassadors, and so on) of the monarch, could today probably be as well performed by a non-hereditary and nonroyal head of state, as they are by governors-general and presidents in other parts of the Commonwealth. It does not follow, however, that it makes no difference to British politics that the head of state is in fact royal.

To abolish the monarchy would necessitate, among other things, far-reaching changes in the legal status of ministers and all other public servants who at present rank as servants of the crown, wielding its traditional and vaguely defined powers. To make these changes would probably produce a corresponding change in the whole atmosphere of government which would not necessarily be for the better.[10] Socially it is likely that the introduction of republicanism would have some effect upon the

---

basically similar constitutional rules in the various contemporary European monarchies, there seem to be appreciable differences in the range of activities permitted to the sovereign in, say Belgium, Greece, and the United Kingdom.

[9] See W. Bagehot's famous statement that a constitutional monarch has "three rights—the right to be consulted, the right to encourage, the right to warn." *The English Constitution* (London: Oxford, first published in 1867), Chapter 3.

[10] This is not a subject about which it is easy to be precise. One possible change, however, might be a more arrogant approach by governments who no longer would need to give public deference to a person with a stronger claim to embody, even if not actively to represent, the nation as a whole.

class system, in that hereditary positions in the social hierarchy might be undermined and the prestige of the House of Lords decreased. In and of itself, however, it is much less likely that republicanism would weaken social differences than it is that a more egalitarian society would lead to a less socially exclusive royal entourage. The monarchy, indeed, has proved itself very adaptable socially as well as politically to national developments and, on the whole, is now more affected by social changes than it is likely to determine them.[11]

The most obvious function of the monarchy is to provide color and pageantry in a society wherein neither otherwise predominates. Less worthily, but no less usefully, the royal family seems to provide vicarious splendor and spaciousness for many people whose personal lives are cramped and drab. If at times the members of the royal family seem forced into a glamorous role from some light opera, and at others simply to provide "bread and circuses," yet behind the publicity and occasional artificiality lies an important and genuine symbolic status. They symbolize the continuity of British society, provide a personal embodiment of the nation rather than "the state" (a word with a slightly foreign ring in British ears, and hence rarely used except in a pejorative sense), and are expected to represent the virtues of the British way of life. British history as taught in the schools is divided into dynasties and reigns whose dates are the first to be learned, and whole periods are named after the ruling monarch. To identify with royalty is therefore easy, and to cheer a queen or princess a permissible outlet for national self-love.

It is extremely unlikely that any elected figure with a political past nowadays could attract the same emotional loyalty. What is even more to the point, for a political figure to do so would probably be dangerous. Indeed, it might be said that the greatest contribution made by the modern monarchy is that it attracts to itself some of the deepest nonrational feelings toward authority. It may thus help to preserve the political life of the country both from capricious withdrawals of support and from excessive yearnings for a "strong man." In itself monarchy may seem, at best, an anachronism in a modern democracy. Nevertheless, it is

---

[11] Not even the most ardent royalist need share the evident worry of the Duke of Windsor about the fact that "the decline in the fortunes of the landed gentry has tended to leave the monarch and his court more or less marooned" (see his *The Crown and the People 1902–1953* [London: Cassell, 1953], p. 10), for there is every sign that the court and monarch are seeking a wider social basis, and no reason to doubt the possibility of success.

possible that, in Britain, cabinets owe more to the monarchy than their legal powers, and democracy, more than its institutional forms.

In recent years, it must be recorded, the monarchy has attracted heavy criticism—on the one hand, for not giving a firmer lead to the people; and, on the other, for diverting attention from serious problems. This may be taken as symptomatic more of a growing discontent with certain developing aspects of modern life (the commercializing and cheapening of values over a wider range than merely the monarchy) than of republicanism per se. The monarchy seems now to be dissociating itself from these things and to be emphasizing more serious concerns, including its link with the other members of the Commonwealth, the republics as well as the monarchies.[12] It is too soon, however, to attempt to delineate the effects of present changes upon the character of the monarchy. But if the past is a reliable guide, it may be said that the institution will continue to survive new conditions by adapting itself to them.

The Prime Minister

If any single person today occupies a position of supreme governing power, it is the prime minister. He is principal adviser to the crown and thus also the principal inheritor of its powers. He is usually leader of the majority party as well as head of government. Above all, he it is who appoints the other members of his governmental team. Even if a prime minister retires for personal reasons which do not involve any change in the party situation, it is generally understood that every member of the administration places his office at the disposal of the incoming leader in order to give him a free hand in the construction of *his* government, as it will thenceforth be regarded. Similarly, the prime minister may at any time call upon any member to resign, or may move him to a new post, either to fill a chance vacancy or as part of a more extensive change in personnel (a so-called reshuffle).

Gladstone, the famous nineteenth-century Liberal leader,

[12] There is not space here to examine the nature of these links with the Commonwealth, nor the problems associated therewith. A discussion of them may be found in the present author's "The Crown and the Commonwealth," *Parliamentary Affairs,* XI (2, Spring, 1958), and in the Note to Chapter 10 below. On the more general questions see also his "The Crown and Parliament," *ibid.,* X (3, Summer, 1957).

once said that the first duty of a new prime minister, when deliberating upon the appointments to be made, was "to reach for the butcher's knife." No prime minister, however, can be as free politically as he is constitutionally. He must have an eye not only for the effectiveness of his administration and its inner harmony, but also and above all to its ability to attract and hold the support of his party and the public. For this reason he cannot pass over the other leading figures in his party. There are always some others whom he must include in the cabinet because of the support they command, and not only, if at all, because of their administrative ability. It may be possible to pass over one or even two prominent party leaders, and it may be essential to ignore some of the claims of those who expect office, but the prime minister cannot, politically, ignore all of them, even if he should wish to.

Nevertheless he continues to have the freedom to decide which particular post should go to each of his senior colleagues. His actual freedom will be greater, of course, when he comes to fill the less important posts. In general, it may be said, he is free to build as he wishes so long as the administration as a whole is reasonably representative of the principal political forces within the party and so long as he does not leave any sizable body of influential people outside the administration in a position to make trouble. It follows from this that his powers, certainly in peacetime, will be more restricted in a coalition than in the normal one-party government.

The prime minister's powers extend far beyond those to appoint and dismiss, crucial as they may be. His special status continues throughout his tenure of office. No one who has ever served on any committee can ignore the importance of the prime minister's position as chairman and his power to draw up the agenda. He is frequently the arbiter of disputes between ministers. Subject to cabinet ratification, he may make important decisions on his own and, by announcing them publicly in his capacity as chief spokesman for the government, make the ratification more likely. And, of course, upon his ability and energy depends the general efficiency and morale of the whole administration, a fact which is generally recognized, both by politicians and by the general public.

In part his powers derive simply from administrative necessity: someone must be chairman, prepare the agenda for meetings, supervise the general conduct of affairs, ensure that there is adequate preparation of business before the final decisions are

taken, be prepared to take immediate action, on his own if necessary, and so on. A cabinet of fifteen to twenty members is too
large effectively to direct all the functions of modern government
in formal conclave. (Hence the need for committees and an inner
council as well as for firm leadership from the prime minister.) [13]
There is little doubt that the efficiency of government is seriously
impaired by weakness or indecision on the part of a prime minister. But considerations of efficiency alone rarely suffice to confer and sustain a position of power.

More fundamentally, he draws his strength from the twin
sources of party and public support. As party leader he becomes
both a focus for party loyalty and the chief party spokesman
with the final (but by no means only) voice in the presentation
of party policy and the formulation of the election platform. It is
in his capacity as party leader, too, that he acquires his influence
upon the careers of his colleagues. This influence is, of course,
important even when in opposition (particularly in the Conservative party, as we have seen), but may be crucial when a party
is in office.[14] A Conservative leader, by tradition, has the additional right to nominate to the most important offices within the
party organization (including those of chairman and treasurer),
positions which are filled by election in the Labour party.

It is also because he is party leader that, normally, he becomes prime minister and thus the most important national
leader. As the latter, he is the automatic spokesman for the
nation in international and domestic affairs, the person to
whom people instinctively turn in times of crisis or upon formal
state occasions for an authoritative expression of policy and
opinion. Above all, as national and party leader he is news and,
more than any other politician, will benefit from that tendency
to personalize ideas and organizations which characterizes modern
society. For many, the prime minister *is* the party, *is* the government and, at times, may become the personification of the political nation, as Churchill symbolized and articulated the national resolve to continue the fight in 1940 and after.[15] With

[13] See below.

[14] It is not confined to the filling of ministerial posts. The patronage at
the disposal of a prime minister extends, directly or through other ministers,
to many other positions, including bishops in the Church of England, membership of innumerable committees and boards of all kinds, including the
boards of nationalized industries, and, of course, inclusion in the honors
lists (of peerages, knighthoods, and lesser ranks).

[15] Only rarely is the nation sufficiently united politically for this last
to be possible. It is the monarch, of course, who symbolizes the deeper and

justice Sir Ivor Jennings has described the prime minister as "the keystone of the Constitution." [16]

Great as his powers may be, however, they are by no means unlimited. Political and constitutional necessity combine to ensure that, for the most part, the powers are wielded with respect for the wishes and interests of others. We are not, therefore, confronted with an example of irresponsible power used in defiance of public opinion. Quite apart from the controls exercised by the electorate and public over the activities of government in general, there are others operating within the framework of government upon the discretion of the prime minister in particular.

No powers are legally vested in the prime minister as such, but only in individual ministers or in the crown. Occasionally a prime minister will also take command of a department,[17] but normally his only other position is that of First Lord of the Treasury. This was at one time the most important ministerial position politically because it controlled the crown's powers of patronage, so important in managing the Commons. It now carries with it responsibility for that side of the Treasury's work concerned with regulation of the civil service, but is important primarily just because it is the office usually filled by the prime minister.[18] It is as chief adviser to the crown that the prime minister exercises governing power. With this may be contrasted the position of the American president, in whom alone, by the letter of the Constitution, is vested responsibility for the executive power of the federal government. To a greater extent than a president, therefore, the prime minister is constitutionally constrained to work with and through others. These others must, in virtue of this fact alone, place some limit to the prime minister's power, and thus share the burden of responsibility—a fact which may assist him in carrying the load of office as much as it may frustrate his personal wishes.

Their share is the greater because the prime minister is also

---

more lasting bases of national and social cohesion, the "way of life" rather than political co-operation. See the discussion of the monarchy above.

[16] *Op. cit.*, p. 173.

[17] Ramsay Macdonald was his own Foreign Secretary in 1924, and Churchill was his own Minister of Defence during the war and again in 1951. The practice is rare.

[18] For which reason it also carries with it a salary of £10,000 against the ordinary cabinet minister's £5000. The general powers of those few prime ministers who have not been First Lord, however, have not been sensibly diminished.

dependent upon their allegiance for his political strength. He
owes his selection to his ability to secure a majority in the House
of Commons. Effective government thereafter depends largely
upon the willingness with which that majority continues to
support him. Under the prevailing two-party system this means
that he must carry his own party with him, although on occasion he may feel, as Sir Robert Peel did when repealing the Corn
Laws in 1845, that some problem is so important that he must
tackle it even at the cost of splitting his own party.[19] The cabinet, as we have seen, includes most if not all the other party
leaders, each of whom will probably have some personal following. Under normal circumstances no prime minister could hope
to survive the resignation of all or even a majority of his senior
colleagues without himself forfeiting the support of his party.
Mr. Macmillan in 1958 survived the successive resignations of
Lord Salisbury, the Conservative leader in the House of Lords
and for long a powerful voice in the party, and of Mr. Thorney-
croft, the Chancellor of the Exchequer (traditionally a pre-
eminent post in governments); but had they resigned together
over the same issue and been joined by one or two other senior
ministers, the Prime Minister's position would have become
critical. The prime minister must therefore act in conjunction
at least with the more important members of the cabinet, who
thereby become able to control his activities. More positively, the
prime minister's colleagues can always stage a "palace revolution" and, by collective action, force him to resign. It was thus
that Lloyd George became prime minister in 1917, as the culmina-
tion of mounting dissatisfaction inside the cabinet with the way
in which Mr. Asquith had been conducting the war. Lloyd George
in his turn was unseated in 1922 by a revolt among the rank-and-
file M.P.'s in the Conservative party, who thereby forced the party
to leave the coalition which had continued after the end of the
war. Lloyd George thus lost his majority in the House of Commons and had to resign.

The prime minister, given his status as party and national
leader, is normally the least dispensable member of the govern-

[19] Peel carried through the bill he wished only, of course, because he
was able to obtain a majority by the support of a sufficient number of
members of other parties to supplement those of his own who remained
loyal. The action of Ramsay Macdonald in 1931, when he became prime
minister of a coalition government composed almost entirely of Conservatives
and Liberals and opposed by almost all his former Labour party colleagues,
provides another example of an occasion when a prime minister may successfully dispense with the support of his own party.

ment, but as the foregoing examples show, he is not indispensable. Should he differ too greatly from the majority of his supporters and colleagues, or should they come to think that he is a liability to the government and party, then he will be forced to resign. Pressure of work, personal indolence, or other factors may at times lessen the influence of the cabinet as a whole and increase that of the prime minister or the inner council. Nevertheless, it always exerts some influence. When Franklin Roosevelt and Winston Churchill met and drew up the Atlantic Charter in 1940, it was significant that Roosevelt needed to consult no one, whereas Churchill was in constant touch with the cabinet in London and secured its agreement before signing the charter. On one occasion Abraham Lincoln is reputed to have announced the results of a vote in his cabinet as follows: "The *noes,* seven, the *ayes,* one; the *ayes* have it." No British prime minister has comparable power over his cabinet.[20]

Underlying the legal and political restraints on the prime minister's personal power, and bolstering them, are the conventional principles of ministerial responsibility. We must therefore resume our examination of this doctrine.

Collective Responsibility

To say that a minister is "responsible" for some action may mean several different things. It may mean that he is the actual agent, the person deserving praise or blame therefor; in other words, the *author* of the action. Alternatively, it may mean no more than that he is *accountable* for the action in the sense that he is the proper person to be visited with the constitutional consequences or that he is the person under whose authority it was taken. In either case the responsibility may be legal or conventional. In fact, as we have seen, ministerial responsibility was originally primarily a legal concept. Moreover, even up to the eighteenth century ministers were accountable for their governmental acts through the judicial process of impeachment by the Commons before the House of Lords. Nowadays, however, impeachment is never resorted to and must be regarded as unnecessary as well as archaic, following upon the development of

[20] Formal voting in a British cabinet is rare. If a vote is necessary to discover the opinion of the majority because of an almost equal division, the chances are that an attempt will be made to compromise. In other situations, it is the nature and intensity of disagreement rather than its numerical extent which is important. In neither case would a mere counting of heads be very helpful.

the newer conventions about ministerial responsibility. Using the word "responsibility" primarily, but not exclusively, in the sense of "accountability," it may be said that ministers both share in a collective responsibility for the general policies and record of the government and bear an individual responsibility for the actions and record of that portion of the administrative machine placed directly in their charge.

In accordance with these conventional rules about collective responsibility, all members of the administration are expected publicly to support its policies and its actions, regardless of their private feelings on the matter. Should they for any reason no longer be prepared to do so, they must resign their offices (although not, usually, their seats in Parliament). Constitutionally, they cannot acquiesce in a decision and then, at some later stage when, for example, it becomes unpopular, claim that they were opposed to it and thus seek personally to escape the political penalties. In the words of Lord Melbourne, they must all "tell the same story." By the same token, it is impossible for the House of Commons to vote for the removal of a particular member of the government without also voting against the whole government, unless it is clear that the government is prepared to sacrifice that individual either as a scapegoat or because no collective responsibility is involved.[21] Just as, at an election, the voters must judge the government's record as a whole, so must they (and the House of Commons) judge the government as a whole. In short, the administration must stand or fall together. All its members must submit its policy to Parliament, must defend that policy, and, without exception, must resign or submit themselves to a general election if the House of Commons refuses to support it.

To say that the Administration is collectively responsible in the sense of "accountable" is not, however, to say that they are all equally enthusiastic in their support of any particular decision. Within the government as well as outside it, the political choice facing an individual is rarely a simple one of *yes* or *no* to a single question. As with decisions about emigration, divorce, or a change of job, so with one about political allegiance: the choice is never (or hardly ever) between total satisfaction and total dissatisfaction. The principle of collective responsibility does not deny this, nor does it involve the pretense that no arguments or compromises ever take place amongst ministers. It requires only that the arguments be conducted in private. Sig-

[21] See next section on Individual Ministerial Responsibility.

nificantly, the minutes of cabinet meetings (which are themselves confidential) record only the outlines of discussion and disagreement and refrain from naming the individual members who put forward particular arguments. Nevertheless, it is usually possible to obtain a reasonably accurate idea of the general division of opinion on major issues, if not on more detailed ones, from political gossip (often based on some indiscretion), press reports (often based on political gossip), and above all, from the previous political record of the people concerned. This can be of great political and historic, if not constitutional, importance. Because of it, for example, widespread support could be given to Winston Churchill when he became prime minister in 1940, despite his having been a member of the immediately preceding Chamberlain government, whose conduct of the war had just been found wanting.

Collective responsibility does not mean, either, that all members of the administration share equal authorship in that they play an equl part in the decision-making process. It has already been pointed out that the cabinet is the ultimate director of government policy. Other ministers usually attend cabinet meetings when the affairs of their departments are being considered, but this does not mean that they share the general powers of the cabinet. Less obviously, but as significant, there may exist an uneven division of responsibility (authorship) within the cabinet itself. For one thing, the cabinet nowadays makes extensive use of standing committees: on defense, legislation, home affairs, and the like, as well as *ad hoc* committees set up as circumstances require.[22] In most cabinets, moreover, there exists a small "inner council," to use Lloyd George's terminology, consisting of the prime minister and those of his colleagues whom he finds most sympathetic or stimulating, or whom he deems most important. One essential function of this group is to make quick but vital decisions when it is impossible to call a full cabinet meeting in time, and when the prime minister is not prepared simply to act on his own.[23] But its role does not end

[22] The details are never made public at the time, and not always afterward. But for a description of the committee system in the Labour cabinet of 1945–51, see Francis Williams, *The Triple Challenge* (London: Heinemann, 1948).

[23] Today it is not necessary, in order to make swift decisions, for a prime minister to act without consulting his colleagues—although he still may, even on important matters. In the nineteenth century, before the invention of modern means of communication, it might sometimes be imperative—as with Disraeli's famous Suez Canal share purchase.

there. The inner council will tend to take the initiative in all major issues and, *when its members are fully in agreement with each other,* will probably be able to carry the rest of the cabinet with it. Many decisions will thus, in effect, be taken before appearing formally upon a cabinet agenda. On other occasions, particularly in the realm of foreign policy, it is not unknown for a major decision to be taken in this way, and not to be discussed in the cabinet until it is too late to reverse or modify it.[24] The special position of the prime minister, which we have already discussed, represents a further inequality among cabinet members.

It would be a mistake, nevertheless, to conclude that collective responsibility, taken as a statement about the authorship of the administration as a group, is a myth. The above qualifications to the principle mean only that there are degrees of authorship, ranging from the extensive responsibility of the prime minister to the minimal amount borne by the most junior ministers. We have already seen that the cabinet in particular and, to a lesser extent, all members of the government are able to restrain a prime minister. By the same token it may be said that the cabinet is dependent upon the continued co-operation of other ministers. The very fact of joint accountability, moreover, is an inducement to all cabinet ministers to concern themselves with what their colleagues are doing, just as it confers upon them the constitutional *right* to be informed and to express a judgment about the whole range of government business. For their attempts and their failures to control the prime minister and their colleagues the cabinet must be responsible (in the sense of being the authors), as the administration as a whole must be responsible (in the same sense) for supporting or failing to support the cabinet. The degree of authorship may vary, but even in this sense it is impossible to deny the reality or importance of collective ministerial responsibility.

The principle of collective responsibility thus limits the powers of individual ministers, of the cabinet as a whole, and of

[24] One example was the development of the Anglo-French alliance in the years before World War I, when a few members of the government committed the country to a much closer relationship than many others knew of or, when they were informed of it in 1914, were prepared willingly to accept. Another was the conduct of much of British foreign policy by Mr. Chamberlain in 1938–39 (Duff Cooper, *Old Men Forget,* [New York: Dutton, 1953]). It has been suggested that Sir Anthony Eden's Suez policy in 1956 provides another example; it is established that he did not consult all the normal Foreign Office and diplomatic officials, but it is not clear exactly how far and at what stage the cabinet as a whole was kept informed.

the prime minister. It helps to channel the ambitions of politicians and make them less disruptive of that group co-operation which is essential to effective and responsible government. Even the most ruthless "lone wolf" must secure the co-operation of other party leaders if he is to reach the top and, once there, he cannot dispense with them. On the other hand, the principle has also served to increase the power of the cabinet as a whole: against the monarch originally, thereby depriving him of the freedom to play off the leading statesmen against each other, and latterly against the House of Commons, which is thereby constrained to judge and support governments as a whole rather than individual ministers.[25] By the same process, however, cabinets have become more directly dependent upon and accountable to the electorate which, through the party and electoral systems, chooses the government and not, as, for example, in the Third and Fourth French Republics, simply the members of an assembly who then must bargain and compromise between themselves before providing a government.

The principle has other important effects. The coherence of the government exercises a strong pressure upon the opposition to unite in the presentation of a clear alternative set of policies and ministers, for only thus can it make a serious claim to provide an alternative government. Both the government and opposition parties are thus led to seek internal compromises at deeper levels of agreement than might otherwise be the case. While "horse-trading" is probably an inescapable aspect of political life, it cannot form the only basis for co-operation when those concerned must be prepared publicly to defend both sides of any "deal." There is thus more chance that the parties will put forward programs embodying a coherent policy and not simply a compendium of miscellaneous responses to particular pressures. Any democratic government must probably do some things solely in response to such pressure. Yet when every major demand and all important policies must be accepted by a cabinet collectively answerable to a national electorate, then all demands and all policy proposals must at least be dressed up in terms of some potentially national interest. The result of this may, at times, only be to encourage hypocrisy and deception, but in general it must serve to limit the demands made on governments and the policies accepted or pursued by governments.

Vital and beneficial as the British system of collective

---

[25] But see the next section on Individual Ministerial Responsibility.

cabinet responsibility is, its continuance and well-being are not automatically ensured. In 1931 there took place a famous departure from the general rule in the form of an "agreement to differ" about tariffs among the members and supporters of the newly formed National Government. The Conservatives were convinced of the need for import duties to protect industry from the slump. The Liberals were equally convinced that any departure from free international trade would be disastrous. Compromise was clearly ruled out by the nature of the conflict, and ordinarily the result would have been for one or the other to resign from the government. Both sides, however, were still convinced that their continued participation in the government was necessary to combat the financial crisis which had called the coalition into being. They therefore agreed to differ and leave the decision to a free vote of the House of Commons. Tariffs were imposed. (In the following year an extension of the principle and the adoption of discriminatory tariffs in favor of Commonwealth producers—the system of imperial preference—was too much for some of the Liberals. They resigned; the rest continue their conservative alliance as Liberal Nationals until this day.)

Had the agreement to differ become a general practice, and had cabinets continued to stand for both sides of major disputes, it is easy to see that the whole system would have broken down. How, for example, could the government be judged upon its tariff policy when it was both for and against it, and how was a supporter to know just what he was supporting when voting for the government? This experience suggests that the system works best when a cabinet rests upon some genuine agreement on principles, as may be expected only when it is formed from one group of party leaders or, as in wartime, when some single objective obviously transcends all other considerations and the principal means to its attainment are dictated by the objective itself. The cabinet and party systems are thus mutually dependent. In one other way, too, this is true. It is at least arguable that the "agreement to differ," like other unsatisfactory features of British politics in the nineteen thirties, escaped retribution largely because the opposition party was too small, divided, and unattractive to provide a genuine alternative government. Once again it must be stated that in Britain government is the product of the conflict and interplay between government and opposition.

Individual Ministerial Responsibility

It is not only collectively that ministers bear responsibility for the conduct of government. Each minister is also understood to be responsible individually for his own decisions and for all the actions of the government department or office under his control. The general formula to be found in statutes granting powers to the government is that "the minister may . . ." or "the minister will . . ." and not, "the department or ministry may or will . . ." [26] One minor result of this is that letters from a department, even on very trivial matters, frequently begin with some such wording as "I am directed by the Secretary of State to inform you . . . ," a statement which is patently improbable. (It is, of course, possible.) Legally and constitutionally a government department is its minister's responsibility, and its civil-service staff is there simply to do the minister's bidding and carry out his policy.[27]

The actual "cash value" of the concept of individual responsibility is less easily discerned. Certainly it includes the notion that the minister should be the public spokesman and defender of that part of the administrative structure within his competence. It is he or, in his absence, his junior minister who will explain the policy of the department or of the government insofar as it concerns the department, in Parliament and elsewhere; and upon him falls the task of answering criticisms directed at his department. Anything for which he is technically responsible may be questioned or debated in Parliament. A minister does not feel bound to defend the actions of one of his officials, should that action have been taken in defiance of departmental policy or instructions or have resulted from the purely personal incompetence of a junior official. But in all other circumstances the minister is bound to accept the burden of justifying a departmental action, although, quite obviously, he cannot hope even to be informed of all that is done in his name. Nevertheless, just as the cabinet has the final word in all matters of general policy, so may the minister have the last word in his own department. Admittedly a minister may con-

[26] On the other hand, certain powers are vested directly in the four Scottish departments, set up to administer certain services within Scotland in answer to strong nationalist pressure there. All are under the control of the Secretary of State for Scotland, who also has powers vested in him. He is the only minister normally in charge of more than one department.

[27] See the discussion of the civil service in Chapter 6 below.

tribute little to the running of his department beyond his signature and the ability to say *yes* to the advice tendered by his officials. But even when this is known to be the case, it is still the minister who serves as the public target for praise and blame directed at the record of his department.

Historically, the minister was simply the man appointed by the monarch to run one sphere of the crown's governmental machinery. Once it had been accepted that the minister was chosen on the basis of the support vouchsafed him and/or his colleagues in Parliament, however, he became the means whereby the conduct of administration was made at least responsive to public opinion.[28] For it is through questions and discussion in Parliament that M.P.'s may most surely inform themselves about and then criticize the conduct of administration. This is not, of course, the only source of information, but it is only through the minister that M.P.'s may constitutionally attack the policy of a department and it is only over him that they have any direct power. Just as the monarch could and did dismiss his ministers when they ceased to be loyal, faithful, or efficient servants, so traditional constitutional doctrine states that a minister must resign not only if a whole government is defeated, but also if he or his department individually cease to satisfy the House of Commons. More recently, however, strong arguments have been put forward to suggest that this doctrine has no place, strictly speaking, in the twentieth-century constitution.[29]

There is no question but that a minister will resign in the case of a purely personal indiscretion or blunder, unless his departure from office might undermine the strength of the government even more than his staying. Thus Mr. Dalton resigned in 1947 from the post of Chancellor of the Exchequer following a careless and inconsequential disclosure of his taxation proposals before informing the House, and in 1948 a junior minister resigned when he was discovered to have accepted gifts from people under circumstances which might have appeared to involve a corrupt relationship. There is no doubt, either, that a minister will probably not resign, however unpopular his conduct, if he has merely been carrying out government policy and continues to have the support of his colleagues. These are the limiting cases. The resignation, in 1954, of Sir Thomas Dugdale, Minister of

[28] This was as true in the nineteenth century as it is today, despite the different "publics" concerned.

[29] See, in particular, S. E. Finer, "The Individual Responsibility of Ministers," *Public Administration* (Winter, 1956).

Agriculture, is an example of what may be called the middle ground. It followed a report on the administrative mismanagement of a case about which the minister personally knew nothing until late in the episode, and connected with powers compulsorily to purchase land about which his party was not enthusiastic. Admitting responsibility for tolerating the procedures which made the case possible, Sir Thomas also outlined steps taken to end those procedures before resigning. Against this it may be permissible to cite Mr. Strachey's failure to resign from the Ministry of Food after the collapse of Labour's "ground nuts scheme" in West Africa, or Mr. Lennox-Boyd's continuance as Colonial Secretary after the disclosure of negligence in the Kenya prison administration which led to the death of eleven prisoners at the Hola Camp early in 1959. On the other hand, it is certain that the departmental record of a minister will have an important effect upon his subsequent governmental career, even if, for example, his unpopularity or inefficiency are not cited as reasons for his subsequent departure from office.[30] The fact remains, however, that no modern prime minister has been forced to lose an individual minister merely because this has been demanded in the House of Commons.[31]

Individual ministerial responsibility today therefore appears to be no more meaningful in Britain than in the United States, in that the House of Commons seems to have no more power over a minister's tenure of office than has Congress. (If any weight be attached to the Senate's power to withhold ratification of a cabinet appointment, then the Commons seems to have even less power than Congress.) In neither case, however, is the power negligible. Prime ministers and presidents will both, on occasion, remove the political heads of departments because their continuance in office is the cause of more political difficulties than they are willing to face. Despite these resemblances, however, the situations in the two countries are not identical. Congress's inability directly to force the resignation of a secretary is founded

[30] Officially it may be "to make way for a younger man," for "private reasons," or for reasons of "health" or "business." These will, of course, in many cases be the true explanation.

[31] The resignation from the Foreign Secretaryship of Sir Samuel Hoare in 1935 after public anger over his Ethiopian policy was long thought to be such an example. It now appears that he resigned because he was not prepared to join with the cabinet in repudiating past policy. This case is therefore an example of collective rather than individual responsibility. See his autobiography, Lord Templewood, *Nine Troubled Years* (London: Collins, 1954).

on the constitutional principle of the separation of powers, whose spirit Congress's indirect power may appear to violate. The inability of the House of Commons results rather from the extension of the shield of collective responsibility to protect individual ministers from a legitimate exercise of the House's powers. But one must not press this line of argument too far. The very existence of the concept of ministerial responsibility influences behavior. It helps to shape the attitudes of the House and the cabinet, and hence the determination with which they will attack and defend any individual; it provides legitimate grounds for a prime minister to dismiss a colleague, should he desire to, whether because of his record or as a sop to critics of the government; and it is impossible to assess how many mistakes would have been made, or bold ventures initiated, but for the belief that a minister's personal position would suffer therefrom.

At this stage in British constitutional development the accountability of individual ministers directly to Parliament may have been weakened, but that to his party and colleagues has been strengthened at least as much. Indeed, it is probably correct to say that a minister's security today depends almost entirely upon his relations with his party, his colleagues, and his leader. Since their attitude is likely to be influenced by the minister's showing in the House of Commons (of which they form the bulk), it is not clear that the change has relieved ministers of much anxiety or lessened their need for alertness. The individual minister can never be certain, should trouble arise, that the protection of collective responsibility will in fact be extended to shield him from the traditional obligation to resign.

Cabinet and Commons

Hitherto it has simply been stated that the cabinet can normally count upon the continuing support of its majority in the House of Commons.[32] The statement must now be explained.

The rules of the constitution establish an apparent balance of power between the two bodies. Without the support of the Commons for its legislation and its financial requirements, no government could govern. Should a majority therefore express its lack of confidence in the government, either by passing a formal vote of censure or by failing to pass a measure demanded by the government, it must resign—or take the issue to the country by

[32] The House of Lords is unimportant so far as a government's tenure of office is concerned, as we will see in the following chapter.

dissolving Parliament. Thus, as it used to be said, the power of the Commons to dismiss the government is balanced by the power of the government to dissolve the Commons, and it is this second power which, more than any other factor, prevents M.P.'s from voting against a government which hitherto they have supported. This may well have been a correct statement of the facts at least until the late eighteenth century. A new election, at which the influence of the crown or the local magnates could be brought to bear upon the voters, would often result in returning a majority more sympathetic to the crown.

Party loyalty is rightly given pride of place by most modern writers. But they also suggest that "the extent of party discipline" and the power of dissolution are important, if only because "an Election contest will cost the individual member time and money, and at the end of it he may not be returned." [33] This language tends, however, to give a misleading impression of the contemporary situation with its predominantly two-party system.

To appreciate the position, attention should initially be focused upon the factors motivating those among a government's supporters who have decided, or might decide, to support it no longer. There have been many such defecting groups, usually small in number, but only twice in this century have their votes resulted in a change of government: late in 1924, when MacDonald lost an election held because the Liberals had withdrawn their support from his minority Labour government; and in May, 1940, when the adverse votes of thirty-three of Chamberlain's supporters, and the abstention of another sixty, led him to resign, despite the fact that he still secured a majority of eighty-one votes. It is noteworthy that the only actual defeat occurred during a year when no single party had a majority in the House, when in fact a three-party system existed, and that Chamberlain's resignation took place at a period when national unity and a government with wide support were vitally necessary.[34] Neither government was saved by the existence of the power of dissolution.

It may be argued that it is only when the two-party system

[33] The quotations are from Wilfrid Harrison, *The Government of Britain,* 6th ed. (London: Hutchinson, 1960), pp. 36 and 35. Similar statements can be found in most textbooks on British Government. See, for example, Sir Ivor Jennings, *op. cit.,* p. 474, where dissolution is referred to as "a big stick," or B. E. Carter, *The Office of Prime Minister* (London: Faber, 1956), p. 274, where it appears as "this terrifying power."

[34] The debate took place just after the final withdrawal of British troops from Norway and the completion of the German occupation of that country.

is functioning "normally" that the power is effective (when, one might suppose, it is least necessary). If so, there is nothing to indicate that it is effective for the reasons usually given. Few M.P.'s now pay their own election expenses, which are borne largely by the parties. The financial argument, indeed, applies principally to the party organizations and leaders, and is almost always one *against* threatening an election for disciplinary or any other reasons. It is true that an election campaign is or may be exhausting for the individuals concerned, but not dramatically more so than the everyday work of a parliamentarian—except in the case of the prime minister and leader of the opposition, who feel impelled to undertake national speaking tours. Both these points, in other words, are reasons why a prime minister should attempt to conciliate potential defectors rather than threaten them with an election. In order to substantiate the third argument, that defectors are deterred by the possible loss of their seats, it would be necessary to show both that the great majority of rebels have had large majorities, while those in "marginal" constituencies are models of regularity, and that no other explanation can be found for this correlation. The evidence has never been produced.[35]

At best, however, the power to dissolve, as presented, can provide no more than a small part of the explanation of party voting, if only because the reasons put forward apply exclusively to members of the government majority, whereas party voting also characterizes the opposition, even if to a slightly lesser extent. Another approach is therefore indicated if one is to understand why it is that British M.P.'s vote the party line so much more consistently than do, for example, their American counterparts.

Paradoxical as it may seem at first, it is the power to dismiss governments or, rather, the fact that governments nowadays consider that any adverse vote, unless immediately reversed, is tantamount to dismissal, that prevents M.P.'s from defecting. To defect in numbers sufficient to abolish a government's majority may result in the other party's being put in power either immediately or after a new election. Party loyalty, the natural preference for a government drawn from one's own party, is therefore the principal sanction. Party rebels, accordingly, even when sufficiently incensed to vote against their party or abstain from voting, are normally careful to see that their numbers are

[35] Incomplete researches by the author have, at the time of writing, failed even to establish the correlation.

small enough not to imperil the government's majority. After the 1956 Suez invasion fifteen Conservative M.P.'s refused to vote for their government's decision to withdraw from Port Said. They probably would not have done so had the Conservative majority been very small, since the Labour party, the only alternative governing party, would have been even "softer" toward Egypt, and thus, from their point of view, even less worthy of support. Only where all the other differences between the two parties are less important than the question at issue, or when two or more possible coalitions are almost equally desirable or undesirable, is one likely to see any group defecting under circumstances where this would involve dismissing a government.[36] Even then the likelihood of such a revolt will also depend upon the rebels' estimate of the effects of rebellion upon their own futures. These are likely to be adverse since, as we have already seen, third parties and small groups usually fare badly at British elections. (This would, of course, be true whether or not governments had the power to dissolve Parliament, so long as elections continued to take place at all.)

Other forces, internal to the party, reinforce loyalty in help- ing to maintain "discipline," the word normally (if misleadingly) used to designate all the reasons for party solidarity in the House. The fact that M.P.'s are elected in their capacity as party members and supporters, their feelings of community with at least some of their party colleagues, and their reluctance to break old ties and personal associations all play their part. So, too, does ambition. No M.P. who has left one party and joined another has been re-elected since 1945, though Winston Churchill, early in his career, managed this feat twice. The politician with ambition for office will normally tread carefully, therefore, but not too carefully: there are instances of men receiving promotion be- cause of as well as despite rebellion and a proper show of inde- pendence. There is, too, the ultimate possibility of expulsion from the party in Parliament, a sentence which is comparatively rarely passed, but which, if permanent, carries with it the cer- tainty of personal defeat at the next election. None of these factors, and particularly expulsion, is trivial, but not even ex- pulsion can effectively or too frequently be applied against a large group without damaging the fortunes of the party, possibly

[36] Examples include, respectively, the defection of a large group of Liberals to the Conservatives over the question of Irish Home Rule in 1886, which led to the downfall of Gladstone's second administration, and the with- drawal of Liberal support from the first Labour government in 1924.

irreparably. To the other reasons given for voting conformity on
the part of M.P.'s must therefore be added the continuous efforts
of the party leadership to avoid putting too great and too constant a strain upon the loyalty of their supporters.

In contrast to the picture just given, it is often imagined—
and to talk loosely of party discipline rather than loyalty encourages the misconception—that M.P.'s are simply cowed or
coerced into supporting the government with their votes. In one
sense only is this view tenable. No government need resign
except upon formal verdicts of censure and no-confidence or
the rejection by the House of the basic principles of essential
legislation. In recent decades, however, governments have come
more and more to regard any vote, even upon questions of apparently minor detail, as votes of confidence. Indeed, unless it is
formally announced beforehand that a question is being left to
a so-called free vote, it is now assumed as a matter of course that
any defeat in the House of Commons must be reversed or else
lead to the government's resigning or dissolving Parliament. It is
to this point, if anywhere, that criticism of the power of the government should principally be directed.

The common misconceptions of the nature of party regularity are further encouraged by reference to the activities of
the whips, whose very name conjures up visions of a reign of ter-
ror within the party. The whips are, in fact, the M.P.'s appointed
to manage the affairs of the party in each House of Parliament,
the government ones being paid a salary. Their duties are wide,
and include much of the administrative work of arranging parliamentary business as well as purely intraparty work. Their
primary functions, however, are to act as the intermediaries between the party leaders and their followers, keeping each in
touch with the feelings and attitudes of the other. As such, they
will advise the leaders on appointments, tactics, and policy, and
will attempt, conversely, to persuade and cajole M.P.'s to accord
their full support to the party's leaders. They will also, of course,
advise upon questions of promotion or of possible action against
M.P.'s who have been particularly "difficult." But their principal
role is simply to keep the internal party machinery well oiled, so
that the natural forces for loyalty may continue to do their work.
One of their tasks, therefore, is to circulate information about
forthcoming debates, indicating when votes are expected, how
party members should vote (not always easy to appreciate, given
the language of many motions), and, by the number of under-
linings, how important each vote is. These printed instructions

are also referred to as "whips"—a "three-line whip," for example, being one wherein a particular vote is trebly underlined as one of major importance which a member should attend if humanly possible. The printed "whips" are also used to summon members to party meetings of all kinds.[37] It is perhaps a fair summary to say that the main concern of the party whips is to help maintain party cohesion, occasionally by pressures and threats, often by persuasion, and mainly by pointing out to members how best to demonstrate the loyalty which they naturally feel, and to the leaders how best to earn that loyalty.

The situation is a little different when a party is in opposition, since the object in view is to obtain rather than retain office. Defection then has less obviously and directly damaging results. But insofar as it makes the job of the government easier (a divided opposition is less dangerous), and the likelihood of attracting electoral support less, such signs of disunity are still kept in check. Most members would accept Mr. R. A. Butler's statement that "we are here in a struggle for power," [38] and therefore continue to support their own side with loyal regularity (one might almost say "monotony"). The forces which operate within a party also continue to have their influence. Nevertheless, M.P.'s may usually indulge their personalities more freely when in opposition, without incurring disfavor, simply because less is at stake. At all times, too, the Labour party seems more frequently to experience open rebellion or the threat of it than do the Conservatives. It may be that this reflects the greater emphasis in the latter upon the need to stay in office if anything is to be accomplished and the presence in the former of more people who place "purity" above power, as well as the natural tendency of reform parties to embrace a wider range of opinions than one more concerned with preservation.

To argue, as we have done, that the standard account of the power of dissolution is misleading (when applied to the contemporary situation) is not, however, to say that the power is unimportant. In at least two ways its existence may exert a strong influence upon behavior. In the first place, it means that within the limits of the present maximum period of five years between elections it is the government which decides[39] when to hold a

[37] Hence the use of the phrase "to withdraw the whip" as a synonym for expulsion from the party in Parliament.

[38] In the House of Commons, January, 1958. Mr. Butler was speaking as Conservative Secretary of State for Home Affairs and Leader of the House.

[39] Subject to what has been said above or will be said shortly about the monarch's prerogatives.

general election, and which may thus choose the circumstances (or even create them) which appear most favorable to its own chances.[40] Others will be able to venture intelligent guesses about the probable date, but they can never *know*. This uncertainty may well have a "disciplining" effect. Potential rebels are less likely to defect if they think there will be an early election, because of the stronger feelings of party loyalty and the greater desirability of party unity at such a time. The opposition, too, must always bear this possibility in mind. If at times the hint of an election may lead it to intensify its attacks upon the government, at others it will be restrained by the fear of having its bluff called at the polls, and at all times such a hint will encourage it to try to remain united and ready for battle at short notice.

In the second place, the power of dissolution may be important whenever a government depends for its parliamentary majority upon the votes of M.P.'s who belong to no party or to a third party. Such members would probably be vulnerable to the traditional deterrent qualities of a dissolution to the extent that nonparty or small-party members are likely to have small financial resources and uncertain electoral prospects.[41] On the other hand, in such circumstances the monarch would no longer be bound to grant a dissolution to a defeated prime minister. If, for example, the "floating" group were prepared to support an alternative government which could be formed from the existing House of Commons, then the monarch might well refuse to dissolve Parliament. Only, indeed, if all reasonable combinations of parties and groups had been tried would a dissolution almost certainly *be* granted.

To cite the most recent illustration, after the election held late in 1923 the Conservative party remained the largest single party in the House of Commons, but it had fewer seats than the Labour and Liberal parties combined. Mr. Baldwin, the Conservative prime minister, did not resign at once, but waited until the Liberals, who held the balance of power, had voted against him. Mr. Macdonald was thereupon invited to form the first Labour government, sustained by the votes of the Liberals, whose leaders nevertheless did not join the government. Later in the same year (1924) a somewhat confused situation resulted in the

[40] The right is now apparently acknowledged to be the prime minister's. It is up to him to decide whether or not to consult the cabinet.

[41] Even in this case, however, the deterrent value of dissolution is conditional—the M.P.'s concerned might conceivably have adequate finances and a strong electoral base.

Liberals' voting against the Labour government. The only two possible governments had thus been defeated in the life of the same Parliament and, for this reason, despite some doubts at the time, one must defend the king's decision to grant a dissolution to Mr. Macdonald.[42]

It is, indeed, in precisely such a situation that the power of dissolution is most valuable and effective—but not purely or necessarily as a deterrent.[43] Had there been no power of dissolution, the House of Commons would have had to continue for a full term and the country would have had to suffer a succession of minority or coalition governments, none of which might have been any more long-lived or powerful than the Labour one. The Liberal party, furthermore, would have wielded inordinate power during this period and, such was its internal condition, might well have split under the strains involved in holding the balance, thus compounding the instability of the system. As it was, the election of 1924 gave the Conservative party a clear majority which enabled it to remain in office until after the election of 1929, when, it is worth recalling, a situation similar to that of 1923 resulted and the second Labour government was formed.[44] The power of dissolution, it might be concluded, thus rescued Britain from a longer period of governmental instability. What is more, the knowledge that it can do so must help to prevent dissatisfied groups of M.P.'s from defecting in the hope that they could perform comparable balancing roles, or in order to put in the other side for a limited purpose, after which they could restore the former government to office.[45] The existence of the power of dissolution, this is to say, helps to ensure that M.P.'s accept or reject governments as a whole and not merely on a single issue unless that issue is of supreme and overriding importance. But it is not dissolution alone which has this result. The dissolution of 1924, to revert to the example already cited,

[42] See the similar situation which arose in Canada in 1926 and the discussion thereof in E. A. Forsey, *The Royal Power of Dissolution of Parliament in the British Commonwealth* (London: Oxford, 1943), pp. 131–250.

[43] The situation in 1924 was too confused, and Mr. Macdonald's actions too unpredictable, for this incident to be conclusive as to the deterrent value of dissolution or the threat to dissolve.

[44] The Labour party in 1929 was the largest single party, as it was not in 1923–24, but it had still to depend upon Liberal support for office.

[45] As, for example, the left wing of the Conservative party might have wished to put Labour in office in 1956 to prevent, or end, the Suez invasion, and subsequently restore the Conservative government to pursue the rest of its policies.

led to stable government because *the resulting election produced a clear majority* for a single party. On the other hand, as we have seen, the elections of 1923 and 1929 (exceptionally) did not produce such a majority. It is, therefore, only in conjunction with the existing electoral system and voting patterns, and with the other social and political forces which tend to produce a substantially two-party system, that the power of dissolution may be relied upon to assist in stabilizing and strengthening governments.[46]

The cabinet, backed by a loyal party majority in the House of Commons, is clearly the most powerful organ of government. Doubts have sometimes been expressed, however, as to its ability to wield its powers in the most efficient manner possible. In particular, it is suggested that cabinet ministers are too burdened with administrative duties to be able to devote enough attention to the formulation of long-term policy. Holding cabinet office appears also to be an ever-increasing physical strain which none but the most robust can sustain for long. Since the *Report* of the Haldane Committee in 1919 many people have favored the idea of a cabinet of "co-ordinating" ministers largely freed from departmental routine. But neither this nor the wartime device of having very small cabinets of less than ten members has been adopted in peacetime.[47] Rather does the problem seem to have been tackled pragmatically by increasing resort to cabinet committees in which other ministers, and even officials, may participate. In this way, it is argued, the cabinet at least avoids the main danger inherent in more radical schemes, namely too great a separation between policy-thinking and the administrative experience on which it should be based.[48]

The risk still cannot be entirely discounted, however, that cabinets will either govern largely in the light of the thinking

[46] It follows from this analysis, I think, that the power of dissolution would have made little, if any, difference to the stability of governments in the Third or Fourth French Republics, or at least that the case for believing otherwise must rest upon stronger foundations than unqualified references to the strength of British cabinets.

[47] Mr. Churchill made a limited and not noticeably successful experiment with ministerial "overlords," 1951–53, which has not been repeated.

[48] See the various opinions expressed in, for example, the *Report* of the Haldane Committee, cited in the first footnote to this chapter; L. S. Amery, *Thoughts on the Constitution* (London: Oxford, 1947); H. J. Laski, *Reflections on the Constitution* (Manchester: The University Press, 1951); Sir John Anderson, *The Machinery of Government* (London: Oxford, 1947); and H. Morrison, *Government and Parliament*, 2d ed. (London: Oxford, 1960).

carried out while in opposition, or will rapidly exhaust their inspiration and thereafter simply drift, or will become almost totally dependent upon advice from the civil service—than any of which, of course, many worse fates can be imagined.

The British cabinet system represents a fusion rather than a separation of powers. It also embodies a concentration both of power and of responsibility, most noticeably while it rests upon the two-party system. Even so, the cabinet is not all-powerful. As we will see, it is subject to continuous influence from Parliament and guidance from its senior civil-service advisers, not to mention the constant activities of pressure groups and the decisive power of the electorate. But it is at all times armed with sufficient constitutional power to function effectively as Her Majesty's Government and to serve as the focal point of all political endeavor. It is impossible to talk of government policy, or a government decision, unless that policy or decision has implicitly or explicitly been approved by the cabinet. At worst, a cabinet will therefore be like a dam, containing and channeling the political forces which produce national policy; while at best, it will be more like a generating-station, driven by the waters of national life, but transmuting their energy into new and more potent forms.

5 - Parliament

Sovereignty

The sovereignty of Parliament is normally cited as a fundamental principle of the British constitution.[1] Parliament is sovereign, it is said, in that it can amend or abolish the constitution by the same legislative processes as it can (say) regulate betting on horse races. It can also override previous legislation at will, prolong its own life indefinitely, proscribe any or all

[1] See the classic statement of the principle in A. V. Dicey, *Introduction to the Study of the Law of the Constitution* (London: Macmillan; 10th ed. by E. C. S. Wade, 1960), Part I.

religions (or authorize but one church as official), make criticism of the government a penal offense, and, in short, do anything except bind succeeding Parliaments, all without *legal* let or hindrance.

The situation is, of course, much less sinister than this might suggest. The principle does not, for one thing, imply any political power to do whatever Parliament feels like or give any indication as to the likelihood of Parliament wishing to pass such laws. It is simply a legal principle which is more accurately stated in other terms. What it amounts to is that the courts have adopted the practice of accepting validly made Acts of Parliament as supreme law, the provisions of any statute being superior to other legal rules (for example, those of common law), including rules laid down by previous Acts. The sovereignty of Parliament is therefore itself an example of case law. It is also one on which there are remarkably few cases, so that some doubt exists as to its precise implications and, in particular, as to how closely judges will examine an Act to ensure that it is in fact "validly made." [2] By "Parliament" is here meant the queen-in-Parliament, which is to say that valid statutes must be assented to by the queen and both Houses of Parliament and that, for example, a resolution of the House of Commons alone will have no general legal force.[3] The main *political* effects of the doctrine are, first, that a Government with the support of Parliament knows that it possesses or can acquire all the legal powers necessary to carry through its program and, second, that political disputes must be argued in political and not legal terms, in contrast to American experience, where the institution of judicial review sometimes has the opposite result.

The House of Lords

In everyday discussion "Parliament" is normally used to denote the House of Commons only, or primarily. This usage reflects the legislative inaction of the monarchy and the subordinate position of the House of Lords. Convention progressively limited the powers of the House of Lords in the nineteenth century. For example, the rule came to be accepted that the Lords should automatically agree to financial legislation already

[2] See G. Marshall, "What is Parliament? The Changing Concept of Parliamentary Sovereignty," *Political Studies,* vol. II (1954), pp. 193–209.

[3] See *Stockdale vs. Hansard* (1839). Account must also be taken of the limitations upon the powers of the House of Lords (see below).

passed by the Commons. After the second chamber rejected the budget of 1909, however, its powers were limited by the Parliament Act of 1911. As amended in 1949, it declares that an Act may legally be passed without the approval of the House of Lords if it is agreed to twice by the House of Commons in separate sessions, provided that a year should elapse between its acceptance in principle for the first time and its final acceptance after passing through all the procedural requirements for the second time. Legislation to extend the life of Parliament beyond its present maximum must, however, receive the assent of the House of Lords. Financial legislation, on the other hand, may become law within one month of its being passed by the Commons, regardless of the attitude of the Lords.[4] The first Parliament Act was violently opposed by the Lords, who passed it only when told that the king had agreed to create enough new peers to secure a favorable majority. The second Act, which established the one-year period of delay for ordinary legislation in place of a two-year one, was passed under the provisions of the first Act. They were introduced by, respectively, a Liberal and a Labour government against the opposition, in both cases, of the Conservative party which, in this century, has been able to count on a permanent majority in the House of Lords. This majority, combined with the nonelective basis of membership, provided the main reason for the limitation of the Lords' powers as well as for a whole series of proposals to reform the composition of the upper chamber.

The House has almost 900 members, about 800 of whom are hereditary English and United Kingdom peers of varying rank.[5] The remainder consists of royal princes (who take no part in governmental proceedings), the two archbishops and 24 senior bishops of the Church of England, representatives of the old Irish and Scottish peers (i.e., peers bearing titles conferred before Ireland or Scotland had united with England), nonhereditary life peers and peeresses (created under an act of 1958), and nine Justices appointed for life to discharge the House's duties as the supreme court in the country. Peerages are conferred by the monarch on the advice of the prime minister.[6]

[4] Financial legislation is officially defined as legislation certified to be such by the Speaker of the House of Commons. Speakers, to date, have been very cautious and have frequently refused to certify budget legislation because it contained matter not strictly financial.

[5] In descending order of precedence: duke, marquis, earl, viscount, baron.

[6] Principally upon inhabitants of the United Kingdom, but also occasionally upon people from other parts of the Commonwealth.

Over one-half the membership in 1957 consisted of the holders of peerages created since 1906, and about one-fifth, of the first holders of a title. Of the 380 titles conferred between 1916 and 1956, almost all have been given as a reward for some kind of public service, primarily in politics (193 were former M.P.'s) and in business (70).[7]

The average attendance in the House is small, rarely exceeding one hundred, and is largely made up of those who are or have been ministers, supplemented by the first holders of titles. Procedure is highly informal, and most debates are not followed by a vote. This is to say that the House of Lords confines itself principally to discussion and to the minor revision of bills, about three-quarters of which have already been passed by the House of Commons. What changes it makes, moreover, are frequently requested by the government, which has decided further to modify legislation after, or even because of, the discussion in the House of Commons. Its most important function in this respect, however, is often to discuss clauses in a bill which were passed by the Commons without any debate due to shortage of time. Frequently, too, the Lords will hold debates on general problems about which government action is either contemplated or desired—the subjects ranging, for example, from deer poaching in the Scottish Highlands to foreign policy or from the installation of parking meters to the introduction of commercial television. In all these ways the House now performs useful if ancillary functions. For the most part the Lords do not press their disagreements with the House of Commons, but acquiesce, sometimes under protest, in the decisions taken in the popular chamber. For these reasons one no longer hears much talk of abolishing the House of Lords. Nevertheless, in 1948 there was an all-party conference which tried, without success, to secure agreement about reform and, in 1958, the Conservatives passed legislation authorizing the creation of life peerages (the most revolutionary feature of which was the decision to include women among their recipients).[8]

Without being the cause of strong political feelings, the House of Lords is criticized both from the left and the right.

[7] See P. A. Bromhead, *The House of Lords in Contemporary Politics* (London: Routledge and Kegan Paul, 1958), p. 26.

[8] But as Lord Home said on behalf of the government: "Taking women into a parliamentary embrace would seem to be only a modest extension of the normal functions and privileges of a peer." House of Lords, October 30, 1957.

On the left dissatisfaction is voiced both on social and political grounds. Socially, the objection is against the system of titles in general[9] and, in particular, against the principle that membership of any governmental organ should rest upon a hereditary claim. Politically, it is objected, above all, that the House of Lords is predominantly and apparently permanently conservative in character, and that no guarantee exists that it will always act with forbearance in the face of left-wing legislation and never obstruct the implementing of a reform program. After assenting to the various Acts nationalizing transport, fuel and power (other than oil), and the Bank of England, the Lords jibbed at taking over the iron and steel industry and, by their opposition, delayed its implementation by at least two years, thus provoking the Parliament Act of 1949. Again, in 1956, after a free vote in the House of Commons in favor of abolishing the death penalty, the House of Lords rejected the bill in an unusually well-attended debate, whereupon the Conservative government took no further action on behalf of a cause with which, it must be said, it had no sympathy.[10] No major measure actively supported by the Conservative party or government has been rejected in the past century. If one were rejected today, it would be a startling action by a House, only one-ninth of whose members admit to supporting either the Labour or Liberal parties.[11]

That there is any right-wing discontent with the present position of the House of Lords may seem surprising. It stems, however, from an uneasy feeling that it is difficult to justify even the present powers of the second chamber as it is now constituted. A reformed House, it is felt, would be more capable of acting as a brake upon "radical legislation," if only because to impose delay might then seem more disinterested. Such a brake is desirable, the argument usually continues, because, at least toward the end of a five-year term of office, a radical government should do nothing radical without again consulting the people at an election. (This endorsement of the theory that a government is bound by its "mandate" from the electors to

[9] A system of titles and other honors, although not necessarily hereditary ones, may nevertheless be one of the less pernicious forms of political or official reward and patronage.

[10] For a discussion of the bearing of this case upon the doctrine of ministerial responsibility, see G. Marshall and G. C. Moodie, *Some Problems of the Constitution* (London: Hutchinson 1959), pp. 74–77.

[11] Between them, these parties obtained close to 50 per cent of the popular vote in the 1959 election.

implement its electoral program and nothing else is not balanced
by any suggested provisions whereby a reformed House of Lords
would be able to make a government *act,* rather than do nothing, in the face of real or alleged public demand.)[12] The Life
Peerages Act may be seen as a first move in the direction of
making the House of Lords less obviously unqualified to exercise significant influence in a nonpartisan way.

In the space at our disposal it is not possible to pursue the
controversy further. It may safely be said, however, that there
are severe limits to the type of reform desirable. To institute an
elected House of Lords would either pose a threat to the authority of the Commons or, if this threat were disposed of, lead to
the election of relative nonentities. The second is obviously undesirable and would involve a signicant regression from the
existing state of affairs. On the other hand, in any way to increase the real powers of the House would be to upset the whole
relationship between the government and Parliament to the
extent that the government may be faced with conflicting majorities in the two Houses. Were this eventuality made impossible, moreover, then the point of having a more powerful second
chamber becomes doubtful.[13] At present, as for the past century
or more, the complexion of the government depends entirely
upon the party strengths in the Commons, and its tenure of
office is unaffected, constitutionally speaking, by the degree of
support it obtains from the Lords. These facts both reflect and
in part explain the relative weakness of the upper chamber. The
remainder of our discussion of Parliament may therefore confine itself almost exclusively to the House of Commons and its
place within the constitution.

The House of Commons

It has already been remarked that government in Britain
proceeds by way of an organized confrontation of government

[12] The theory of a definite "mandate" to a government from the electorate
has received little respectable backing outside this context. In practice it is
cited primarily as a weapon whereby to attack the other side or to defend
one's own actions. The electoral studies discussed in Chapter 3 above lend
little support to the doctrine. Nevertheless, the mere fact that the theory
is bruited with reference to parties and governments in Britain tells one
something important about British politics. To the author's knowledge
there is no corresponding notion in French politics or, except possibly with
reference to a president, in American.

[13] The objection against the existing House, with relatively few powers, is
not so much that its majority may differ from that in the Commons as that it
never changes.

and opposition. It has also been suggested that Parliament can in no way be said itself to govern the country. The principal function of the House of Commons, and therefore of Parliament, is rather to sustain the government and the official opposition and provide the principal "oratorical battleground" [14] for the conflict between them. It is, of course, easy to imagine a government's being able to survive and function without the continuing presence of the Commons. It is necessary only to assume the grant of sufficiently wide legislative and discretionary powers. But for several reasons the existence and satisfactory functioning of the Commons are well-nigh indispensable to the effective operation of an opposition party and hence, except possibly in the very short run, to the maintenance of *good* government. It is in the House that the best opportunities exist for extracting the information about the government's plans and actions which is necessary properly to evaluate and criticize or even fully to understand them. It is there, too, that governments are not only expected to explain and defend their policies, but also to justify them in the face of critical cross-examination. Equally, of course, the opposition parties will be called upon to defend and justify the alternatives which they propound. The extent to which the mere need to offer a public justification for an action serves to control and limit a party cannot be measured, but is obviously a vital constituent of free democratic government. Too often it is overlooked in assessments of the power of Parliament, which is therefore sometimes underestimated. At all times, finally, the House of Commons serves as an indispensable avenue for the expression of discontent and the airing of grievances (perhaps its most basic traditional function). Although the opposition parties play the most obvious role in these respects, thus to control the work of government is one of the principal concerns of government supporters as well.

In discussing and assessing the work of the House of Commons it is important to avoid passing judgments based upon the mistaken notion that its purpose is to legislate or otherwise to govern rather than to criticize those who do govern. Nor should it be forgotten that throughout almost all its history the latter has been Parliament's essential role. If there exists any fundamental separation of powers in British government, it consists not of a separation between legislature and executive but of one between the doers and the controllers, between those who initiate

[14] Jennings, *Parliament*, 2d ed., p. 529.

policies and take action on the one hand and, on the other, those who criticize the actions and attempt to ensure that the policies adopted are broadly acceptable to the community. The methods whereby Parliament discharges its duties are continuously evolving as circumstances change and, with them, the demands placed upon government. But the principal innovation of the modern constitution has been to superimpose the further task of providing and sustaining the government. Even this, however, was no sudden development. For centuries the House of Commons has been a training ground as well as a testing ground of ministers.

Organization and procedure

The physical layout of the House is itself informative. The chamber is rectangular in shape, with rows of benches banked along the longer sides of it, like the choir stalls in a cathedral. As in some cathedrals, the benches are divided into two groups facing each other across a floor. On one group sit the government and its supporters, and on the other sit the members of the opposition party or parties. Physically as well as politically the government and alternative government sit permanently confronted and divided. There are no cross-benches for independent or minor-party members who neither support nor oppose the government consistently; they, too, must sit either with the government or with the opposition party. At one end of the floor is the "bar" of the House through which members enter, and at which offenders against the privileges of the House may be arraigned or petitioners may attend. At the other end is a table for the clerks of the House, who (it may be said) handle the paperwork of the Commons. The table extends some way along the central floor of the House and separates the front benches on which sit the leaders of the government and of the opposition. Customarily the leaders speak from this part of the table. All other members of the House speak from wherever they happen to have found room for themselves. Beyond the table, on a dais, sits the Speaker, wigged and gowned, facing the bar of the House, with the government to his right and the opposition to his left. The position of his chair, elevated and separated from the parties by the clerks' table, symbolizes both his authority over the conduct of the House and the tradition that he be impartial in applying and interpreting the rules and, indeed, in the discharge of all his duties as chairman of the House. Despite the fact that the Speaker is elected by the House from among its members, rarely is his impartiality impugned. Rarely, therefore, is the election contested and, once elected, the Speaker is normally re-elected automatically for as long as he wishes. Customarily the government, in whose gift the speakership lies, will consult with the opposition before nominating a member better known for his moderation and committee work than for his partisanship and debating prowess.[15]

The manner of selecting a Speaker is typical of the way in which all the business of the House is arranged. The rules of procedure consist in part of customary rules dating back to the seventeenth century or beyond and in part of standing orders formally adopted at later dates and comprehensible only with reference to the older rules which they modify or supersede. Most of the later rules have been adopted in the last hundred years and are designed to expedite business or limit the scope for pure obstruction.

All the rules are applied by the Speaker, and round them there has now grown up a considerable body of "case law" in the shape of Speakers' rulings. Within the chamber the Speaker's decisions about the meaning or application of any rule are final, but the power to decide what the rules should be lies with the majority, which is to say, with the government. If a government were so minded, it could, therefore, deny to the opposition or its own supporters any opportunity to question or to criticize. But governments are not so minded. Conscious of the possibility that, after the next election, they may themselves be in opposition, conscious, too, that by abusing their power they may contribute to this result, their members always try to take the other side with them in any proposed changes in procedure. They do not always succeed. Nor do they necessarily accept the proposals coming from the all-party select committees on procedure which normally precede any substantial change. But they usually feel it incumbent upon themselves to produce respectable reasons for procedural innovations, and not to depart too far from what would be generally acceptable.

In arranging the order of business and the agenda for the House, governments again consult with the opposition (the "usual channels" for negotiation being the party whips) about the amount of time to devote to particular items as well as when to debate them, or even whether to debate them at all.

[15] Exceptionally Speaker Morrison, who retired in 1959, had been a minister. His appointment was not, therefore, universally welcomed, but in fact he seems to have upheld the tradition with distinction.

Thus, for example, the government may agree to provide time for a debate upon a recent government decision in the realm of foreign policy if, in exchange, the opposition will help to secure the speedy passage of legislation on building standards. It is understood that the government is there to govern and that the opposition should therefore not attempt continuously to obstruct its legislative program. In return, the government attempts to ensure that there will always be some opportunity for discussion and criticism, and respects certain traditional rights belonging to the opposition—for example, that the opposition decides which estimates of expenditure should be debated in full,[16] and that the opposition always is given time to move and support a formal vote of censure upon the government. In this manner a balance is maintained between the demands of government and the freedom to criticize.

This balance is constantly shifting and, at times, is severely strained by the expanding role of modern governments, but few would say categorically that it has yet been destroyed. Clearly, however, the whole system depends for its successful working upon the continuation of at least some mutual confidence between government and opposition and upon their both continuing to respect the parliamentary tradition itself. Both conditions have been undermined on occasion, and might, for example, have been totally submerged early this century by the passions associated with Irish Home Rule, woman's suffrage, and developing trade unionism, had not the First World War occasioned a re-emphasis upon national unity. Today, however, the prestige and satisfactory working of the House of Commons seem threatened more by the predominance of both front benches to the detriment of the ordinary back-bench member, and by the increasing tendency to take important decisions off the floor of the House entirely, than by militant party antagonisms.

Members and their powers

The ordinary back-bench Member of Parliament, by comparison with a United States Senator, or even Congressman, seems unimportant and powerless. He is literally neither. Nevertheless, he is relatively limited both in his opportunities for initiative and in the effectiveness of his efforts.

It has been estimated that during the period 1945–55, less

---

[16] It being impossible to discuss them all and still have time for any other business during the year.

than one-fifth of the average session was devoted to business initiated by Private Members (an official category which includes opposition front-benchers as well as all back-bench members). The one hundred fifty-eight working days which made up the session were apportioned approximately as follows:

Government program	75 days	(47.5%)
Business initiated by opposition	41 days	(26.0%)
" " " Private Members	29 days	(18.3%)
Other	13 days	(8.2%)[17]

The third category includes only the time devoted to bills, motions, and debates initiated by back-benchers. It does not include, for example, time devoted to questions, nor is account taken of the numerous small committees appointed by the House. In both these spheres ordinary members can make important contributions to the work of Parliament. All members, likewise, have the right to take part in debates and discussion initiated by either front bench. But in practice the priority traditionally granted to official party spokesmen and privy councillors[18] may empty this right of much value—for all that members known to have distinctive views or to be particularly well informed may also find it comparatively easy to "catch the Speaker's eye."

Except in the official questioning of ministers, however, the back-bench member is made constantly aware that he must follow a long way behind the two front benches in determining what is to be discussed in the House. During the war and for several years after, for example, he was completely deprived of the times normally set aside for his bills and motions, which, in 1960, received ten days each per session. Even within these times the back-bencher is aware that the outcome of any debate is largely preordained by the government's attitude, as the support

[17] See Sir Thomas Erskine May, *Treatise on the Law, Privileges, Proceedings and Usage of Parliament,* 16th ed. by Fellowes and Cocks, 1957, pp. 312–15. This is the standard work on the procedure of Parliament and the bible for Speakers, Members, and scholars throughout the Commonwealth. It is normally referred to simply as "Erskine May."

[18] The Privy Councillors are mainly ministers or ex-ministers. Membership of the Privy Council is now largely a formal matter, although attended by important legal consequences, including an oath of secrecy and a right of personal access to the monarch. Several committees of the Privy Council, however, may be important, as is the Judicial Committee, which is the supreme court of appeal for certain territories within the Commonwealth. Some modern departments, Education included, began life as committees of the Council.

and attitudes of the parties usually make all conclusions virtually foregone; but not entirely so. The Chamberlain government resigned in 1940 in large part because of the expressed and critical opinion of its back-bench supporters; governments frequently undertake to appoint committees of inquiry or royal commissions because of back-bench pressure; in 1957, to take but one example, the government withdrew a bill about the opening hours of shops in answer to back-bench opposition, and many bills may receive important amendments for the same reasons. As Sir Alan Herbert showed before the war, and Mr. Roy Jenkins has shown since, it is also possible for a Private Member to secure the passage of a bill to which the government was initially hostile or indifferent.[19] It is, furthermore, impossible accurately to assess the importance of "prenatal" back-bench influence which may prevent a government from introducing certain legislation at all. A determined government, however, so long as it commands the general support of its followers, can always have its way. Fundamentally the position of the back-bencher is a function of his political power and his relationship to the formal and informal channels of access to the government and administration. Without examining them, it is impossible to understand the nature and significance of the House of Commons today.

In addition to his rights as a member, chief among which are those to raise questions and air grievances on the floor of the House, the back-bencher has two principal sources of power: as a party member he is, in association with his colleagues, the ultimate arbiter of the party's leadership; and he is the elected representative of his constituency. Of these, the first is probably the most important, although, of course, it confers direct power over the government only upon the government's supporters. This power is limited. As we have already seen, individual members are constrained by the fear of expulsion from and the hope of promotion within the party, and members may be collectively restrained by a reluctance to dismiss a government or precipitate a damaging party split. But it must be emphasized that these weapons are rendered necessary by the back-benchers' power over their own leaders and have not, probably could not, neu-

---

[19] See A. P. Herbert, *The Ayes Have It* (London: Methuen, 1937), for an account of his Matrimonial Causes Act, and Roy Jenkins's account of the struggle for his Obscene Publications Act in "Obscenity, Censorship and the Law," *Encounter* (October, 1959), pp. 62–66.

tralize their power. Back-bench influence is continuous, if not always obvious.

An M.P. "represents" his constituency in two main senses. He is there in their stead, formally assenting to legislation and accepting the burden of taxes on behalf of all the commons. (Bills are passed, in law, by the House of Commons, not by the members who happened to vote with the majority, so that all citizens are deemed to have concurred in and accepted the resulting obligations.) The M.P. is a representative, secondly, in the sense that one of his duties is to make representations on behalf of his constituents, particularly with reference to purely local or individual interests and grievances. (It is customary for an M.P. to emphasize, once elected, that he regards himself as the representative of all the voters and not only of his own party followers. This claim is normally substantially justified.) He is not, however, a representative in the sense of being a copy or mirror of the political divisions or ideas within his constituency. At most it can be said only that he will support or oppose the government on behalf of the party which won the largest number of votes, although he cannot be forced to resign should he change his allegiance after being elected. Nor is he necessarily a "representative" (i.e., typical) example of his constituents. It cannot even be claimed, as we shall see, that M.P.'s as a group are typical of the people they "represent." On the other hand, he must be *responsive* to the opinions and interests of his constituents adequately to fill his two representative roles and, above all, to maximize his chance of re-election.

His principal concern today, however, is with his party, for it is this which primarily decides whether he will be elected. It is the general standing of the party nationally and locally, along with the social composition of the constituency which, more than any other factors, will win or lose his seat. An M.P. can and must, of course, attend to the wishes of his local party and his constituents. He dare not forget that his adoption as a candidate lies within the discretion of the local party militants and that, even after entering Parliament, his re-adoption, although usual, cannot be guaranteed. Naturally, his constituents decide whether he will be elected. He is, therefore, controlled by these local groups in some degree. If this were not so, he could with less justice claim to speak for them in the House of Commons and in the wider circles of his party.

The essence of the back-bencher's position may therefore

be said to consist of its being intermediate between the front
benches and the voters. His relation to each, moreover, is in
part determined by his relation to the other. The front bench
cannot ignore him because he may air issues in the House, because he is in close touch with his constituency, and because he,
with his fellows, has the ultimate power over the destiny of the
leaders. For these reasons, too, he is guaranteed access to his
leaders, directly or through the whips, and regardless of his
party, to the administrative departments. His constituents may
depend upon him to intercede on their behalf with the government and administration in order to secure the redress of their
grievances. But they wield power over him as voters. In virtue
of this power inherent in representative government, the citizen
is assured of a hearing from the M.P. and, through him, of at
least one point of access to the government; indeed, in the case
of the ordinary citizen, it will be the only assured point of
access.

The back-bencher's influence is not necessarily confined to
that derived in these ways (and from his own capabilities) any
more than the voter is restricted to this one channel of access
to government. Their relationships to pressure groups must also
be taken into account.[20] It is through them that the variety of
interests and opinions seek their primary expression, thus making good any failure of M.P.'s to "represent" them. A back-
bencher who is known to speak for an important interest or
pressure group will gain in influence thereby, just as he will from
any other special qualification or expertise which lends weight
to his views. The services of a back-bencher, in turn, may be as
useful to pressure groups as to constituents, and for the same
reasons: his access to the administration, his right to air points
in public, and his share in the policy-making processes of his
party. But back-benchers are useful above all to groups which
have not yet fully established their public position and therefore
whose right automatically to be consulted on matters affecting
them has not yet been conceded by the government and administration.

For established groups and for groups drawn from the major

[20] The term "pressure group" is here used to cover any group, whatever
its primary *raison d'être*, other than a political party, which attempts de-
liberately to influence the conduct of government in pursuit of some common
aim. A similar definition is adopted in one of the best studies to date of
British pressure groups, namely, Harry Eckstein, *Pressure Group Politics:
The Case of the British Medical Association* (London: Allen and Unwin, 1960),
especially pp. 8–11, 15–39, and 151–63.

social interests (employers, trade unions, and the national churches, for example), direct parliamentary representation is less important than the close relations with the administration which accrue to them naturally because of their powerful positions in society.[21] The leaders of pressure groups know, better than most people, that the decisions important to them are taken not by or in the House of Commons, but by the administration. Conversely, the facts that back-benchers may hope only to *influence* the decisions taken by their leaders or by the civil service, and that they must normally work within the broad limits of their party's policy, help to confer immunity upon them from the worst types of political pressure. This is one possible reason why students of British politics long tended to deny that pressure groups existed at all. Another reason, probably, was that these groups are so built into the system that their operations need be less public and less strident than they are in, for example, the United States. It has simply been taken for granted that the major interests in the community should be represented in Parliament. For centuries they have in fact secured representation, directly by means of patronage, the sponsorship of candidates, or through the desire of men successful in one walk of life to embark upon a political career, and indirectly through the many formal and informal channels of access to members of both Houses.[22] In this way, too, party leaders as well as back-benchers are linked to the complex of pressure groups, although the demands of their leadership role and the need to concern themselves with party policy and a national electorate normally prevent them from being direct or overt pressure-group spokesmen to the extent possible for a back-bench member.

Some indication of the groups and interests now particularly favored may be gathered from the available statistics relating to the occupational and educational backgrounds of members of the Commons and of the cabinet.[23]

[21] It is indicative of the established place of trade unions today that, in November, 1959, complaints were voiced by some trade union M.P.'s that they were increasingly being by-passed by their own unions in dealings with government.

[22] See Samuel H. Beer, "The Representation of Interests in British Government," *American Political Science Review*, September, 1957.

[23] The first two tables are adapted, by permission, from those given in D. E. Butler, *The British General Election of 1955* (London: Macmillan, 1955), pp. 38–46. For the third table, and for supplying the percentages in the others, the present author alone is responsible. No significant changes took place as a result of the 1959 General Election.

Occupational background of M.P.'s elected in 1955

	Conservative*	Labour*	Total
Professions	159 (46.2%)	100 (36.1%)	259 (41.7%)
Law	77	36	
Armed forces	47	3	
Teaching	4	39	
Business	101 (29.4%)	34 (12.2%)	135 (21.7%)
Small	0	9	
Company director			
or manager	78	6	
Clerical	7	14	
Miscellaneous	83 (24.1%)	46 (16.6%)	129 (20.8%)
Private means	11	0	
Politics	17	7	
Journalism, etc.	19	27	
Farmer	31	5	
Manual work	1 (0.3%)	97 (35.0%)	98 (15.8%)
Skilled	1	29	
Miners	0	33	
TOTAL	344	277	621

* It may also be noted that of the Conservatives, 105 (30.6%) were either in business (not clerical) or had private means, while 96 (34.7%) Labour members had been sponsored by trade unions. There were also 9 members who belonged to neither of these parties and who are therefore excluded from this and the following tables.

The House of Commons thus does not, and to an even lesser degree does the cabinet, provide a cross-section of the public in terms either of education or occupation. This is explicable, probably, in terms of such factors as the attitudes of constituency selection committees (including deference to success or ability, as well as, and at times superseding the desire to be represented by someone like themselves); the inclination to enter politics of people already accustomed to making decisions and to influencing others verbally; and the filtering effect of financial necessity, which favors sponsored candidates and those who have skills or occupations which can still be used, after an M.P. is elected, to supplement the relatively low salary of a back-bencher. The result, it might be argued, is that the House primarily reflects and ·maintains the existing unequal distribution of prestige and power within British society. Certainly, access to government through Parliament, as in other ways, is more easily attained by "respectable" groups, organizations, and classes than by others. Not that it is denied to all others: securing representation in the House, indeed, may be one way of increasing a group's prestige and power, as it has been for organized labor. No list of occupational and educational backgrounds, moreover, can provide a complete guide to the interests, attitudes, or affiliations of members, for all that it may be indicative thereof, nor do such factors necessarily outweigh the need to satisfy a very mixed electorate.

Whatever the ability, electoral backing, or pressure-group allegiance of a back-bencher, however, the fact remains that until and unless he is promoted to the front bench, he cannot hope to do more than influence the decisions taken by others. In his speeches, conversations, or otherwise, the back-bencher's purpose can therefore only be to persuade rather than decide. His targets within the House are the government, the leaders of the opposition, and his colleagues. Outside it, they are his constituents, his party, and the general public. In other words, his purpose is to persuade the actual or potential governmental decision-makers directly or through those with power over them. Only thus can he hope to further his aims and ambitions.

While the major decisions on policy may often be taken in

Full-time education of M.P.'s elected in 1955

	Conservative		Labour		Total	
Elementary only	52 {8	(15.1%)	157 {94	(56.6%)	209	(33.7%)
Secondary only	{44		{63			
Public school only	74	(21.5%)	10	(3.6%)	84	(13.5%)
Secondary and						
university	32	(9.3%)	58	(20.9%)	90	(14.5%)
Public school and						
university	186	(54.1%)	52	(18.9%)	238	(38.3%)
TOTAL	344		277		621	
Universities:						
Oxford or						
Cambridge	182	(52.9%)	46	(16.6%)	228	(36.7%)
All other	36	(10.5%)	64	(23.1%)	100	(16.1%)
Public schools:						
Eton	78	(22.7%)	4	(1.5%)	82	(13.0%)
Harrow or						
Winchester	32	(9.6%)	5	(1.8%)	37	(6.1%)
All other	150	(43.5%)	53	(19.2%)	203	(32.7%)

Education and occupational backgrounds of cabinet ministers

	Conservative (November, 1959)	Labour (October, 1947)
Occupation		
Professional	8 (4 lawyers)	9 (7 education, 2 lawyers)
Business	7	1 (small, previously manual)
Miscellaneous	2	2
Manual	0	5
	—	—
TOTAL	17*	17
Education		
Elementary only	0	7
State secondary	1	2
Public schools:	16	6
Eton	7	1
Winchester	2	1
Other fee paying	2	1
	—	—
TOTAL	19	16*
Universities:	16	8
Oxford or Cambridge	15	6

* It has not been possible to obtain information about the occupational background of two Conservatives or about the education of one Labour minister.

areas remote from the back-bencher, there are other spheres of government in which the able and conscientious individual makes an important and useful contribution. He is constantly being called upon to intercede between the citizen and the official. Frequently, it is true, his work could be as well performed by anyone with some familiarity with legislation and some confidence in dealing with bureaucracy. Indeed, much could be done to lighten the M.P.'s burden of work by extending public advisory services or by providing each member with permanent staff concerned with such routine "welfare" work.

This could the more easily be done because it seems that members' letters to government departments "do not win any special favours for those on whose behalf they are written." [24] The same can probably be said of all personal or direct interventions by back-benchers. But, should it be a matter of rectifying an injustice or of bringing to light an abuse of power, then a

[24] P. G. Richards, *Honourable Members* (London: Faber, 1959), p. 170.

member is in the unique position of being able to raise it in the House, in question time most notably, but also on other suitable occasions.[25] About the effectiveness of this type of action there can be no dispute. Many a minister, or even government, has been harried into changes in administrative practice, or even legislation, as a result of back-bench persistence, while even a single question in Parliament will induce a careful review of its subject matter.

But where more is required than merely publicizing the government's actions in order to secure some change or redress or to set in motion the forces which could secure them, the back-bencher is virtually powerless. Whether or not any immediate results are obtained, the back-bencher can, however, perform much useful educational or propaganda service at question time and on those less frequent occasions when he can propose a motion or introduce a bill.

It is in the many parliamentary and party committees that the back-bencher has the widest opportunities for initiative in other respects than the airing of specific points. Governments generally are more amenable to persuasion on points of detail than basic policy or principle, and are therefore more ready to accept amendments at the committee stage of any bill.[26] They know, too, that standing committees pose no fundamental challenge to them, since any adverse vote can later be reversed on the floor of the House. The smaller size of the standing committees and the resulting more intimate atmosphere also are particularly favorable to the back-bencher member. Until the postwar period, moreover, the party whips tended to take less interest in what transpired in these committees. Since then, however, party "discipline" in the committees has been strengthened.

The power of the back-bencher is also being reduced as, for several reasons, ministers become increasingly resistant to amendments. In the first place bills contain less and less detail over wide areas of government (social and economic in particular).

[25] See the bibliography for some of the many books wherein the details of procedure are readily discoverable.

[26] The committee stage comes after the first general debate on the principles of a bill (second-reading debate) and is taken either on the floor of the House itself, in the case of short, urgent, financial, or constitutional legislation, or in one of the standing committees of twenty to fifty members, chosen in proportion to party strength. In the latter case the whole House has an opportunity to propose and discuss detailed amendments when the committee reports back to it (as it always does). For more information about the committees of the House, see the Note at the end of this chapter.

More and more they take the form of skeleton bills whose most important provisions simply enable or empower the minister to make regulations and otherwise to take action in order, for example, to establish a national health service or reorganize secondary education on certain very generally defined lines. Bills, therefore, may consist almost entirely of "policy" provisions, all the details (on which concessions might be more forthcoming) being left over for administrative action. Much of the substance of legislation is therefore now to be found in the volumes of statutory instruments (as the products of delegated legislation are called) rather than in the less bulky volumes of statutes.[27] In other cases, detailed provisions of a bill have already been negotiated with interested groups before being submitted to Parliament, possibly as the price of securing essential co-operation in administering it, and are thus excluded from the area of parliamentary compromise. Nevertheless it is still possible for a knowledgeable back-bencher, or one supported by influential or powerful opinion, to make a real mark on legislation in committee.

Select committees provide another important avenue of back-bench activity, even if affecting very small numbers at any given time.[28] They are nowadays appointed mainly to examine and report upon some particular problem or some specific aspect of the work of government. For the most part their terms of reference preclude them from examining questions of policy. They have the power to examine witnesses (including civil servants) and documents. Governments have therefore feared that, unless their jurisdiction were limited, the committees might infringe upon ministers' relations with their departments and with Parliament. Select committees nevertheless perform valuable services in scrutinizing the estimates and accounts of public expenditure, the reports of the nationalized industries, and certain formal aspects of delegated legislation or, intermittently, in reporting on questions of parliamentary privilege. But they do not constitute highroads to political power and fame as do, say, U.S. Congressional investigating committees.

For the back-bench member who wishes to influence policy, the most important committees are those set up by and within the political parties. Both major parties maintain a series of

---

[27] On average there are three annual volumes of statutory instruments to one of statutes, and even they do not include all the rules made by the departments under their delegated powers of legislation.

[28] See Note at the end of this chapter.

"standing" committees specializing in particular areas of government. The Conservative ones are loose and informal: they are
open to any back-bencher who wishes to attend (although their
meetings are normally attended only by a nucleus of members
with a continuous interest in the subject concerned). Ministers
or front-benchers attend by request only (but are always informed of what happens by the attendant whip), and no motions
are moved nor votes taken (although the sense of the meeting
may carry as much weight as any formal resolution). The
Labour ones, by contrast, are chaired by the front-bench member who is the official party spokesman in the area covered; their
membership tends to be less "open"; they make formal reports
to the whole party; and they are frequently consulted before
any member tables a motion in the House on any topic within
their jurisdiction.

The differences between the party committees reflect the
different styles of the parties rather than any profound difference
in the functions and powers of their rank-and-file members. In
both parties the committees provide the principal channels of
communication between the appropriate front-bench minister or
spokesman and the back-benchers most interested in a particular
subject; in both, the committees provide machinery for more
intensive and more knowledgeable back-bench pressure than
would be possible for the same people working entirely as individuals; and in neither party have the committees the "last
word" on policy—that lies with the leadership, acting in conjunction with the whole body of M.P.'s.

The strength of the party committees lies in their relative
expertise and in the claim this confers upon them to the support of their less-expert party colleagues, although they are influential also to the extent that they reflect the feelings and
prejudices of those colleagues. Given the ascendancy of the two
front-benches in the House and the virtually automatic majority
behind the government, it follows that the most vital debate on
important questions of policy may take place in these party committees, at whose meetings no reporters attend and of which
(too often) only distorted reports may reach the public. The
prestige and interest of Parliament suffer from the existence
and importance of the committees, but, on the other hand, the
power of back-benchers is thereby increased. To put it another
way, it may be said that the influence of back-benchers who are
active in any committee is increased, to some extent at the expense of the front-benchers, but also of other back-benchers who

do not belong to the committee in question. But it is quite clear, as is indicated also by the proliferation of other *ad hoc* party and interparty committees, that on questions of policy back-benchers are important primarily when participating in collective action, and hardly at all as individuals. It cannot be said that this is always or entirely regrettable.

The party committees only go part of the way to making good the basic weakness of the back-bencher's position. His decline in prestige since the mid-nineteenth century, and that of Parliament as a whole, does not stem simply from the greater dominance of party, as is so frequently alleged, nor even from the growth of direct communications between the executive and outside groups. More important are the growth in the range of government activity and, above all, in its complexity and technicality. In the first half of this century the number of non-industrial civil servants (i.e., those concerned with general administration) increased about tenfold, and the proportion of the national income taken in taxation was quadrupled,[29] to give but two rough indices of the changes which have taken place. During the same period the interconnection of different spheres of government has become closer and increasingly recognized, while even such "traditional" government concerns as defense, foreign affairs, and fiscal policy, not to mention such newer ones as scientific research, community development, and atomic energy, have become less and less intelligible to the average layman, M.P. or not.

It is increasingly obvious that, in these circumstances, the pay and conditions of work of the back-bench member are no longer adequate for him properly to perform his traditional role of critic and watchdog. In 1911 M.P.'s received, for the first time, a "minimum allowance"[30] of $1,200 (£400) per annum, which, by 1957, had been raised to $4,900 (£1,750). Apart from free stationery, copies of parliamentary (not all government) publications, travel to and from their constituencies, and telephone calls in London when the House is in session, this is their total remuneration. When one remembers that many members must keep up two residences, that $2,100 (£750) is the *average* figure for deductible expenses approved by the tax authorities, and that a well-known member may have to spend over $560 (£200) a year on postage alone, the occupational bias of members be-

---

[29] See, for example, P. E. P., "The Growth of Government," *Planning*, XXIII (December 16, 1957).

[30] As it was described by Lloyd George, then Chancellor of the Exchequer.

comes more understandable. The legal profession, journalism, and certain types of business may be practiced on a part-time basis to supplement the parliamentary salary on the one hand and, on the other, sponsorship by a trade union or comparable organization may carry with it financial, secretarial, or other forms of assistance. The "full-time" M.P., however, especially if he has a family to maintain, cannot hope for more than a very modest standard of living, and may well, for example, be unable to travel in the United Kingdom outside London and his constituency, not to speak of traveling abroad; nor is he entitled to an adequate pension (as opposed to a relatively small allowance on proof of need) upon retiring or being defeated. None but the wealthiest M.P., moreover, can afford to employ any or sufficient secretarial, administrative, or research workers to relieve him of essential routine chores (dealing with constituents' problems above all) or to provide all the leisure and facilities needed for independent thought and investigation. The staff of the House Library helps in every way it can, but it is too small. The physical amenities of the House are also grossly inadequate for the needs of a conscientious back-bencher.[31] One potentially alarming result of all this is that the ordinary member is unduly dependent on, or at the mercy of, what information he can himself extract from government and other public sources for the necessary factual basis on which to criticize and evaluate the policy and record of the government.

In practice the bulk of the work of the House, and especially of attendance at House committees (which meet in the mornings), is performed by some two to three hundred members who, for whatever reason, may be regarded as "full time." Because they are already overworked, they, as well as the "part time" members who wish to remain so, tend to resist suggestions for a greater use of committees for purposes of scrutiny as well as legislation. (These proposals are also resisted on other grounds, among them the fear that they might detract from ministerial responsibility to the whole House[32] for the work of their departments.)

[31] There are no offices for back-benchers, there are not even enough tables and desks to supply every member with a place to work, and the small lockers available provide little room for storing papers or other belongings. On this point and the whole question of working conditions of M.P.'s, see B. Crick, *Reform of the House of Commons* (London: Fabian Society, 1959).

[32] It has always struck this author as peculiar that so much weight is

This problem, too, is closely linked to the level of pay and, in particular, to one of the main reasons why it has not been increased. It is believed, principally by Conservatives, that there is something reprehensible about full-time M.P.'s (identified pejoratively with "professional politicians"). It is argued that, individually, they would be "careerists" (as if there were none to be found among the independently wealthy), and that, collectively, their presence would deny to the Commons the existing contacts and "outside experience" obtained by the simultaneous pursuit of some other occupation. The cogency of these arguments is open to doubt. They must also be set against the extent to which financial anxiety deters many people from entering Parliament at all. What is not open to doubt is that unless considerably better amenities and much higher salaries (and pensions) are given to members, the present trend to a diminution in the prestige of Parliament and to an increase in the discretion of the executive (to the benefit, often, only of the civil service and sectional interests) will not be reversed, and may not even be contained.

That the prestige of Parliament is declining is widely argued —at least among many back-benchers and outside observers.[33] It may also be significant that the names of many M.P.'s are better known to the general public for their journalistic writings or their (not necessarily political) appearances on TV than for their contributions to the work of Parliament, which may well suffer for such "extramural" activities.

It is important, all the same, not to exaggerate the pace and extent of the "passing of Parliament." [34] The collective power of private members, if and when invoked, is still formidable. The story of British policy toward the Suez Canal throughout the mid-1950's, for example, would be quite otherwise but for the influence (for good or evil) of the rank-and-file members

---

attached to this objection, since the proposal is designed largely to make good the increasing deficiencies of that very principle as a means of rendering government responsive to the public. For an excellent discussion of the issue, see Crick, *op. cit.,* and G. Marshall, "Anglo-Saxon Platitudes," *The Listener,* September 15, 1960.

[33] See, for example, the views of the following: B. Levin in *National Review,* October, 1957; R. H. S. Crossman in the *New Statesman,* April 2, 1955; C. Hollis in the *Spectator,* February 20, 1959; and Michael Foot in the Sunday *Observer,* January 11, 18, and 25, 1959.

[34] The phrase forms the title of a well-known and bitter analysis of Parliament's waning powers by Professor G. W. Keeton (London: Benn, 1952, with a second edition in 1954).

of both major parties. Such influence, moreover, is not exclusive to the government's own supporters. On great and critical occasions particularly, there frequently develops a distinct "feeling of the *House*" which no minister or government dares ignore. The ablest and most successful political leaders in Britain are almost all peculiarly sensitive to the mood and feelings of the Commons and almost automatically will attune their arguments and even their policies to it. The trouble is not so much that the Commons is unable to affect events as that it is primarily effective only upon the deepest levels of policy and upon matters of unimportant and irritating detail (as they may seem to governments) which impinge on an important political principle or ideal. There remains a large and vaguely defined middle ground where, for reasons of time and complexity, back-bench influence may be slight, where back-bench interest is sporadic or ill informed, or where the subject matter is not intrinsically dramatic enough to touch off any widespread public indignation. But when all is said and done, the facts remain that the Commons is still the most important forum of and focus for public political debate, that it can still, on occasion, speak loudly and clearly for the British people, and that, to the citizen in trouble, the best advice to give is still "write to your M.P."

Notes

Legislative procedure in the House of Commons

Bills fall into two categories: public and private. The latter are defined in Erskine May as "bills for the particular interest or benefit of any person or persons." In modern times they are primarily desired by local authorities seeking special powers additional to those granted by general legislation. They are considered under special procedures in which very small committees play the main part, whilst the right of the House to make the final decisions is reserved. Private bills should not be confused with Private Members' bills. The latter are "private" only in origin, being legislation proposed by a nonministerial M.P. They are in fact public bills subject to substantially the same procedure as ones introduced by the government. Public bills themselves are officially and simply defined as all bills which are not private ones. The terminology may be reminiscent of a Gilbert libretto, but the principles of classification are reasonably straight forward.

Public bills are considered and debated in a series of stages.

These are: (1) first reading: the bill is introduced by title and the motion "that this bill be given a first reading" is normally carried without discussion. The full text is then ordered to be printed. The function of the mover at this stage is primarily to give notice of pending legislation on a particular subject; (2) second reading: a full-scale debate takes place on the general principles of the bill as a whole. If they are accepted, possibly on the promise of some amendment, the bill proceeds to (3) the committee stage: the bill is discussed clause by clause, detailed amendments to which are in order. This stage is held either in a standing committee or in Committee of the Whole House (see below); (4) Report stage: the Committee reports back to the House, which may accept or reject the changes made and make new ones; (5) third reading: a final general debate at which further verbal amendments may be proposed, but none of substance. Thereafter the bill will be sent to the House of Lords for consideration in similar stages or, if the bill originated there (as do about one-quarter of all public bills, few of them of major political significance), for consideration of the Commons' amendments. If the Lords persevere in decisions differing from the Commons', the government must give way, allow the whole bill to lapse, or invoke the provisions of the Parliament Acts of 1911 and 1949 and thus override the wishes of the Upper House.

Committees of the House of Commons

COMMITTEE OF THE WHOLE HOUSE. Sitting under special rules, the whole House of Commons will take the committee stage of urgent or very short bills, bills of constitutional or great political significance, and, indeed, any others so decided by the government. The whole House will also discuss the estimates of expenditure as "the Committee of Supply," and directly authorize expenditure or discuss revenue proposals as "the Committee of Ways and Means."

STANDING COMMITTEES. As many of these as necessary are appointed, but rarely more than five or six. They are known simply by letters of the alphabet, *A, B, C,* and so on, with the exceptions to be mentioned shortly. They consist of a nucleus of twenty members, to whom an additional thirty may be added for the purpose of considering each particular bill. All are appointed in proportion to the strengths of the parties in the House. They are purely legislative and, in principle, are nonspecialist—that is, they are intended to represent the whole House and, like it, to consider any bill put before them. In practice, however, the additional members at least will serve because of some special interest or experience. The minister in charge of a government bill is always a member of the appropriate standing committee. One of the exceptions referred to is the Scottish Standing Committee, drawn entirely from M.P.'s for the Scottish constituencies, which conducts the committee stage of purely Scottish legislation. It is not to be, but often is, confused with the Scottish Grand Committee, consisting of all seventy-one Scottish members and twelve others, which may discuss the Scottish Estimates, other purely Scottish affairs, and the second reading of Scottish bills. There also exist Welsh Standing and Grand committees which by early 1961 had still to meet for the first time. The chairmen of all committees are drawn from a panel of back-benchers appointed by the Speaker.

SELECT COMMITTEES. They are so called because the members are selected and named at the time each committee is established. They normally consist of fifteen members, although the one on Estimates has thirty. They are set up as required to investigate and report upon a specific problem or topic, which may be a question of privilege, or the management of the Palace of Westminster (the Houses of Parliament building), or some other problem which the House itself wishes to study. These committees have power to send for papers and persons. Certain select committees are regularly re-established: those on public accounts, estimates, statutory instruments, and the nationalized industries (reports and accounts), being the most well known.

The first of these is assisted in its work of scrutinizing the amount and manner of public expenditure by the Comptroller and Auditor General, a senior official appointed by, and responsible to, the House of Commons to audit the national accounts. The Committee on Statutory Instruments is assisted by the Speaker's Counsel, trained and experienced in constitutional and administrative law. Both committees render invaluable service in bringing to light and querying irregularities within their jurisdiction. The Committee on Estimates, despite pressure of time and lack of staff, by extensive use of subcommittees has carried out useful checks on selected items in the annual estimates of government expenditure. None of these three, however, may raise questions of policy. The youngest is the one on the nationalized industries, being established in its present form in 1956. Its principal function is to obtain and order the information necessary to evaluate the reports and accounts of the nationalized industries, but it also pronounces on the operations and organization of those industries insofar as they affect those matters for which a minister is responsible. (The appropriate ministers are, broadly speaking, entitled by statute to issue general directions to the managing boards, which they appoint, but not to make decisions about the day-to-day running of the industries. They are responsible, naturally enough, only for those aspects of the industries about which they are able to make decisions.) About all four committees it may be said that they do not so much extend the range of parliamentary scrutiny as they make it more meaningful and concrete.

6 - Administration and Civil Service

Organization

In June, 1956, 3,700,000 people were employed by the central government and other public undertakings, not counting members of the armed services. Listing all the government and public offices and their most senior members of officials took ninety-seven double-column pages of small type in Whitaker's *Almanack* for 1959.[1] The most important of the organizations are the twenty-two departments headed by political ministers who, with their ministerial colleagues,[2] are also in some degree responsible for the direction of the myriad other public offices and authorities. Of these latter bodies, some are controlled directly by a nondepartmental minister or a ministerial department. Others, like the boards of the nationalized industries and the University Grants Committee, have been subjected only to a limited degree of ministerial control in order to insulate their work from direct or continuous political involvement.

[1] See A. M. Carr-Saunders and others, *Social Conditions in England and Wales* (Oxford: The Clarendon Press, 1958), Table 8.4, p. 97; and Joseph Whitaker's *Almanack for the Year of Our Lord 1959* (London: Joseph Whitaker, 1959), pp. 355–450.

[2] Ministers like the Law Officers of the Lord Privy Seal have offices, but not departments, under them.

It is in the departments that almost all the 600,000-odd nonindustrial civil servants work.[3] Only a tiny fraction of these are *politically* important. In 1956, for example, 472,000 out of 618,000 were concerned entirely with routine administrative, technical, or post-office work, or were employed as typists, messengers, cleaners, and porters.[4] Their work is, of course, administratively essential, and they are the people who have the most frequent face-to-face contact with the public. But for our present purposes they must largely be ignored.

The system of recruitment to the higher levels derives from two fundamental principles which were first clearly accepted in 1870: that the service be designed to offer a "career open to the talents" as they emerge from the educational system; and that a basic division of labor should be recognized within the service.[5] Among the general administrators there exists a three-fold classification into administrative, executive, and clerical, adopted in 1920. The last is concerned with the detailed routine work of any large administrative machine and, in its work, is closely guided by instructions from the classes above it. At the top is the administrative class, whose duties may be described as the formation of policy and the general management of the administrative machine. The work of the executive class may be most conveniently defined as covering everything between the work of the other two classes—it performs responsible work, demanding good judgment, but it does so within the broad framework of policy decisions made elsewhere.[6]

Each class is further subdivided into grades, each with their

---

[3] The standard definition of civil servants is "those servants of the Crown, other than holders of political or judicial offices, who are employed in a civil capacity, and whose remuneration is paid wholly and directly out of monies voted by Parliament." See W. J. M. Mackenzie and J. W. Grove: *Central Administration in Britain* (London: Longmans, 1957), p. 11–13. This definition includes "industrial" civil servants who work in Admiralty dockyards or government arsenals, for example. The majority of public servants, e.g., those in nationalized industries, do not fall within this definition, in most cases because their remuneration is either not paid from "monies voted by Parliament" or is so only in part or indirectly.

[4] Carr-Saunders, *op. cit.*, table 9.4, p. 111.

[5] The modern civil service was largely inspired by the famous *Report on the Organisation of the Permanent Civil Service* by Stafford H. Northcote and C. E. Trevelyan, published in 1854. For an excellent brief discussion, see Wyn Griffith, *The British Civil Service 1854–1954* (London: H.M.S.O., 1954); also K. C. Wheare, *The Civil Service in the Constitution* (London: Athlone Press, 1954). The text of the *Report* is reprinted in *Public Administration* (1954).

[6] See the definitions quoted in Mackenzie and Grove, *op. cit.*, pp. 62–63.

appropriate levels of pay and responsibility. Most civil servants will in fact spend their working time within the class to which they are first recruited,[7] on the broad assumption that each class demands, and obtains, different kinds and levels of capacity. Certain specialist classes (professional, technical, and legal) exist separately and alongside these three general ones. The principal avenue of entry is by open competitive examination and interview directly into each class, supplemented by promotion from a lower class and by limited competitions. The open examinations for the administrative classes are designed primarily for recent university graduates, and those for the executive, for people leaving a grammar school or its equivalent at about the age of eighteen. (The professional, scientific, and technical grades are recruited on the basis of their qualifications, plus interview. The examinations for the lower, clerical and subclerical, classes are designed for people leaving school at the national minimum school-leaving age [fifteen in 1960] after attending any type of secondary school.)

Recruitment is organized by a body of six civil service commissioners, appointed by the crown, and their staff. In the actual conduct of examinations and interviews they act quite independently of all departments and of any direct ministerial supervision. Candidates for the main nonspecialist classes may offer almost any subject, so that no student of ability shall be barred from sitting the examinations; to insist upon candidates offering subjects with a real or assumed relevance to their future work would, it is believed, result in curtailing the field. This principle is further defended on the ground that general intelligence and the ability to take responsibility are more important to a high-level administrator than, say, a training in economics which may in any case be outdated by the time it is most useful. The only essential qualities, it is argued, are good judgment and the ability to use and evaluate the expertise of others.

Selection on the grounds of general rather than specialized qualifications has an additional justification. Both for the sake of the service and to offer the greatest possible career opportuni-

[7] For example, a new recruit to the administrative class will normally begin at the lowest level as an assistant principal. The other grades, in ascending order, are: principal, assistant secretary, under secretary, deputy secretary, permanent secretary. In 1955 there were 1,259 principals, 673 assistant secretaries, 214 under secretaries, 63 deputy secretaries, and 23 permanent secretaries.

ties to civil servants, great emphasis is placed upon the ideal of a unified civil service. Thus almost all the three and a half thousand administrative civil servants are members of the one Treasury or General Administrative Class. The sole exception is the Foreign Service "A" Class, which is separately recruited and trained to fill some of the top positions within the Foreign Office and its overseas branches (embassies, U.N. delegations, etc.). More than half of the over sixty thousand executive civil servants are, similarly, members of the Treasury Executive Class. Members of the general classes are technically recruited to the civil service first, and only thereafter allocated to particular departments or offices. Throughout their subsequent careers they remain at least eligible for transfer between departments. The separate departmental classes are maintained partly from a sense of reverence for tradition but principally because special training and experience is required (for example, in the collection of taxes). They are linked with the Treasury classes so far as possible in order to secure comparable pay and status for comparable degrees of responsibility, and thus to emphasize the common qualities in civil service life.

The labeling of the common classes as "Treasury" classes calls attention to the role of the Treasury as the "department of departments," the department which is primarily responsible for the personnel and machinery of government. The system of Treasury control[8] has grown from the Treasury's financial responsibilities for the whole field of government and administration. It is now responsible also for all major questions of establishment, including the most senior appointments, and civil service organizations and method, as well as for the general coordination of financial and economic policy. In its former capacities it must be regarded as the prime minister's department,[9] and only in its latter capacities as coming under the Chancellor of the Exchequer. For obvious and natural reasons, these institutions have not abolished departmentalism among

[8] For a brief account by a former civil service Head of the Treasury, see the lecture by Sir Edward Bridges, *Treasury Control* (London: Athlone Press, 1950). See also Samuel H. Beer, *Treasury Control* (London: Oxford, 1957).

[9] It will be remembered that the prime minister almost invariably holds the office of First Lord of the Treasury. The Chancellor of the Exchequer and five junior lords make up the rest of the board. In fact, the junior lords have no Treasury responsibilities, but are junior government whips serving under the chief whip. The latter is officially known and paid as Parliamentary Secretary to the Treasury, and formerly held the title of Patronage Secretary.

civil servants. Nevertheless, the ideal of a unified service, if un-attainable in full, remains operative and influential.

Constitutional Status of Ministerial Departments

The constitutional status of ministerial departments may be said to rest upon two basic principles, the first of which is that of ministerial responsibility.[10] From the point of view of the civil servant this means that it is the minister, the man at the top, who has to bear the brunt of criticism for any short-coming within the department, and, as a necessary corollary, that the minister's decisions (which may in fact be taken by the cabinet) must be accepted and acted upon by the department. One of the primary duties of the civil servant, therefore, is to try to keep his minister out of trouble, especially, but not ex-clusively, where the "trouble" is accidental rather than the foreseeable outcome of conscious decisions on policy. Indications of the seriousness with which this duty is taken may be found in the care with which a department's officials will prepare answers to parliamentary questions and in the fact that their preparation takes absolute priority over any and every other work. Thus, through its minister, a department is kept in touch with and responsive to Parliament and the electorate. But ministerial responsibility is more than a control mechanism. It is also, for the civil servant, a defense mechanism. The principle is so in-terpreted as to shield individual officials from public criticism and direct political involvement. Even in their appearance before select committees, for example, officials maintain the roles of their departments' spokesmen and servants, talking in terms of depart-mental, not personal, policy and practice. Through ministerial representation, too, officials are assured of the opportunity to defend their actions against inevitable criticism in Parliament and elsewhere, as well as to provide authoritative explanations of their intentions, without which their work might be seriously hampered by public ignorance or misunderstanding.[11]

The second basic principle governing the constitutional posi-tion of ministerial departments is that their officials be the civil *servants* of the crown. Legally, this means that they have no

[10] See Chapter 4 above.
[11] Nineteenth-century experiments with independent boards administer-ing controversial services (like the Poor Law) were not persevered with, partly because of the administrative inconveniences attending the lack of an authori-tative parliamentary spokesman.

rights against their employer, to be paid, pensioned, or retained in service, and that the conditions of their employment are governed not by statute[12] but by Treasury regulations or Orders-in-Council. In fact, of course, for reasons intimately connected with the general standing of the government as well as in the interests of efficiency and recruitment, their positions are more secure and assured than any other outside the universities and the courts of law. The other implications of this principle are therefore of more importance. What they amount to, in brief, is that the political and administrative virtues of the ideal civil servant are much like those of the perfect butler or valet of tradition. He should be discreet, unobtrusive, loyal, tactful, and fully capable of running the entire household, including his master (so long as the last quality is not apparent outside the family). In particular, the civil servant is expected to refrain from personal comment on political questions or the affairs of his department and, in short, to do nothing in public (other than to resign) which might imply any personal, as opposed to departmental, opinion upon public issues. At no time, either, must he disclose information about the internal operations of his department or its affairs without authorization. This rule is, clearly, a necessary corollary of the principle of strict ministerial responsibility and a condition of the official's being able to serve a succession of political masters with different personal and party policies.

For long these considerations were held also to require that all civil servants confine their political activities exclusively to the ballot box. Since 1953, however, the prohibition has been greatly relaxed. Very broadly speaking, it was then agreed that political activity be denied only to the administrative and executive classes (and members of comparable specialist grades) and to "those who work in local offices and deal directly with the individual citizen in relation to his personal circumstances." [13] Even these groups may, at the discretion of their department, be allowed to take part in local politics. This permission is commonly granted, except to members of the "higher civil service." [14]

[12] Acts of Parliament are necessary to *enable* salaries and pensions to be paid, and others, e.g., the Official Secrets Act, apply specifically, if not exclusively, to civil servants; but appointments are, in law, made at the discretion of the crown.

[13] From the statement of government policy on *Political Activities of Civil Servants* (London: H.M.S.O., Cmd. 8783 of 1953), p. 6.

[14] All civil servants may belong to any political party, including the Fascist and Communist parties. But see the note on security provisions at the end of this chapter.

The Higher Civil Service

The phrase "the higher civil service" is frequently used to refer to the most important members of the civil service, but little agreement exists about its precise connotation.[15] Essentially, however, the higher civil service consists of the chief policy advisers to ministers and those in most regular personal contact with ministers. The group will be larger or smaller, depending on whether or not one includes the lower levels of the administrative class (who, as they are promoted, will become increasingly involved in making policy) and on just where one draws the line separating policy from other matters. But at its largest it will consist only of the administrative class and certain individual civil servants drawn from the most senior levels of the executive classes (possibly), of the inspectorates, and, increasingly, of the professional, legal, and scientific groups. At most, therefore, it will include something in the region of three thousand people. More realistically, from the point of view of policy-making, it will probably number about one thousand and will certainly include no more than fifteen hundred people, of whom the largest single group will be drawn from the administrative class, but with a growing proportion from the specialist groups.

The duties of the higher civil service range at least as widely as those of the government it serves and advises. Ministers— relatively inexperienced and impermanent—are necessarily dependent upon their permanent expert advisers for knowledge and guidance. As in all countries, too, one of the primary tasks of civil servants is to act as filters for their superiors, ensuring that only the most important matters (but all of them) should be placed before ministers. Inevitably, therefore, civil servants must take many decisions without reference to the minister—even on important matters of "policy." By all accounts they do so, insofar as they can, only in accordance with the known preferences and principles of the minister, just as they always consult the minister before deciding questions in which they know him to be specially interested. Moreover, because of the doctrine of ministerial re-

[15] For example, the *Report* of the Royal Commission on the Civil Service (London: H.M.S.O., Cmd. 9613 of 1950), includes within its scope all civil servants above the salary level of a principal (nearly 3,000 people); R. K. Kelsall, in his *Higher Civil Servants in Britain* (London: Routledge and Kegan Paul, 1955), on the other hand, limits it to home administrative civil servants of and above the grade of assistant secretary (1,045 people in 1950). See also the excellent "insider's" account, H. E. Dale, *The Higher Civil Service* (London: Oxford, 1941).

sponsibility, even the most senior members of the higher civil service in Britain will play a much less public and much less "political" role than many of their American counterparts.

It is not possible for an outsider accurately to measure the extent or nature of civil service influence upon the conduct of government—and particularly upon the formation of policy, which is our principal concern—yet some general remarks can be made. Some ministers will be little or no more than the spokesmen for their permanent officials. But unless a minister is capable at least of stating his department's view in dealings with other ministers or the cabinet, and of seeing that his department works within the confines of government policy, he is unlikely to remain in office for long. Others will make a decisive impact upon the whole work of their departments. Even the strongest minister, however, must leave all but the most important decisions to his officials. These considerations apart, the extent to which departmental policy is made by its higher civil servants or by its political head will depend upon the personalities involved and the degree to which the minister and the cabinet are dependent upon those officials for their knowledge and ideas. This dependence will tend to increase with the complexity and technicality of the issues, their remoteness from ordinary experience, and the shortage of time and facilities available to those other than the official. On all these grounds it may be surmised that the influence of the civil service is increasing in the mid-twentieth century.

If the role of the civil service raises certain doubts about the sufficiency of ministerial responsibility as a control mechanism, the principle itself nevertheless remains intact and unchallenged. Civil servants in fact take pains to keep their ministers out of trouble by careful and responsible work, by attempting to forestall and to meet criticism, and, it must also be noted, by resort to "the pathological secretiveness of British government." [16] Ample testimony also exists to the integrity of civil servants and their ability to serve successive political masters and policies.[17] The principle is also invoked to help the civil servant resist particular pressures. He is the one who normally conducts the extensive and continuous negotiations and discussions with other departments and with outside interests and organizations, but he

[16] The phrase is quoted from Brian Chapman, *The Profession of Government* (London: Allen and Unwin, 1959), p. 321.

[17] See, for example, that of Lord Attlee in his "Civil Servants, Ministers, Parliament and the Public," *Political Quarterly*, XXV (1954), pp. 308–15.

can always fall back on the defense that the final decision must rest with the minister.

Anxiety is often voiced about the power vested in the civil service—particularly with regard to the extensive legislative and semi-judicial powers delegated to them by Parliament.[18] As we have suggested, there exist solid grounds for it. But it may be possible to quiet the doubts without fundamental reorganization. If, for example, the House of Commons were to be equipped with specialized scrutiny committees, and ministers with a larger personal staff (drawn from within or without the civil service) to aid them in their administrative duties, the problems might dwindle almost to insignificance.[19]

It is even more difficult to write with assurance about the nature of civil-service influence. But it is too important a question timidly to pass over. British officials seem to fulfill very well two desirable functions of any bureaucratic organization: they represent the claims of continuity in government as the repositories of administrative tradition and experience; and they embody the principles of administrative "rationality" as against the claims of political expedience. In these ways, as well as through their unrivaled knowledge of many of the weaknesses in existing laws and administrative practices, they have saved ministers from embarrassment and, not infrequently, enhanced ministerial reputations. If account is also taken of their ability, discretion, and remarkable degree of incorruptibility, it is easy to understand how the higher civil service should exercise a beneficial as well as indispensable influence upon the formulation of policy and the conduct of government. Yet the other and less generally acceptable side of their influence must also be noted.

In general, higher civil servants are detached rather than enthusiastic. They are concerned with "good government" rather than self-government, while tending to see government largely in terms of administration. The conditions and nature of their work

[18] See the reports of the (Donoughmore) Committee on Ministers' Powers, Cmd. 4060 of 1932, and of the (Franks) Committee on Administrative Tribunals and Inquiries, Cmd. 218 of 1957, of the Select Committee on Delegated Legislation, H.C. 310 of 1953; also see Chapters 5 and 7 of this text.

[19] The case for the former change is well argued in B. Crick, *Reform of the House of Commons* (London: Fabian Society, 1959). On the latter suggestion, see the discussion of ministerial cabinets and "posts of confidence" in B. Chapman, *op. cit.*, pp. 275–81. These ideas are mentioned here to illustrate the magnitude of the problem of civil service power, and not because they are generally agreed to be desirable.

and their recruitment must often tend to nurture in them the feeling that they are a governmental as well as an undoubted administrative elite, and that they are endowed with superior wisdom as well as undoubtedly greater experience. This tendency is likely also to be strengthened by their predominantly middle- and upper-middle class social origins and by their educational background. In 1950, for example, about 70 per cent of home civil servants above the rank of assistant secretary were the children of fathers from the "top" 5 per cent of the population. That is to say, the fathers belonged to the registrar-general's occupational classes I and II.[20] Almost 80 per cent of the group, moreover, attended fee-paying schools, including 24 per cent who had attended the more expensive and exclusive public schools— the proportion being higher among entrants by open competition and lower among other entrants.[21] The social composition of the higher levels of the civil service is not necessarily indicative of party political allegiance: after all, Burgess and Maclean (the two Foreign Office officials who fled to Moscow in 1951) both had impeccable social and educational origins.

In normal times, at least, it seems that governments may confidently rely upon the political neutrality of civil servants. But these facts about the social composition of the civil service do indicate the groups which have the readiest *informal* access to civil servants and which therefore have most influence upon their general outlook; and they support the view that, as a whole, higher civil servants are unduly removed from the outlook and way of life of the majority of the population. It is probably true, also, that a reforming government must rely less than may a conservative one upon its civil-service advisers for its policy inspiration. It must be emphasized, however, that this exclusiveness (which is admittedly less striking in 1960 than it was in 1900, or even in 1939) is largely the reverse side of the civil service's brightest coin. Whatever its shortcomings, the civil service has for long succeeded in maintaining a high place among the professions as a worthy and honorable career, and

[20] The same proportion was found among entrants to the administrative class by open examination in 1949–52. Such entrants accounted, however, for only a half of all entrants; those recruited by promotion or by competition limited to the civil service, who form the bulk of the remaining entrants, usually include many whose fathers were in Class III, and a few from Classes IV and V, which include the bulk of the population and constitute the bottom of the scale.

[21] See Kelsall, *op. cit.,* tables 16 and 25, pp. 128 and 153. And see the discussion in Chapter 2 above.

partly for this reason, in recruiting some of the ablest graduates of the educational system. It is primarily a result of the educational system, and of the social structure which it reflects, that the higher civil service should be so largely cut off from the experience and intellectual resources of much of the population.

The defects of the higher civil service in modern Britain assume much of their significance simply because of the shortcomings of parliamentary and ministerial control. Were these made good, relatively minor changes would suffice to ensure that the civil service itself would continue fully to deserve its high reputation.[22] Dr. Kenneth Wheare has said that "if Civil Servants appear . . . at times to act as Ministers in disguise, does not the remedy lie in stronger Ministers and a more independent and vigilant House of Commons rather than in weaker Civil Servants?"[23] This comment may be applied to other criticisms of the civil service than allegations of excessive influence.

Notes

"Security"

By the terms of the Official Secrets Act and various Treasury and departmental regulations, civil servants are under the strictest obligations not to disclose information pertaining to their work. Since March, 1948, steps have also been taken to try to prevent unauthorized disclosures by removing from "sensitive" posts individuals believed to be politically or (since 1956) personally unreliable. They must be transferred to nonsensitive posts, or allowed to resign without official discredit, or (only as a last resort) dismissed. Appeal lies to an independent committee of two retired civil servants and a trade-union official. Procedures are informal, not judicial. The accused person, but not the committee, may be denied access to all the evidence. Up until March 1957, 158 cases were heard, as a result of which 81 people were transferred, 24 were dismissed, 23 resigned, and 30 were reinstated after inquiries.

Workers in private firms engaged on secret government contracts are also liable to investigation and dismissal, subject to fewer safeguards. This, combined with the wider definition of "unreliability" adopted in 1956 (among other things, the relia

---

[22] See the suggestions contained in, for example, the works of Dale and Kelsall already cited and in H. R. G. Greaves, *The Civil Service in the Changing State* (London: Harrap, 1947).

[23] K. C. Wheare, *op. cit.*, p. 30.

bility of an employee's family also became "relevant"), and grounds for doubting the type of evidence considered, must worry any person anxious to preserve liberty. On the other hand, the absence of public hysteria, together with parliamentary interest in individual grievances, serve at least to limit the number of individual injustices involved in the quest for "security."[24]

The University Grants Committee

The University Grants Committee (U.G.C.) is an exceptional body, and one which has attracted a great deal of attention and even envy elsewhere.[25] It is unique in two principal respects. (1) It is appointed by the government to allocate public money to the universities, which are private institutions, but its twenty members are drawn almost entirely from those who work or have worked in those institutions. The chairman and secretary (the only full-time members) are both civil servants, but even the former was, until his appointment, the head of an Oxford college. (2) Despite the fact that the U.G.C. is responsible for spending large sums of public money (over $140,000,000 in 1958–59), its accounts are not audited by the Comptroller and Auditor General. The normal procedure is that the U.G.C. makes recommendations to the Treasury, on the basis of which the latter provides the money necessary to cover grants to the universities both for their running expenses (recurrent grants) and for approved items of capital expenditure (nonrecurrent grants). All grants are made from annual Treasury allocations, but the amounts are usually fixed with reference to general decisions made for successive five-year periods. How exactly the grants should be distributed to particular universities, and for what purposes, however, is decided by the U.G.C. in consultation with the universities themselves, and *not* by the Treasury or the Minister of Education.[26] The government, of course, is ultimately

[24] See Mackenzie and Grove, *op. cit.*, pp. 152–155; H. H. Wilson and Harvey Glickman, *The Problem of Internal Security in Great Britain, 1948–53* (Garden City, N.Y.: Doubleday, 1954); the *Statement on the Findings of the Conference of Privy Councillors on Security* (London: H.M.S.O., Cmd. 9715 of 1956); and the remarks about the police and security in the following chapter.

[25] It has, for example, been copied in India. See an invaluable American study: H. W. Dodds and others, *Government Assistance to Universities in Great Britain* (London: Oxford, 1952).

[26] He, like the Secretary of State in Scotland, has no jurisdiction in university affairs except for the provision of grants to students. (In 1958–59 80 per cent of all full-time students received financial assistance from central- or local-government grants.)

responsible for university policy to the extent that it decides how much money to make available to the U.G.C. for what *general* purposes. But the U.G.C. makes all detailed decisions and is invariably consulted by the government upon all questions of higher education. It is to preserve this division of responsibility and to safeguard the U.G.C.'s role as mediator and defender of academic freedom that successive governments have resisted pressure from the House of Commons Committee on Public Accounts for stricter control by the Comptroller and Auditor General and thus by Parliament.

In 1958–59 the Treasury paid $99,400,000 in recurrent grants and $46,200,000 in nonrecurrent grants. The Treasury now provides about 70 per cent of the total income of the twenty-four universities and university colleges in receipt of grants. Nevertheless, there has been no suggestion that university education has become a mere plaything of governments or a victim of partisan political interference. On the contrary, British universities are probably at least as free from external pressures upon their academic policies as any in the world, public or private. It cannot be doubted that the U.G.C. has played a major part in maintaining this state of affairs, even in the postwar period when its terms of reference were enlarged to include a duty to advise on "the preparation and execution of such plans for the development of the universities as may from time to time be required in order to ensure that they are fully adequate to national needs." [27] Whether the U.G.C. has been able to exercise these wider powers to the best advantage and whether it is the best body to undertake the preparation of long-term plans for development are further questions into which we cannot probe here.[28]

It is also at least debatable how far the U.G.C. is an "exportable" institution. It has worked well in Britain where the Treasury civil servants have similar social backgrounds to a substantial proportion of M.P.'s and to the members of both the U.G.C. and the principal governing bodies of the universities, where the university world is fairly small and not notoriously radical in outlook, and where the political tradition readily permits much of the business of the U.G.C. (in its own words) to be "dealt with informally between persons well known to each

[27] To quote from the terms of reference adopted in 1946.

[28] But see the discussion in the present author's *The Universities: A Royal Commission?* (London: Fabian Society, 1959), and some of the other sources cited there.

other." It might not work as well where these conditions were absent.

7 - Law and Order

The British people have become accustomed to a reasonably high standard of honesty and competence among their public servants. The latter, in turn, seem to rely upon a reasonably high standard of law-abidingness among the British people. Key figures in the day-to-day interaction of the public and authority are the members of the police. In all societies public attitudes toward policemen are likely to be ambivalent. In Britain, it may be said, feelings of respect, even affection, generally outweigh more negative attitudes. The sentimental picture of the police constable, armed solely with whistle and baton, walking his solitary beat, becoming acquainted with everyone in his "parish," and helping old ladies across streets, is, however, becoming outmoded. Today account must also be taken of the anonymous mobile patrol and increasingly frequent reports of violent behavior on the part of an overworked and undermanned force.[1] Nevertheless, police relations with the public continue to be predominantly peaceful and relatively amicable; the police have never become closely identified with any political movement, although they appear to have a natural affinity for the right rather than the left, and at no stage have they been a privileged (or alien) group set apart from the rest of society. For this state of affairs the institutional context in which the police work is largely responsible.

There are about one hundred and sixty regular civilian police forces in Britain, organized on the basis of existing local government areas (the counties, county boroughs, and Scottish

[1] Whether there has been an increase in anything other than the number of incidents which are reported in the press may be decided by the Royal Commission on the Police, whose formation was announced in December, 1959, and whose terms of reference include the question of public complaints as well as problems of pay and constitutional status.

cities, or amalgamations thereof, being the appropriate units).[2] The Metropolitan Police in London is under the control of the Home Secretary, acting through a commissioner appointed by and responsible to him. Elsewhere the constitutional position is more complicated. Each police force is commanded by a chief constable who is appointed and may be dismissed by the appropriate committee of his local council, subject to the approval of the Home Secretary, in England and Wales, or the Secretary of State for Scotland.[3] He then assumes primary responsibility for running, recruiting, and organizing the local force. It must be kept up to certain minimum standards of efficiency laid down by the central government, to which end it is subject to periodic inspection by H.M. Inspectors of Constabulary; but so long as the chief constable is in office, he exercises considerable discretion in matters of law enforcement.

His legal relationship to the local police authorities is not entirely clear, but he has been described as an officer of the crown whose "authority is original, not delegated, and is exercised at his own discretion by virtue of his office." [4] He is, however, dependent upon the local authority for finance as well as for his office. On the other hand the authority depends upon a grant-in-aid from the central government, which may be withheld or reduced if it is not used properly. The Home Secretary, in deciding whether to do this, will take account of reports from the chief constable as well as from the local authority and the inspectors. The policy followed by any police force is thus the outcome of the interactions of the chief constable, the local committee, and the central government, whose day-to-day relations are conducted by means of discussion and suggestion rather than by issuing orders. The responsibility for the investigation of particular cases, however, is entirely a matter for the local police. So are the decisions to prosecute—although the latter are subject to

[2] See the following chapter for an account of the structure of local government.

[3] The administration of the police, as well as the whole legal and judicial systems, are separate and distinct in Scotland. Space does not permit a description of them, but occasional reference will be made where the difference of principle seems of special interest or importance. In general, however, what follows applies directly only to England and Wales.

[4] Viscount Symonds in *Attorney General v. New South Wales Perpetual Trustees Co.* (1955) A.C. 457, quoted in an excellent discussion of the subject, Bryan Keith-Lucas, "The Independence of Chief Constables," *Public Administration*, XXXVIII (Spring, 1960).

general guidance from the office of the Director of Public Prosecutions (a legal official of the central government).[5]

These arrangements are partly accidental in origin and partly the product of continuous public watchfulness against any danger that the police should come under too much government control or should become too independently powerful. The second of these dangers is guarded against by public opinion itself (the police being the first to acknowledge their dependence upon public co-operation), strongly reinforced by the law and the courts. Thus, by law, the police must whenever possible obtain a warrant from a local magistrate before entering any premises without the occupier's permission; must lay specific charges against any arrested person before a magistrate within (usually) twenty-four hours of arrest, and produce some good reason for his continued detention, or else release him; must bring the accused person to trial within a further limited period; and must adhere to strict rules, imposed and enforced by the courts, about the manner of obtaining and producing evidence (including "confessions" and statements from the accused). Once trial commences, they appear only as witnesses, subject to no special privileges or immunities.[6]

The power of the police is further contained by the established criminal-law principle that any person accused shall be deemed innocent until proved guilty beyond reasonable doubt. The practice of leaving questions of fact to be determined by a jury in all serious criminal trials may also, if less confidently, be seen as a safeguard against arbitrary police power. The opportunities for injustice to result from police incompetence or excessive zeal are thus severely restricted, if not yet reduced to the human minimum, so far as the ordinary police and the criminal law are concerned.[7] The same cannot be so boldly asserted of the increasing demands upon the police, whether of the

[5] Private citizens may also initiate a criminal prosecution. In Scotland the decision to prosecute or not rests with the Procurator-Fiscal locally, and nationally with the Lord Advocate, both lawyers (the former a civil servant and the latter a member of the government), and not at all with the police. No private prosecution has taken place in Scotland since World War I. See Sir Patrick Devlin, *The Criminal Prosecution in England* (New Haven, Conn.: Yale University Press, 1960).

[6] Occasionally in an English Court of Summary Jurisdiction a police officer will conduct the prosecution personally, but it is more usual for this work to be done by a lawyer retained for the purpose.

[7] For a critical account of police procedure in one case, see Ludovic Kennedy, *10 Rillington Place* (London: Gollancz, 1961).

ordinary or the special branch, to investigate and report on "security" cases. It is doubtful, in particular, how far they are qualified or trained for the very difficult political evaluations required. This appears also to be true of the section of military intelligence concerned with this work.[8] What is most alarming, perhaps, is the apparently total exclusion of this type of investigation from the purview of the courts.

At first sight British practice seems to violate the principle of the separation of judicial and executive power. The head of the judiciary, the Lord Chancellor, is a member of the cabinet and presides over the House of Lords. All judges and magistrates are appointed by or on his advice.[9] There might thus seem to be close political supervision of the judiciary. In fact, it is completely independent of political pressure or interference. It was so even in the nineteenth century when, according to Professor Laski's studies, the great majority of senior judgeships were conferred as a political reward.[10]

All superior judges are appointed "during good behaviour subject to a power of removal by His Majesty on an address presented to His Majesty by both Houses of Parliament"—to quote the phrase used in the Judicature (Consolidation) Act, 1925, and derived from the Act of Settlement, 1701. The security of tenure thus granted (for the removal procedure has never been used in Britain) provides the first explanation of judicial independence. Another lies in English history and tradition: in the facts that the courts and Parliament were allies during the seventeenth-century struggles against royal power, and that those struggles seemed, to both of them, to be on behalf of the common-law rights of which the judges provided the surest defense. Parliamentary and public opinion continue to be highly sensitive to any suggestion of "political" (which means, in this context, executive) interference with the work of the courts. For the most part, indeed, to vest the appointment power in ministers who are accountable to Parliament is regarded as a safeguard against possible abuses of irresponsible power.

The fact that the courts accept the supremacy of Parliament

[8] The dangers, illustrated by case histories, are disturbingly set out in *The Secret Police and You,* a pamphlet published by The Campaign for the Limitation of Secret Police Powers (no date).

[9] Except in the old royal possession of the Duchy of Lancaster, whose chancellor appoints magistrates and county-court judges, and in Scotland, where appointments are the responsibility of the Secretary of State in all cases. Both these men are ministers.

[10] H. J. Laski, *Studies in Law and Politics* (London: Allen and Unwin, 1932), pp. 168–73.

English courts of law

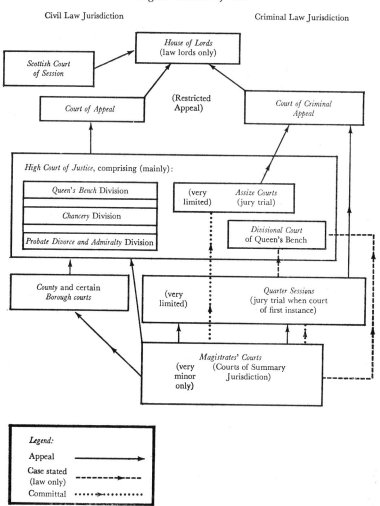

Civil Law Jurisdiction   Criminal Law Jurisdiction

House of Lords
(law lords only)

*Scottish Court
of Session*

(Restricted
Appeal)

Court of Appeal

*Court of Criminal
Appeal*

High Court of Justice, comprising (mainly):

Queen's Bench Division

Chancery Division

Probate Divorce and Admiralty Division

(very
limited) *Assize Courts*
(jury trial)

Divisional Court
of Queen's Bench

County and certain
Borough courts

(very
limited)

Quarter Sessions
(jury trial when court
of first instance)

(very
minor
only) *Magistrates' Courts*
(Courts of Summary
Jurisdiction)

Legend:

Appeal

Case stated
(law only)

Committal

in the law-making field is also an important bastion against political pressures. It means that an unpopular decision results in pressure upon Parliament for legislation and not upon the courts directly or through those who appoint the judges. Thus the decision of the House of Lords in the famous Taff Vale case,[11] which destroyed well-established beliefs about the legal rights and status of trade unions, and which seemed to imperil their very existence as effective organizations, resulted in a political campaign by the unions for the return of sympathetic M.P.'s and not, as might have happened, in lasting hostility to or defiance of the courts.[12]

Possibly the single most important factor in any explanation of the position of the judiciary in Britain is the organization of the legal profession itself. The profession comprises two distinct branches—barristers and solicitors. The former have the exclusive right to plead in the higher courts and, in fact, specialize in advocacy. The latter, who form by far the greater part of the profession, are responsible for most other types of legal work, including the interviewing of clients and, possibly, appearing for them in magistrates' and county courts. But it comprises only two branches; for, by law or custom, the judiciary and the legal ministers (except for the Secretary of State for Scotland—and in judicial matters he is advised by the Lord Advocate, who is a lawyer) are all appointed from barristers of some years' standing. What is even more important, perhaps, is that they continue to be members of the Inns of Court, the ancient bodies responsible for organizing, disciplining, admitting, and in part educating members of the bar.[13] The legal minister and the judiciary are thus members of a tightly organized and largely self-governing profession, jealous of its traditions and with a strong vested interest in the maintenance of its independence.[14]

[11] *Taff Vale Railway Co. v. Amalgamated Society of Railway Servants* (1901), A.C. 426.

[12] The result was the passage of the Trades Disputes Act, 1906, by the newly elected Liberal government. The Taff Vale campaign also undoubtedly helped secure the election in 1906 of the thirty independent Labour M.P.'s who formed the Parliamentary Labour party.

[13] For a brief, informative, and very readable account of the profession, see R. M. Jackson, *The Machinery of Justice in England,* 2d ed. (Cambridge: University Press, 1953), pp. 203–21. This book should be consulted on all the points, other than the police, discussed in this chapter.

[14] In Scotland the position is similar. There is a twofold division also, into advocates and solicitors, the former being organized in the Faculty of Advocates, which performs functions comparable with those of the Inns of Court. In both countries, too, the solicitors are largely self-governing, if less tightly organized.

The rule of law is a concept which is difficult to define with precision. Nevertheless, it is customarily listed among the basic principles of the British constitution.[15] If by this phrase is broadly meant an absence of arbitrary and unregulated public power, it is clearly safeguarded in Britain by the nature and powers both of the police and of the judiciary. More specifically, too, it is maintained by certain well-established principles of British law, among them: that the citizen may not be punished except for a specific breach of a definite rule of law; that, while officials or public persons and organizations may be granted special powers, they do not escape judicial scrutiny to ensure that they act only within those powers; that, in their individual capacities, officials do not escape from the general obligations imposed on ordinary citizens; and that, in general, so far as judicial rules and procedures can ensure it, there exists equality before the law. This is not to say, however, that there are no grounds for anxiety.

In Britain, judges rightly have a high reputation for impartiality and the ability to weigh evidence.[16] It is less certain, however, that the system has been able to eliminate a social bias rooted both in the individualism and conservatism inherent in the common law and in the finances of justice in Britain. Money is important in two different ways. To become a lawyer, and particularly a barrister, is difficult if not impossible for anyone without at least a small private income. For the most part, therefore, the legal profession is composed of, and mixes socially with, people from the higher social classes. As Lord Justice Scrutton has said: "It is very difficult sometimes to be sure that you have put yourself into a thoroughly impartial position between two disputants, one of your own class and one not of your class." [17]

Money matters also to the extent that for a client to obtain justice is a costly affair in terms of court and lawyers' fees. In a big case, these may easily run into the tens of thousands of pounds. The government has assumed some responsibility for helping those in need. Under the Poor Prisoner's Defense Act of

[15] See A. V. Dicey, *Introduction to the Study of the Law of the Constitution*, 10th ed., Part II (London: Wade, 1960), and such modern works as Wilfrid Harrison, *The Government of Britain*, 6th ed. (London: Hutchinson, 1960), pp. 26–28.

[16] As is evidenced, for example, by the heavy demands upon them and, to a slightly lesser extent, upon barristers, for service upon arbitration boards, royal commissions, and other committees of inquiry, usually as chairman.

[17] 1 *Cambridge Law Journal*, p. 8, cited in Jackson, *op. cit.*, p. 234.

1930 the courts are empowered to ensure that a poor prisoner
obtains a solicitor and, if necessary, a barrister to undertake his
defense in criminal cases. A fairly strict means test is applied,
but the vast majority of applications are granted.[18] The Legal
Aid and Advice Act of 1949 provided that public assistance also
be available in some, and eventually all, civil actions (for
plaintiff as well as defendant), the scheme being administered,
under the direction of the Lord Chancellor, by the Law Society.[19]
As general economic conditions have improved, the Act has
progressively been implemented—the latest section to be brought
into force being the provisions establishing a system of free oral
legal advice. The result is that legal aid may be obtained, subject to a means test, to bring any but the more trivial civil actions, or to defend any action outside the magistrates' courts
and except for certain specified categories of proceedings—among
them defamation and breach of promise of marriage—in the
county courts and above. The principle has thus been accepted
that money should not bar access to the courts even if, perhaps,
the level of the means test is still low enough to hinder the full
application of that principle. It is too soon, however, properly
to assess the efficacy of the scheme or its impact upon ignorance
and the fear of legal procedures which may still prevent many
people from obtaining full judicial defense of their legal rights.

It is partly because of this social bias in the legal system
that there has been a proliferation of special administrative
tribunals appointed by ministers to decide, originally or on
appeal, cases arising out of the application of social policy to
particular persons, places, or circumstances.[20] Other reasons have
included the desire for speedier and more informal procedures
than are normally obtainable in the courts, and the claim that
many of the issues which present themselves involve too many
questions of "policy" to be suitable subjects for judicial deter-

[18] See Jackson, *op. cit.*, p. 129, for a table of applications and refusals.
[19] That is, by the professional association to which most solicitors belong.
[20] Examples of such tribunals, which vary widely in their power, procedure, and composition, include: the Licensing Authority for Public Service
Vehicles; the Special Commissioners of Income Tax; rent tribunals; and appeal tribunals to deal with pensions, national assistance, and other aspects
of the social services.
    There also exist many private tribunals exercising statutory functions:
for example, the disciplinary committees established by, and with jurisdiction over, members of the legal, medical, and other professions. From their
decisions appeal lies, on points of law, to the Judicial Committee of the Privy
Council.

mination. The existence of these tribunals, their powers, their procedures, and above all the lack, in many cases, of statutory provision for appeal to the courts and the difficulties of judicial review, have given rise to almost continuous disquiet, particularly, but not exclusively, among judges and lawyers. They have, accordingly, been the subject of two major inquiries.[21] The report of the second of these, the Franks Committee, was quickly followed by the Tribunals and Inquiries Act, 1958, which established the general principle of judicial review on points of law as well as providing for numerous procedural reforms on lines suggested by the committee. By this Act, too, a council was set up to keep the working of some thirty named tribunals under constant review and to make reports thereon. It remains to be seen whether this Act will allay all fears that resort to such tribunals constitutes a serious breach in the rule of law, or, more realistically speaking, how loudly the law journals will continue to echo to the eternal conflict between the claims of executive discretion and judicial restraint. At present, however, the conflict is largely confined to such relatively restricted circles. Not even in this respect is the role of the judiciary a major public concern.

8 - Local Government

Local-government authorities are very closely linked to the central administration in their operations, but organizationally they retain their independence. By a "local authority" in Britain is meant, broadly speaking, a local government unit whose powers are vested in a council elected by, and politically responsible to, a local electorate, but which is legally subordinate to, and indeed the creation of, the central organs of government.

Structurally, local government is organized into what is known as the dual system—that is to say, into two sets of authorities which are quite independent of each other. The four major cities in Scotland and over eighty of the largest ones in England

[21] See the *Reports* of the Committee on Ministers' Powers, Cmd. 4060 of 1932, and of the Committee on Administrative Tribunals and Inquiries, Cmd. 218 of 1957.

and Wales (the "county boroughs") are self-contained and independent of the system in the ninety-two administrative counties.
The county councils are responsible for some local-government
services throughout the whole of their areas, but separately
elected councils are responsible for other services in the various
urban and rural districts into which the counties are subdivided.[1]
(This division of authority in the counties constitutes the "two-
tier system.) London has its own two-tier system unlike those
found elsewhere.

Two other principles must be noted. The first is that each
local council, if one excepts the two-tier county system, is the
only local-government body within its area, and is thus a multi-
purpose authority responsible for *all* the powers limited to its
area.[2] The second principle is that of a correlation between range
of function and type of authority—each category of authority
having its distinctive set of powers. Unfortunately, the operation
of this principle is vitiated by a substantial adherence to the
historic boundaries of counties and boroughs. The result is that,
for example, the counties are widely different in area, population, and financial resources (and the same can be said of every
other category), so that it is unrealistic to expect them to
discharge the same functions with comparable efficiency. Local
rivalry and pride also make it very difficult to alter the status of
particular areas to keep pace with population and other changes.
Numerous Private Acts of Parliament conferring greater powers
on particular authorities, and the recommendations of successive
boundary commissions (aimed at rationalizing the structure to
some extent), have not fundamentally altered the position. Its
indefinite continuance seems assured by the reluctance of the
central government to offend the numerous people and organizations whose prestige (or *amour propre*) is deeply involved in the
present system and who cannot be persuaded to agree among
themselves on any alternative.

The failure to reform the structure of local government has
had unhealthy results. None of the existing areas is large enough
to administer certain modern services, with the result that the

---

[1] In England and Wales these lesser authorities consist of borough
councils, urban and rural district councils; in the country a third tier also
exists consisting of the parishes (with very minor functions). In Scotland the
corresponding authorities are the large burghs, small burghs, and the districts (predominantly rural).

[2] There are not, and have not been since the nineteenth century, any
independent *ad hoc* bodies like elected school boards in the field of local
government.

central government has absorbed such formerly local responsibilities as hospital management, gas and electricity supply and
distribution, and public assistance.[3] In allocating powers to
different types of authority it has been necessary either to accept
inadequate performance by the smaller authorities within any
category or else to deny those powers to the larger ones which
could cope with them perfectly well. Increasingly local-government structure has ceased to reflect the actual units of social
existence, particularly in the major conurbations, with deleterious
effects upon the level of public interest,[4] as well as upon the
performance of functions. (Town and country planning is perhaps the most obvious sufferer.[5]) Above all, structural shortcomings must accept some of the blame for the growth of central
control over the day-to-day work of local authorities. Local
authorities still have fairly wide discretion over such matters as
recreational and cultural facilities, child welfare, sanitation, street
lighting, and other minor matters, but over their most important, dramatic, and expensive functions, among which are
education (except universities) and low-rent housing, their discretion has been progressively narrowed by control from above.

The councilors themselves are elected for three-year terms
of office—together or one-third each year, according to the type
of authority—by those local inhabitants qualified to vote in
parliamentary elections.[6] In England and Wales the councils also
appoint additional members, the aldermen, for a six-year term[7]
—but in Scotland all councilors are elected. In all but some coun-

[3] It is often said that the parish was the area appropriate to a time
when walking was the principal means of transport, and the county, when
the horse came into general use, but that neither is obviously the best area
in an era in which all forms of communication have advanced somewhat
beyond these means.

[4] Rarely do more than 40 per cent of the local electorate go to the polls,
and frequently very much less. No one can yet be certain why nonvoting is
so prevalent, but this divorce of the administrative from the social pattern
seems likely to form part of the explanation.

[5] The manifest failures adequately to plan and develop land are not
wholly the result of such local causes as the separation of town and country
or the multiplicity of weak local authorities. The absence of national legislation to deal with real-estate speculation, or of a more definite national
policy on such issues as suburban sprawl, the conservation of agricultural
land, and the development of city centers have tended to frustrate the good
intentions of many local authorities.

[6] Until after World War II the suffrage was restricted to those who paid
local rates (the principal form of local taxation, which will be discussed
below).

[7] Up to one-quarter of the total council may be aldermen.

ties and the smallest authorities, the strong tendency is to conduct elections and all council business on strict party lines, and most usually on two-party lines: Labour versus anti-Labour (the names under which the latter rally vary considerably, but their support is principally Conservative). In those few councils which remain free of party organization the councilor possibly has more scope for personal initiative, but contested elections are fewer and power tends to lie with a local established oligarchy of landowners and farmers in rural, and of shopkeepers and merchants in urban, areas.

In all but the smallest councils the actual work of administration is carried on by committees and subcommittees of the council, the most influential members of which are usually the chairmen, or conveners, who act in particularly close conjunction with the council's officials. By statute certain committees, for example, those on finance and (where appropriate) police, health, and education, must be established and must be consulted. In fact, it is rare for a council to overturn a committee recommendation or decision, although it may remit some matters for further consideration. Officials are the servants of the particular council which employs them and, broadly, occupy the same constitutional position in relation to it as do civil servants to ministers and the cabinet. Increasingly, too, thanks largely to the energetic work of the National Association of Local Government Officers, their conditions of work are approximating those of the civil service—at least in the largest authorities. Elsewhere, it is more difficult to organize regular procedures for recruitment and promotion. Being a local-government officer is thus coming more and more to be regarded as a worth-while career, offering considerable scope for initiative and providing a salary, if not yet prestige, comparable to all but the most lucrative positions in other professions.

Membership of a local council, however, is widely believed to attract fewer men of real vision and ability than formerly. Such a historical comparison is difficult to substantiate, but local government clearly attracts fewer such men than is desirable. Were it not that local-government service is one of the more useful steppingstones to, and training grounds for, a parliamentary career, the position might be much worse.[8] Many ex-

[8] At the 1955 general election, for example, 29 per cent of the Conservative M.P.'s and 56 per cent of the Labour ones had had some local-government experience, while about 50 per cent of the unsuccessful candidates of both parties had at least fought in a local election. D. E. Butler, *The British General Election of 1955* (London: Macmillan, 1955), p. 41.

planations of this state of affairs are commonly put forward. They include the structural weaknesses already mentioned, the general decline in local community life which seems to characterize modern industrial society, the dependence upon unpaid councilors,[9] and the combined effects of increased work and diminished opportunities for the exercise of initiative.

Despite the loss of functions to the central government, local-government expenditure runs at about three times the 1938–39 level. In part this is to be accounted for by inflation, but it also represents the greatly increased demands upon local authorities, particularly in the realms of education and housing.[10] These demands have, however, been accompanied by comparable increases in local-authority dependence, financial and other, upon the center.

The principal independent source of local-authority revenue consists of the rates levied upon land and buildings.[11] As such they have many shortcomings. The main burden falls upon domestic housing and shops, industrial property having been partially exempted from rates, and agricultural land and buildings totally exempted, in 1929.[12] In the modern world rates are a highly regressive and inadequate form of levy. They contribute less than one-third of local-authority income—a similar proportion comes from miscellaneous receipts, rents, and payment for services. What is more, rates tend to be least productive where the need is greatest: for example, in counties with small and

[9] Councilors receive certain allowances for expenses and for loss of earnings while actually engaged on council work. Since neither amount to adequate compensation, the result is to restrict the number of people prepared to serve.

[10] Education now absorbs about one-third of total current expenditure. The increase here is largely the result of the 1944 Education Act (see Chapter 2 above). Housing expenditure has mounted with increased recognition of the need for new houses: for example, despite the construction, 1945–55, of over 2,000,000 new houses, another 2,000,000 were over a hundred years old, and at the time of the 1951 census, almost 5,500,000 had no fixed bath and over 1,000,000 lacked a water closet (while another 2,000,000 households had to share one with up to five or more others).

[11] Real property, after valuation, is given an assessed annual rental. The rates are levied in the form of a poundage—i.e., a demand is made upon the occupier for x shillings for each pound of assessed rental. The average rate levied in county-boroughs, 1958–59, was 18/10d. in the £, so that the occupier of a fairly modest modern house, with an assessed rental of (say) £30, would have paid the average county-borough council £28 5s. 0d. in 1958–59.

[12] In 1956 domestic housing contributed 49.4 per cent and shops 14.3 per cent of rates paid in England and Wales, while offices, cinemas, and other miscellaneous properties paid 27.3 per cent and industrial property only 6.3 per cent.

thinly scattered populations which have to maintain a huge road mileage, or in poor industrial areas where slum property is inadequate to support the necessary expenditure on public health, housing, and schools. Government grants-in-aid are thus required to make good both the inadequacy and the inequities of the rating system, and with financial help must come control over expenditure. Since 1959–60 government aid has been paid mainly in the form of a general grant, plus a special rate-deficiency grant where necessary, with only a few grants specifically allocated to particular services.

The power of the central government to withhold part or all of a grant and to insist that grants be used only for "approved" expenditure clearly amounts to an important form of control exercised, in fact, by central departments. But it is not the only type of control. Local authorities are, of course, governed by parliamentary legislation. Their actions may be challenged in the courts as being *ultra vires* or otherwise illegal. And they are subject to various forms of nonfinancial administrative control. The relevant department must approve local-authority proposals in most spheres, including education, highway construction and maintenance, town planning, smoke abatement, fire services, and the police. Sanction must be obtained for raising loans for capital expenditure (and this in addition to approval of the actual scheme on which the loan is to be expended), and new by-laws must be confirmed. The appointment or dismissal of certain officials (the medical officer of health, for example) must also be approved. Local authorities are governed by departmental directions and regulations on many subjects; and in practice it may be hard to distinguish between regulations contained in statutory instruments—directions issued by a minister under his statutory powers—and suggestions or recommendations contained in circulars and memoranda.

To this list of controlling agencies must be added two important groups: inspectors and district auditors. Departmental control, financial or other, frequently operates upon the basis of reports from itinerant inspectors.[13] They are experienced, qualified, and often specially trained officials who, in addition to their controlling functions, perform invaluable services as transmitters of knowledge and opinion among local authorities as well as between them and the departments. The district auditors

[13] Those of education, constabulary, and housing and planning being perhaps the best known.

examine the accounts relating to most local-authority expenditure for the purpose, mainly, of detecting illegal and unreasonable expenditure or misappropriation of grants; they have the power to disallow such items and to surcharge those responsible, subject to appeal to the Minister or the High Court. Their functions are thus semi-judicial and, despite their being civil servants, they in fact operate independently of ministerial control.

Even were local authorities financially independent, they would not be entirely free agents. Fundamentally, this is because the public would not tolerate marked local differences in the standards of education and other essentially national services. Financial weakness, allied to structural deficiencies, only provides a supplementary reason for central supervision. In many respects local authorities thus come close to being mere agents of the central administration; but they are unlikely ever to be that alone. At no point yet have they sunk to this status—even if, for example, the salaries, qualifications, and conditions of service of teachers are nationally determined, yet the crucial powers to hire and fire rest with the appropriate local council. It is, indeed, unlikely that any department could, or would wish to, impose such a strict control. It is also easy to exaggerate the present degree of strictness: many of the regulations affecting local authorities, for example, are the product of the continuous formal and informal consultation which takes place between central and local government. Moreover, the existing powers of central control are divided between several departments, each concerned only with one or a few aspects of local government.[14] Above all, local councils, with all their weaknesses, are still the centers of more or less independent political interest and avenues for the politically ambitious. As such the councils constitute what are probably the most effective spokesmen and defenders of purely local interests that could be devised, and ones which in fact government departments treat with considerable respect.

[14] With the exception of the Secretary of State for Scotland, in whom is concentrated almost all the central powers over Scottish authorities.

9 - Government and the General Welfare

With very few exceptions all governments at all times have been concerned to promote "the general welfare" in some sense of the words. Today we tend to talk of welfare policies in a narrower sense than the pursuit of the "national interest" (however defined). Rather do we mean to contrast them with economic and social laissez faire. Economically we mean to describe thereby certain types of government action to regulate, temper, or supersede the simple operation of the market and the price system. In the social context we refer thereby to government actions designed to replace or supplement the operations of privately organized benevolence, charity, or insurance in alleviating human hardship. It is with welfare in these more specific senses that we are concerned.

British governments have long pursued such welfare policies in some degree. The earliest legislation about public health, hours and conditions of work, and urban amenity was passed in the nineteenth century (customarily regarded as a golden age of laissez faire). The foundations of the present system of national insurance were laid by the Liberal government of 1906–14 with their Acts to establish health and employment insurance. Such examples could be multiplied indefinitely. At the end of World War II a new era of welfare policies began, but its roots are deep, and even now political argument is about how and at what speed the government should act rather than about the extent of its responsibilities.

The fundamental commitment of any British government today is to maintain a high and stable level of employment. It was first accepted, very tentatively, in the wartime coalition government's statement on *Employment Policy* issued in 1944.[1] There, however, "a high level" was defined as being compatible with an unemployment rate of 8 per cent of the labor force. Once

[1] (London: H.M.S.O., Cmd. 6527).

the Labour government came to power, the target was raised to that of "full employment"; since then the electorate has come to regard even a 3 per cent unemployment rate as verging on the intolerable. The second major commitment is to provide, through the social services, at least a bare minimum of economic security to every individual. It is realized, of course, that full employment (or something like it) is a basic social as well as economic necessity. From these two goals follow certain other economic responsibilities which also would once have been thought to lie outside the government's proper territory. They include, in particular: the continuous expansion of production; the control of inflation; and the balancing of Britain's international payments and receipts both for the sake of a high standard of living and to stabilize the international value of sterling. To achieve these objectives and fulfill these responsibilities, governments must now manage and regulate the economic and financial systems to an extent unprecedented except in time of war.

Underlying these commitments is a widespread and continuous public demand upon society. There exists a general expectation that the government must provide, subsidize, or supervise any service or organization to the extent required to make good the deficiencies or remedy the abuses of private enterprise and voluntary action. Disagreement is acute about how exactly and to what precise extent the government should intervene, but its basic responsibilities are now questioned only in the margins of political controversy.

After the experience of World War II, when the whole of society was mobilized by the government to a degree which seems to have been unequaled by any other participant except the Soviet Union, no party in office could expect to convince the electorate that a return to mass unemployment or poverty of the kind familiar between the wars was anything but a reflection upon itself. But whereas the Labour party, broadly speaking, welcomes this fact and is anxious to assert the supremacy of public control and public action through governmental and other social machinery, the Conservative party seems anxious rather to use the powers of government only in conjunction with private organizations and only to the extent which seems necessary for private enterprise to survive and for the party to remain in office. Thus, while the extreme (left) wing of the Labour party tends to criticize its leaders for advocating too little public ownership and control of industry, the extreme (right) wing of the Conservative party criticizes its leaders for continuing to exercise too much.

In practice, since 1945, the Labour government used physical controls and powers of direction, as well as fiscal and monetary measures, whereas the Conservative governments have largely dispensed with the former and concentrated upon the latter. It is all too easy to exaggerate the differences, however. The Labour government came to power immediately after the end of the war, inheriting a mass of wartime powers and controls, and had to supervise the adjustment from a wartime to a peacetime economy; yet it progressively dismantled much of the apparatus of control. The Conservatives, governing under generally more favorable circumstances, carried the dismantling process much further, but when faced with mounting unemployment in the winter of 1958–59, reintroduced certain powers to coax industry into the worst-hit areas and, at times since 1951, have been prepared to make drastic use of such fiscal devices as manipulating the rate of interest. The Conservatives in office have not indulged in any wholesale dismantling of the social services, and have returned only two[2] of the nationalized industries to private ownership. Nevertheless, the Conservatives remain more attached, emotionally, to the ideas of the market, the price mechanism, and "self-reliance" or "voluntary action"; are more prepared to leave (or give) things to private enterprise, so long as the latter is able to do the job; are more easily convinced that private enterprise is in fact doing the job socially and economically—and have won more elections than the Labour party.

Administration and the Economy

Within the administration the primary responsibility for the general supervision of the economy lies with the Treasury, serving the Chancellor of the Exchequer.[3] In October, 1956, this concentration of responsibility, which had begun in 1947,

---

[2] More precisely, they have returned most of the iron and steel industry and over half the long-distance road-haulage industry. They have also sold two individual firms which had been taken into public ownership during the war.

[3] For a description and discussion of the administrative arrangements, see D. N. Chester and F. M. G. Willson, *The Organisation of British Central Government 1914–1956* (London: Allen and Unwin, 1957), pp. 39–53, 94–122, and 321–40; and W. J. M. Mackenzie and J. W. Grove, *Central Administration in Britain* (London: Longmans, 1957), pp. 349–59.

was marked by the creation of a second permanent secretary. He is chairman of the Economic Planning Board and the chief financial and economic adviser to the Chancellor (the other permanent secretary being chief civil-service adviser to the prime minister, secretary to the cabinet, "head of the civil service," [4] and directly in charge of the establishments and machinery of government sections of the Treasury). Attached to the planning board is a group of economists and statisticians who formerly composed the economic section of the cabinet. Its transfer to the Treasury may be seen as a further symbol of the acceptance of some degree of economic planning (or at least of economic guidance) as a normal and permanent responsibility of government. The cabinet is still the body which takes the most fundamental decisions in this, as in other, spheres; but the general supervision of the economy has been absorbed into the normal administrative machinery.[5]

The Treasury is the obvious department in which to concentrate this responsibility, if only because of the central place of the budget in modern conceptions of economic regulation. Through its scrutiny of the estimates of expenditure submitted by the other departments, moreover, the Treasury is in a position directly to influence their activities and their future plans. Its powers to prune or guide expenditure are limited by, among other things, the general policy decisions of the government and the ability of the chancellor to carry the cabinet with him in case of friction with other departments. But at the very least it is usually in a position to see that the other departments adjust their expenditures and intentions to meet the requirements of general cabinet policy.

The Treasury is also, traditionally, the department with the closest and most continuous connections with the banking and credit systems, while the Chancellor is the minister responsible for the nationalized Bank of England, which is the central bank for the whole sterling area. Such vital matters as the rate of interest, the level of commercial bank reserves, the foreign exchanges, installment-plan rates of payment, the level of investment funds available to the nationalized industries, and, of course, the levels of taxation, are thus all controlled and co-

[4] A purely customary title.

[5] The Central Statistical Office, primarily concerned with the compilation of statistics relating to the work of the government as a whole rather than a specific department, continues to lodge with the cabinet office.

ordinated by the one government department.[6] What is more, the department knows that once its decisions are approved by the cabinet, it may act upon them without fear that they will be seriously dislocated by public or parliamentary pressures. This is not to say that it need pay no heed to outside opinion—indeed, it is clear that the Treasury pays considerable heed at least to opinion in the "City" [7]—but only that, if the will is there, the government has the power and the administrative machinery to control the general level of economic activity in the country within the limits prescribed by economic knowledge, the international situation, and the general nature of the economy.

Britain does not, however, have a "planned" economy in the sense that the Soviet Union does, nor even in the sense that Britain did during and immediately after the war. The controlled distribution of scarce resources, the direction of industry, licensing systems for building or investment—except for certain foreign-exchange restrictions, even these physical controls are now almost totally lacking. The investment and output policies of the nationalized industries, it is true, are subject to general directives from the appropriate ministers and have been an important variable in the Conservatives' battle against inflation or recession, but otherwise direct government control is invoked only to meet particular crises. Thus, oil and gas supplies were rationed in 1957; in 1959 the government reintroduced moderate powers to induce new industry into areas of exceptionally high unemployment; and, as we have stated, foreign-exchange controls remain to deal with Britain's endemic balance of payments crises. The fact is that experience of the shortages of the war and postwar periods have given "planning," or "controls," a bad name; orthodox economic teaching is strongly in favor of "market" rather than "direct" controls; while even for the present degree of control much essential data is unobtainable (including reliable and up-to-date statistics about balance of payments and currency-reserve movements, or about the state of inventories). The result is that the government's role is in large measure peripheral or possibly residual, while it is left mainly to the forces of private enterprise to determine who produces how much of what, and when.

[6] Technically decisions about the rate of interest and commercial bank reserves are made by the Bank of England, but it is now understood that they are made subject to Treasury control.

[7] The City of London in which the main financial and banking houses are concentrated.

If it is inaccurate to say either that Britain has a planned economy or that British governments pursue laissez-faire policies, it is not entirely helpful simply to apply the customary label of a "mixed economy." The label is accurate enough, but not very informative. Most suitably, it is suggested, one should talk of a system of administered capitalism. To do so is to call attention at one time to the dependence of private industry for its welfare upon government action; to the importance of government expenditure simply because of its size (about one-third of the national income is now absorbed by central and local government); to the growing ability of the largest private business corporations, within these limits, to control their markets, and, as a corollary of all these things, the difficulty in separating public and private administration in ever more areas of social life. This last characteristic is by no means novel to British politics —the relations between government and the legal profession being perhaps the oldest example of a public and private partnership still in existence, while others can be found in such bodies as the University Grants Committee and any royal commission. But only recently has there grown up the extensive partnership between government and economic associations which now seems firmly established.

For this partnership, as for so much government economic policy, World War II was the forcing-house. Every important sector of industry then had its "production authority" among the central departments. The Board of Trade, the Ministry of Supply, and the Ministry of Aircraft Production were particularly closely involved with industry, as controllers, rationers, issuers of licenses, distributors, expeditors, and purchasers. To a gradually lessening extent the system of "production authorities" continued throughout the life of the Labour government, 1945–51. In fact, of course, it was only possible for the departments to discharge this function by incorporating into government administration individuals recruited from the management of the industries concerned.[8] The disappearance of the physical controls upon which this system was built has not led to the complete destruction of the corresponding relationship between industry and the production departments. The latter continue

[8] For details of this and other aspects of the relations between the production authorities and private industry, see A. A. Rogow, *The Labour Government and British Industry 1945–1951* (Oxford: Blackwell, 1955), especially pp. 49–72 and 189–90, and P. E. P., *Government and Industry* (London: Allen and Unwin, 1952).

to act as "sponsors" for different sections of industry, maintaining close informal relations with their protégés. The resulting position has been described "by saying that the department is the main, but not the sole, contact point between its industries and government, that it is expected to know about those industries and to help and advise them as may be necessary. This is an important role, and the very fact that such a relationship continues after direct controls have largely been lifted is a highly significant symptom of the contemporary position of government *vis-à-vis* industry." [9]

The relationship between government and industry nevertheless still takes some very tangible forms. Most welcome to industry are the investment allowances, research and development subsidies, export credit guarantees and loans to foreign buyers, low-rent factories in development areas, supplies of fuel from the National Coal Board at low (and secret) rates, and (as in the case of the cotton industry) grants for capital re-equipment, as well as the fruits of research and development carried out by government agencies.[10] Excluding agricultural subsidies (a special case to be discussed below), it has been estimated that private industry benefits from these services to the extent of some $700,000,000 (£250,000,000) each year. The industries thus assisted include steel, film production, shipbuilding, cotton spinning and weaving, atomic energy, and aircraft manufacturing, but all industry does or may benefit from the work of such bodies as the Department of Industrial and Scientific Research; the National Research Development Corporation, which is concerned primarily with the development of inventions from all sources; or any of the other research activities carried on by or for almost all government departments, both civil and military.

These services have been provided, for the most part, because private industry has been unable or unwilling to fulfill certain national needs without them. Presumably industry must co-operate with the government in return. It appears, for example, that extensive mergers in the aircraft industry in 1959 and 1960 were facilitated, if not brought about, by the government's

---

[9] Chester and Willson, *op. cit.*, pp. 121–22.

[10] According to a 1959 Report of the Department of Scientific and Industrial Research private industry spent less than a quarter of the $840,000,-000 (£300,000,000) spent on research and development in 1955. By 1959, however, its share had risen to almost a third of some $1,260,000,000 (£450,-000,000).

[11] It has been estimated that the total figure for government money spent on aircraft research was $1,680,000,000 (£600,000,000) from 1945–1957; since

known preference for fewer and stronger units.[11] A slightly different sort of example is provided by the government's decision to site a new steel-strip mill in Scotland in 1959: it was opposed by most private steel firms there, but is in fact to be built by and for a private firm, at an estimated cost of $196,000,000 (£70,-000,000), but $140,000,000 (£50,000,000) of that sum will be provided as a special low-interest loan by the government, whose declared policy of bringing industry to Scotland should help to provide a market for the steel strip produced.[12]

The government is not, it would seem, prepared simply to give private industry what it wants, but it is impossible to tell quite how far government is now prepared to go in securing cooperation for its policies nor how far its policies are themselves the products of private industrial pressures. The only outward manifestation of the "big stick" is to be found in the Monopolies and Restrictive Practices Act of 1948 and the Restrictive Trade Practices Act of 1956. By these Acts businesses are liable to investigation and report by the Monopolies Commission, and must register certain stated restrictive practices with a registrar appointed in 1956. The powers of the former, however, were much reduced by the second Act in favor of formal prosecution of offenders before a specially constituted Restrictive Practices Division of the High Court, which includes lay as well as judicial members. The procedure is slow; possibly restrictive agreements continue in being until prohibited by the Court; it is possible for the government to approve a restrictive agreement and thus exempt it from prosecution; and the legislation confines itself to trade practices, leaving unregulated the growth of industrial combination and merger. There is therefore no evidence yet that this legislation has led to any significant liberating of private enterprise, nor that it has cast any shadow over the amicable partnership between public and private administration of the economy.[13]

For farmers, too, the war introduced new and friendlier relations with the government. The need to conserve shipping during the war made it vitally important to produce the maximum possible amount of food at home, as the need to conserve

---

then additional sums have been pledged for aircraft development quite apart from those devoted to rocket research; see, for example, the report in *The Guardian,* July 12, 1960.

[12] A similar loan for the same purpose was promised to a nationally owned steel firm in Wales which by 1961 had still not been bought by private investors.

[13] See, for example, B. S. Yamey, "Restrictive Agreements and the Public Interest: A Critique of the Legislation," *Public Law* (Summer, 1960).

foreign currency since 1945 has argued, if less strongly, in the same direction. The result is that agriculture now receives subsidies and grants of between $700,000,000 and $840,000,000 (£250,-000,000 to £300,000,000) annually. In part this consists of grants and subsidies for fertilizers, drainage, farm improvements, and the like. (The government also runs a free technical advisory service and conducts or subsidizes extensive research programs for agriculture.) The bulk of this sum, however, is devoted to making good any deficiency between the average market price for certain basic commodities and the prices guaranteed to the farmers by the Ministry of Agriculture and Food. The level of these guaranteed prices is determined at an annual review held jointly by the ministry and representatives from the National Farmers' Union, to which nearly 90 per cent of British farmers belong. As a result, the farmers are more prosperous than ever before in peacetime, while they produce about half the nation's food requirements, compared with one-third before the war. On the other hand, it has been suggested, the farmers concentrate too much of their attention upon the annual price review instead of, for example, developing co-operative means of improving efficiency and profitability, while the department has entered into too close a partnership to be able satisfactorily to think out national policy for agriculture under changing circumstances.[14]

In no modern industrial society can government afford to leave the conduct of industrial relations entirely to management and labor, if only because the public interest may be adversely affected by any serious breakdown in the flow of production. The rights of workers to combine, to withhold their labor, and (in varying degree) peacefully to picket has been recognized since the 1870's, while later legislation has granted to trade unions exemption from court actions arising out of trade disputes and the right to contribute to the finances of any political party or movement.[15] Their existence is thus guaranteed by law, but in other respects they are almost completely autonomous and unregulated. Thus despite frequent criticism of the unions on the grounds that their members are apathetic, that their internal government

[14] P. Self and H. Storing, "The Farmers and the State," *The Political Quarterly* (Jan.–March, 1958), pp. 17–27. (This issue of *The Political Quarterly* is a useful special number devoted to pressure groups in Britain.)

[15] Subject to the right of any individual member to "contract out" of paying the political levy. This right, like the others, has undergone a series of vicissitudes in the past century, but there is no space here to recount the history of the trade-union movement so well and fully chronicled in the works of G. D. H. Cole, Sidney and Beatrice Webb, and other writers.

is oligarchic, and that, particularly in the Electrical Trades
Union, the result is domination by a Communist minority, the
government has refused (or has not dared) to legislate about the
conduct of the unions' internal affairs.

Governments have also been similarly chary of intervening
directly in the process of collective bargaining about wages and
conditions of work. The government is, of course, closely involved in negotiations in the nationalized industries to the extent
that they may affect prices and the general financial position of
those industries. Throughout the 1950's, moreover, the attitude
of the nationalized industries to wage claims has apparently
determined the whole climate of industrial relations, with
private employers taking their cue from this indication of government policy. (This may be seen as another indication of the
close relations between government and industry, and their
mutual influence.) In these and other disputes the ministry of
Labour is also prepared at any time to act as a conciliator, and
less often as arbitrator, if and when both sides invite it to. A
major dispute of public importance may be referred by the
ministry to a specially appointed committee of investigation or
court of inquiry, usually presided over by a professional economist or a member of the legal profession. In many industries not
covered by a trade union the government has established some
sixty wages councils (with representatives of management and
labour and at least one "independent" member), which lay
down and enforce wages and conditions for the industries concerned. Probably the most important industries affected are retail distribution, road haulage, and agriculture.

One important result of this freedom of employer and
worker to bargain without government intervention is to make
detailed economic planning even more difficult than it would
otherwise be. Another is that, to a large extent, it helps to
separate the industrial from the political work of the unions.
Particularly since the failure of the 1926 general strike, therefore, the great majority of union leaders have attempted to
influence government policy only by pressure-group methods or
through the Labour party rather than by the strike (not that
one can press this distinction very hard). The comparative readi-
ness of governments to introduce "welfare" measures, relating
both to social security and to such things as factory safety, has
contributed to the same end. Inevitably, one suspects, this
separation has helped limit the bitterness of both industrial and
political dispute.

Social Services

One-third of the government's ordinary revenue is now devoted to the social services,[16] education and the national health service (N.H.S.) being the most expensive. We have already discussed the educational system, which in any case is not generally considered to form part of the "welfare state"; it is not therefore proposed to discuss it further. The health service, however, is perhaps the most radical component of the welfare state in Britain. It is financed from national taxation, supplemented by small flat-rate charges for pharmaceuticals, dental treatment, spectacles, dentures, and surgical footwear (all of which may be met from National Assistance in case of need). Under the N.H.S., introduced by the Labour government in 1948, all residents and visitors are entitled to full medical care, including surgery and hospitalization, at no personal cost other than the charges mentioned. Patients have free choice of general practitioner ("family doctor"), subject only to the doctor's willingness to accept them; through him, they have access to all hospital, specialist, and other forms of treatment. If they prefer, they may also become private patients and be treated in private beds or private hospitals: in which case, of course, they must pay for their attention. Over 90 per cent of the entire medical profession participates, and almost all may conduct a private practice as well, although the sale of such practices is no longer permitted.

The service is administered under the direction of the Minister of Health and the Secretary of State for Scotland by regional boards, on which are represented the medical profession, those universities with medical schools, local authorities, trade unions, and the general public. Shortage of money has prevented its full development: hospital building and the provision of local health centers being the main casualties. In the early years of the service, the accumulation of unfilled need (particularly for spectacles and dentures) almost swamped parts of it. Initially, too, and on occasions since, the medical profession has been strongly opposed to certain features of the scheme.[17] In general, however, there can be little doubt that the N.H.S. has been one of the most successful undertakings of the Labour government,

[16] And another third to defense, which may help to explain why defense and the social services are widely regarded as conflicting obligations.

[17] See H. Eckstein, *Pressure Group Politics: The Case of the British Medical Association* (London: Allen and Unwin, 1960).

which millions of patients, this author included, have had cause to bless.

In 1948, too, legislation introduced a comprehensive system of social security, the heart of which consists of a compulsory scheme of national insurance to provide (principally) sickness and unemployment benefits[18] and a retirement pension, but which also provides for such lesser items, in terms of cost, as maternity benefits. For those employed, there is also an industrial-injuries insurance scheme. The benefits are financed by contributions from employers and employees plus a contribution from the national Exchequer amounting to about 13 per cent of the total. Two further types of grant are made, but not on an insurance basis: a system of weekly allowances for the second and subsequent children in a family; and National Assistance. The latter, administered through local offices of the National Assistance Board (appointed by the Minister of National Insurance, but operating independently of his direction with respect to individual cases), is a system of grants issued (subject to a means test) to those whom the rest of the social-security scheme fails to relieve from serious want.

These schemes, taken together, constitute a great advance on the various insurance systems which existed before the war, but they do not provide a watertight system of social security "from the cradle to the grave." It is possible, for example, for particular families or individuals still to endure very great poverty and hardship,[19] among the chief causes of which are the continuing housing shortage, local unemployment, and lack of knowledge about the services which exist (not all of which have been mentioned here). The level of benefits, even when supplemented by National Assistance, is still such as to allow no more than a subsistence standard of living.[20]

The very real decline in the amount of dire poverty is, apparently, attributable more to relatively full employment than

[18] For employed persons, and sickness benefits for the self-employed. The other benefits mentioned extend to the whole population.

[19] For some case histories, see Audrey Harvey, *Casualties of the Welfare State* (London: Fabian Society, 1960).

[20] By 1957 inflation had reduced the value of the insurance benefits until they could no longer provide even a subsistence standard of living: A. M. Carr-Saunders and others, *A Survey of Social Conditions in England and Wales* (Oxford: Clarendon Press, 1958), p. 190. Despite some increase in benefit since then, the plight of old-age pensioners or of families with many young children is often desperate.

to national insurance.[21] Indeed, the whole system is liable to
financial breakdown in the event of a return to mass unemployment. This is so because, in any strict actuarial sense, it is not an
insurance scheme at all.[22] The situation is rather that "national
insurance" benefits form part of a fairly comprehensive system of
social services, a portion of whose cost is borne by a form of
earmarked tax labeled "insurance contribution." What is more,
it is a completely unprogressive form of taxation, levied regardless of means.

The social services do not, therefore, involve as substantial
a redistribution of income as has generally been claimed. Indeed, it has even been suggested that, if account is taken of the
N.H.S., education, and tax allowances for dependents and private
insurance, then the "welfare state" in fact is of benefit primarily to the middle-income groups.[23] This conclusion becomes
virtually inescapable if the proliferation of private white-collar
and professional pension and superannuation schemes, as well
as other fringe benefits, are included in the reckoning. Under
the Conservative government the trend seems to be increasingly
toward favoring such private projects, to some extent at the expense of the public ones. A similar judgment can, of course, be
made of most areas of government policy.

Inevitably, increased government participation in the
economy must lead to a growth in the formation and activity of
pressure groups. Interests must be more alert to defend themselves from, or improve their position through, government
action, and governments are more dependent upon the experience and co-operation of those interests. It does not follow, of
course, that government becomes merely a register of organized
pressures. The constitution, as we have seen, provides important defenses to a government determined to pursue a
policy which it believes to be in the general interest. The crucial

[21] See W. S. Rowntree and G. R. Lavers, *Poverty and the Welfare State*
(London: Longmans, 1951).

[22] The insurance principle remains important, however, in two respects:
the contributions are paid into an actual fund, where they draw interest;
and those who pay them are entitled to the benefits by right and not at the
discretion of the government (although the latter can vary the level of
benefits and their relations to contributions).

[23] See Brian Abel-Smith, "Whose Welfare State?" in Norman Mackenzie,
ed., *Conviction* (London: McGibbon and Kee, 1958), pp. 55–73. For further
trenchant criticisms of the "welfare state," from the point of view of its
inadequacy to meet the human problems of today, see Richard M. Titmuss,
The Irresponsible Society (London: Fabian Society, 1960), and Peter Towns-
end, "A Society for People," in Norman Mackenzie, *op. cit.*, pp. 93–120.

questions, however, relates to the degree of influence exerted by pressure groups upon the formation of policy. It seems certainly to be increasing rather than diminishing, but quite how far the process has gone, or what form it is taking, is less easy to determine.[24] The shift in emphasis from public to private projects in the sphere of security mentioned above might suggest that recent policy is simply a response to the pressures of the powerful economic interests which support the Conservative party. So, too, might the relative paucity of government aid to the arts and the universities, which between them, at least until 1959, received no more annually than did poultry farmers, despite constant government declarations of devotion to culture and higher education.[25] It is tempting to explain this contrast with reference simply to the greater power and organization of material producers than of artists and educators. On the other hand, there are solid grounds for accepting the view that "if [pressure groups] demonstrated no willingness at all to engage in reasonable deliberation about the public interest they would soon lose the ear of the Government." [26] Moreover, Professor John Kenneth Galbraith has argued that such phenomena are typical of modern Western affluent societies,[27] and it is reasonable to believe that the production of an affluent society in Britain is as much the result of Conservative ideology as of particular pressures. It is also not unreasonable to suppose that the nature and continuance of the affluent society (as depicted by Galbraith) is likely to be the focus for party conflict about the welfare obligations of government in the nineteen sixties and seventies.

In conclusion, two common criticisms of the welfare state

[24] Compare the views of two observers who agree only on the increased role of pressure politics: Samuel H. Beer, "The Future of British Politics: An American View," *The Political Quarterly* (Jan.–March, 1955), pp. 33–43; and Richard M. Titmuss, *op. cit.*, who suggests that Britain has almost reached a stage of being "The Pressure Group State" (p. 12).

[25] See B. V. Bowden, "Too Few Academic Eggs," *Universities Quarterly* (Vol. 14, No. 1), and the comments thereon by N. F. Mott, *ibid.* (No. 3). In 1958–59 the poultry grant was about $133,000,000 (£47,600,000), the recurrent grant to universities $103,600,000 (£37,000,000), while national government grants to museums, galleries, and such bodies as the Arts Council and the British Council amounted to some $20,000,000 (£7,000,000) (see H.M.S.O., *Britain in Brief*, 2nd ed., 1958), although the latter two categories of grant have since been increased by several million dollars.

[26] Peter Self and Herbert Storing, *op. cit.*, p. 25.

[27] In his *The Affluent Society* (Boston: Houghton Mifflin, 1958).

may be dealt with briefly. It is frequently alleged that social security inevitably undermines individual initiative and resilience. It is possible to find cases of individuals who prefer, if they can, to draw benefits rather than work for higher wages,[28] but no evidence has been produced of large-scale indolence from this cause. One should add, for the sake of fairness, that it is not only people with comfortable unearned incomes who assert that receiving national insurance benefits has undermined the national will to work. That British people are often lethargic is not being denied here—only that this is a new phenomenon produced by the welfare state and confined to the recipients of its benefits rather than (say) being a by-product of a national inclination to complacency.

The other criticism which one sometimes hears is that the British welfare state was or is restricting individual liberty. Confining the discussion to the generally accepted civil liberties (freedom of speech, worship, assembly, and so on), one must again reject the criticism. The principal threats to, or inroads upon, civil liberties form part of the security program and have already been discussed.[29] Whether employers (both public and private) refrain from hiring or promoting a man because of his political beliefs is impossible to say for certain, but outside the civil service, this is never the reason given. However, many people *believe* that they should express themselves with care if they wish to get ahead, and this may be restriction enough. On the other hand, there has probably never been an organization or society in which this belief did not exist. And the fact remains that (with these actual or possible exceptions) there are no limits placed upon the right to criticize or express dissent, individually or collectively, in speech or in writing.[30]

In any case, even if one puts the worst possible interpretation upon events, none of the restrictions have stemmed from the introduction of welfare legislation. On the contrary, the provision of a minimum level of material subsistence below which no one may normally fall, if it makes any difference at all, must surely serve to embolden the timid rather than muzzle the critical. At least since the time of Thomas Jefferson it has been

[28] There are also rare cases of people who find it pays to refuse certain very low-paid jobs. This, however, would seem to be an argument against low wages rather than for lowering benefits to well below subsistence level.

[29] In Chapters 6 and 7 above.

[30] Except, of course, for the legal prohibitions on defamation, obscenity, and blasphemy.

recognized that economic security is an important, if not essential, condition of individual liberty.

10 - Foreign Relations

Except that is is "pro-West" and, in general terms, "anti-Communist," it is difficult to describe British foreign policy today. As to what it should be, there are almost as many opinions as there are people interested in the question. The debate has centered, since the late 1950's, upon the problem of defense, and above all upon the problem of nuclear weapons, with opinions ranging widely from the advocacy of total unilateral disarmament to that of building up an "independent" (of America) arsenal of nuclear weapons and the means of delivering them. But the debate is really *about* the whole problem of Britain's place in the modern world.[1]

Britain's international position has changed fundamentally since 1914, when Britain could reasonably claim the status of a major world power, and even since 1939, when the increasing hollowness of that claim was not yet generally apparent. The economic, political, and military changes in the nature of international relations since World War II are too well known to require review here. For Britain, they are symbolized by the fact that it devotes a higher proportion of its national income to defense expenditure (about 8 per cent) than ever before during peacetime, and that it probably obtains less security for its efforts than at any time since Napoleon was finally defeated at the Battle of Waterloo in 1814. Not surprisingly, therefore, it is proving difficult to adjust, or for some people even to recognize the need to adjust, to what must be, at best, a secondary

[1] And, indeed, about the very nature of British society. The movement of social criticism associated with the *New Left Review* and its predecessors, whose blossoming since 1957 has been a remarkable feature of British politics, has close links with the Campaign for Nuclear Disarmament. But the latter is by no means monopolized by members of the "new left."

role in world affairs.[2] For this very reason it is impossible, if one wishes to minimize the risk of being rapidly falsified by events, to describe Britain's foreign relations other than in very broad terms, and in part it is possible only to depict the conflicting pressures upon British policy-makers.

In the nineteenth century British policy was largely determined by the clear national interest in keeping the sea routes open for reasons of trade and empire and, more locally, in ensuring that the English Channel ports remained in unhostile hands. In terms of relations with the major powers, which was to say with other European countries, two of the central themes of British policy can be summarized in the concepts of "diplomacy by conference" and the "balance of power." The former continues to be important, and perhaps has never been more important for British survival. It is often suggested that the latter is, also. Thus an official booklet quotes with approval the following passage[3]:

> The equilibrium established by such a grouping of [equal rival] forces is technically known as the balance of power, and it has become almost an historical truism to identify England's secular policy with the maintenance of this balance by throwing her weight now in this scale and now in that, but ever on the side opposed to political dictatorship of the strongest single State or group at a given time (Sir Eyre Crowe, 1907).

But despite yearnings for such a role, most frequently voiced in support of arguments for the formation of a European or even Commonwealth "third force," and occasional official rhetoric cast in those traditional terms, in fact this policy has had to be seriously modified. Britain has joined one of the two major world groupings, but not only, or even primarily, for traditional "balance of power" reasons. Rather, it is the case that ideological sympathy, historic ties, geographic factors, military weakness, and the urgent postwar need for economic assistance have led Britain to choose the United States of America as its ally and protector. In some respects, even, it would be truer to say that Britain chose America as its international successor.[4] The formal

---

[2] Since the Suez crisis of 1956, it may safely be said, the leaders of all parties at least have come to appreciate the fact that Britain can no longer "go it alone" on any problem which impinges upon American-Soviet relations, i.e., upon any really important problem.

[3] *Britain in Brief,* 2d ed. (London: H.M.S.O., 1958), p. 47.

[4] It will be remembered that the 1947 Truman Doctrine was prompted at least partially by Britain's declared inability to continue as "defender"

cement of this alliance now consists of the North Atlantic Treaty and the Southeast Asia Collective Defense Treaty and their resulting organizations, NATO and SEATO. Military and political alliances now predominate over the earlier relationship represented by the European Recovery Program (the Marshall Plan), whereby Britain, along with most other Western European countries, received massive economic aid from the United States, partly to enable them to recover from World War II and partly, it seemed, to enable them to prepare for or help to prevent World War III.

The American alliance is the most important single feature of Britain's foreign relations, but it does not exhaust them, nor can it solve all problems. Britain is also, above all, a member of two other international groupings: the Commonwealth and (at least geographically) Western Europe. The Commonwealth is not a political or military alliance and involves no treaty obligations. It is better described as a loose and largely informal association of independent states. On the other hand, through continuous consultation, and relying upon certain common political traditions and aspirations, British governments normally attempt to carry Commonwealth opinion with them, or at least not to do violence to it. On many issues, of course, there will be no single Commonwealth opinion—race relations and the American alliance among them—but there tends to be a consensus on many broad and fundamental principles (such as observing treaties, avoiding major wars, defending the freedom of the seas, and adhering to the United Nations). Economically its members are linked by the system of imperial preferences, whereby Britain (and to a lesser extent other Commonwealth countries) discriminates in favor of Commonwealth imports in its tariff policy. A further link for most Commonwealth countries other than Canada is provided by membership of the sterling area, the international currency unit for which Britain acts as the banker; but it is not confined to the Commonwealth.[5]

These extensive international associations are in constant conflict with attempts to associate Britain more closely with Europe. Britain has been and remains a member of the Organization for European Economic Co-operation and its successor,

---

of Greece and the Eastern Mediterranean against foreign pressures. This may help explain the occasional patronizing touch in Anglo-American relations as Britain tries to "teach the new dog old tricks."

[5] See Note at end of this Chapter for a fuller account of the nature of the Commonwealth.

originally established to co-ordinate European economic recovery
under the Marshall Plan, and is linked to many European countries through their common membership of NATO. But since
the war Britain has steadfastly refused to be drawn closely into
the movement for European union, although British leaders
were among its earliest champions. Thus Britain is only *associated* with the Iron and Steel Community and the European
Atomic Energy program (Euratom), while the British refusal
to join seems to have been an important factor in the failure to
create a European Defense Community in 1954. Participation
in the almost powerless bodies which make up the Council of
Europe and Western European Union signifies little beyond
certain vague, if good, intentions. The formation of the European Economic Community (whose six members include France
and West Germany) in 1959, and its refusal to enter into a wider
Free Trade Area on conditions acceptable to Britain, have posed
the problem of Europe more urgently. The eight-nation Free
Trade Association, established soon afterward, provides Britain
only with economic advantages falling short of those promised
by the common market and an uncertain bargaining position
with the six. But at the time it was as far as the British government was prepared to go in the direction of the European
continent.

Since then, however, there have been signs of a strong feeling that Britain could, in fact, have gone much further. Trade
with Europe is likely to prove increasingly attractive to the
other Commonwealth countries, while American opinion has
seemed constantly to favor the idea of European federation. The
two partnerships which have hitherto encouraged British Foreign
Secretaries to see the Atlantic and Commonwealth communities
rather than Europe as their spiritual (and material) homes are
thus not as strong brakes as they may once have been. Moreover,
they are to some extent in conflict with one another. Countries
like India and Ghana tend to be suspicious of American influence, while the United States, to many British eyes, appears
reluctant to concede that the Commonwealth and modern
colonial administration are no longer identical with nineteenth-
century imperialism or even with the overseas policies of George
III.[6]

[6] Since 1945, in fact, all British parties have come, with varying degrees of enthusiasm, to accept economic development and political independence as the proper goals of colonial policy. It is also worth remember-
ing it is usually to Britain that the leaders of colonial nationalist movements

These crosscurrents in British policy on occasion reveal themselves in acute embarrassment at the United Nations. The conflicting Commonwealth attitudes to race relations frequently led Britain to abstain on motions to condemn South Africa's policy of apartheid.[7] The conflict between most Commonwealth opinion on the one hand, and, on the other, Britain's traditional friendship with France and its desire to maintain some freedom of maneuver in its own dependent territories have resulted in abstentions on resolutions condemning France's policies in North Africa. And least palatable of all to much British opinion, there has been the regular abstention on moves to admit the Chinese government to membership of the United Nations and the Security Council, an abstention made necessary, despite Britain's recognition of the Peking government as the legitimate government of China, by American commitment to the Chinese Nationalist government of Formosa. It is particularly difficult for Britons to understand why America should grant recognition to (say) the Falangist government in Spain without, presumably, thereby condoning all it stands for or the way in which it obtained power in defiance of the League of Nations, and should still withhold it from Communist China.

The American alliance is thus the keystone to British postwar foreign policy, but it is also a source of additional conflict in most areas. The example of the two countries' different attitudes toward China is probably indicative of the most reputable basis of the friction between them.[8] This is the relative absence in Britain of the "crusading" attitude against Communism which, to the outside observer especially, seems to have characterized much of America's foreign policy since 1945.[9] In part the British attitude reflects the different climate of opinion existing

---

have come for refuge, when necessary, and the opportunity to continue their political careers.

[7] South Africa's withdrawal from the Commonwealth in 1961 has removed one source of embarrassment—but has not, probably, resolved all the tensions associated with race.

[8] Among the *less* reputable, on the British side, are resentment simply because the United States is now stronger and more important than Britain internationally, dislike of certain features of modern life which are assumed to be American in nature and origin, Conservative resentment at having been "let down" at the time of the 1956 Suez expedition, and the usual assortment of prejudices and stereotypes to be found among most human groups with reference to most other human groups.

[9] See also such American criticisms as those made in George Kennan, *Realities of American Foreign Policy* (Princeton, N.J.: Princeton University Press, 1954).

there. While by no means "soft" toward Communism, a large and influential body of opinion is yet prepared to regard the Soviet Union and China as countries not radically different in kind from others and Marxism as a theory from which something can possibly be learned about the nature of man and society. To this there may be some corresponding group in America, but there seems to be none to the smaller, but still important, group of public figures (like Bertrand Russell) who are prepared continuously to question the whole basis not only of Britain's present alliances and defense policy, but also of the whole Western attitude toward the "cold war." This latter group may never itself be in the position to make British foreign policy, but it arouses sufficient public interest and attention and strikes sufficient response in British society as a whole for its existence not to be totally ignored by those who do make policy. Few people in Britain believe, and even fewer are prepared publicly to admit to believing, that Britain could possibly "win" another major war, and most are therefore prepared to accept the attainment of a peaceful relationship with the Communists as a reasonable, and indeed the only proper, goal in international affairs.

The belief just mentioned reflects the capacities and interests of Britain as much as it represents a way of seeing the world. Successive balance-of-payment and currency crises have brought home the precarious nature of Britain's prosperity, dependent as it is upon international trade and, apparently, the confidence of international monetary speculators. The lesson for foreign policy was sharpened by the particular severity of the financial crises initiated by the Korean Conflict and the Suez expedition. Britain is increasingly conscious, too, that its international trading position is being threatened or "usurped" by Japan and West Germany, and that the success of these rivals may not be unconnected with their relative freedom from the economic burden of expenditure upon defense. As it is, in order to combat inflation at home and loss of confidence in the pound sterling abroad, British governments since 1951 have been trying to cut down the cost of defense, but have still been forced to hold back investment in other spheres in order to meet even their pruned defense budgets. The clear implication is that Britain cannot afford, either economically or militarily, to be drawn into any large-scale military operations. It is equally clear that it cannot possibly defend itself single-handed against any major attack, and probably not even with outside assistance. For the British are coming to grasp the fact, officially acknowledged by the government in 1957, that there is no way of safeguarding the population against nuclear attack.[10]

Britain has, therefore, a vested interest in the peaceful settlement of disputes by negotiation (whether through normal diplomatic channels or international conferences or both) and in international disarmament. Only thus can it hope to survive or to remain politically independent. At present, forced by events largely outside its own control into the attempt to build up strong defenses, it thereby becomes more dependent upon the world economically and less able to pursue its own ends politically. Indeed, much of the argument over the level of defense expenditure in Britain has turned on the issue of the degree of influence thus to be gained with American policy-makers rather than directly on the question of the contribution to be made to Western security. About the need to exert influence on Washington there is no real disagreement. Dispute occurs only about the possibility of having any significant influence or about the best way to obtain it and use it.

Britain is thus in a new situation. Its traditional policies are not obviously apposite, nor does a situation in which lack of room to maneuver is the outstanding feature obviously suggest what new policies should be adopted: hence the multiplicity of opinions referred to at the beginning of this chapter. It is possible to conclude the chapter only by saying that the debate continues.

Note: The Commonwealth

All the members of the Commonwealth were once governed by or from the United Kingdom. This historical experience they share with the United States of America, the Union of South Africa, Eire, and Burma. But, unlike these four countries, they have maintained an association with the United Kingdom. The association is peculiar, however, in that it does not derive from any treaty or formal agreement enforceable at law, and in that

[10] See the statement of policy contained in *Defence: Outline of Future Policy* (London: H.M.S.O., Cmnd. 124 of 1957), and the corresponding *Report on Defence* (London: H.M.S.O., Cmnd. 363 of 1958). Defense expenditure was consuming 10 per cent of the national product in the period 1951–56, before being cut to 8 per cent. See Chapter 2 above for an account of Britain's economic position.

its members are independent sovereign states in all the senses recognized by international law. Their freedom embraces even the right to secede—a right exercised in fact by South Africa, Eire, and Burma.

Until 1949 the chief external badge of association was that the members were "united by a common allegiance to the Crown." [11] The British king was also king of each member state, with the same constitutional function in each (although in what were formerly called "the Dominions" his functions were in fact exercised by governors-general, appointed as his personal representatives by the monarch acting on the advice of the appropriate national government).

In British law the British colonies are colonies of *the crown,* and not of the nation or the government. The development of a nonpolitical monarchy at home was therefore a prerequisite to, and in fact encouraged, the development of self-government abroad in a way which did not destroy every link with Britain. Thus the road to colonial independence may be said to consist of the replacement of legal subjection to the powers of the British crown, exercised through or on the advice of the government in the United Kingdom, by a formal allegiance to the *person* of a nonpolitical monarch whose governmental powers are exercised by or on the advice of separate independent national governments. On the eve of the War of Independence Benjamin Franklin asserted that "America is not part of the dominions of Great Britain, but of the King's Dominions." Fortunately or unfortunately this distinction was then constitutionally unacceptable to Britain and so there existed no alternative to British rule except complete political and legal independence. Today he could have obtained self-government for America while continuing to be, as he acknowledged himself to be, "a subject of the British Crown." But not until the early twentieth century, in fact, did His Majesty's Government in each of the self-governing Dominions[12] become substantially equal in political status to the U.K. government—and even then the Statute of Westminster, 1931, was still necessary before the last legal inequalities could be removed.

After World War II Burma and Eire preferred to leave the

[11] To quote from the definition of the Commonwealth approved by the Imperial Conference of 1926 and generally known as the Balfour Declaration.

[12] In 1926, the year of the Balfour Declaration, they were Australia, Canada, Eire, Newfoundland, New Zealand, and the Union of South Africa.

Commonwealth rather than retain even this formal link with the crown which, to them, was still a symbol of past alien rule. India's later decision also to banish the royal symbol and become a republic presented a more serious challenge. The result, on this occasion, was a further loosening of the Commonwealth bond. A declaration issued by the Commonwealth prime ministers in 1949 agreed that the Republic of India could continue to belong to the Commonwealth of Nations "freely cooperating in the pursuit of peace, liberty and progress," and would accept "the King as the symbol of the free association of its independent member nations, and as such the Head of the Commonwealth." [13] The queen today is thus queen of some member countries, but in India, Pakistan, Ghana, and Malaya (which has its own elected monarch) she is recognized only as the head of the Commonwealth, to which status, as Mr. Nehru has insisted, there is "no function attached."

The only other legal characteristic common to all members today is that they recognize each other's citizens either as British subjects or as Commonwealth citizens, both categories being distinguished from those of aliens or foreigners. However, this is of as little practical significance as the position of the crown. What rights accompany either status in each country is a matter for its own government to decide. The rights vary widely: Australia and India, for example, place severe restrictions on the entry and/or rights of certain Commonwealth citizens, while the United Kingdom, on the other hand, not only gives full rights of entry and citizenship to all British subjects, but also accords the same rights to citizens of Eire and South Africa.

Three other badges of membership deserve notice even in a short discussion: the prime ministers of all the Commonwealth countries meet periodically in special conferences; the member countries exchange high commissioners and not ambassadors; and the United Kingdom gives a tariff preference to imports from other Commonwealth countries, between whom, if to a lesser extent, a similar system of imperial preferences obtains. These badges are important outward manifestations of the twin processes of consultation and co-operation which lend concrete day-to-day meaning to the concept of the Commonwealth.[14]

[13] The full text may be found in N. Mansergh, *Documents and Speeches on British Commonwealth Affairs 1931–1952* (London: Oxford, 1953), pp. 846–47.

[14] See H. J. Harvey, *Consultation and Cooperation in the Commonwealth* (London: Oxford, 1952).

Mr. (now Lord) Attlee, speaking as prime minister in the House of Commons in April, 1946, stated that "it is our practice and our duty, as members of the British Commonwealth, to keep other members of the Commonwealth fully and continuously informed of all matters which we are called upon to decide, but which may affect Commonwealth interests." Prime ministers, high commissioners (those in London meet together regularly with British ministers), finance and other ministers, civil servants, military leaders, and others all play their part in the exchange of information and opinion among the Commonwealth countries. The objects and extent of this must not be exaggerated or misunderstood. The purpose of consultation is to facilitate co-operation, should the members wish it, on any particular point, but there is no duty to agree or to concert policies, nor may any government shift the burden of responsibility for its own policies on to other Commonwealth shoulders. The United Kingdom, furthermore, apparently initiates more consultation and transmits more information than any other member, while communication between the other members is very limited. But even the United Kingdom has departed from its "practice and duty" on occasion: for example, it seems that Britain issued its ultimatum to Egypt in 1956 and subsequently invaded the Suez Canal area without even informing the other members of the Commonwealth of its intentions, let alone consulting them about the wisdom of its policy. Nevertheless, it is probably correct to say, with a Lord Chancellor addressing the House of Lords in 1948, that "the great benefit the Commonwealth brings is the joint consultation, alike in matters civil and military, the sharing of information, and the resulting solution of common difficulties." [15]

Consultation and co-operation, however, must be *about* something of common interest and must be *based on* some shared values or aims if they are not to be empty rituals. Traditionally the essential common interests have been economic and military. The Commonwealth countries have provided the United Kingdom with much of the food and raw materials it needed, while the United Kingdom has provided them with manufactured goods, capital, and the facilities of an established network of financial and commercial contacts. Militarily, it has supplied a world-encompassing navy capable of defending the rest of the Commonwealth, while the latter, particularly in both world wars, has supplied bases and manpower. Inevitably, for-

[15] Lord Jowett, quoted in Harvey, *op. cit.*, p. 30.

eign policy has constituted another principal subject of consultation and co-operation.

The relationship between all the Commonwealth members, including the United Kingdom, has thus rested upon a mutually advantageous division of labor and resources in both the economic and military spheres. But most Commonwealth spokesmen, at least in public, have placed more emphasis on certain shared qualities and values, and especially: British governmental institutions and ideals; a common political vocabulary; a belief in "peace, liberty and progress"; since 1961, opposition to the erection of formal barriers between men because of race, color, or religion; a desire to co-operate with other states, particularly each other; and a tolerance of differing social systems and ways of life.

Merely to mention the bonds of Commonwealth—the crown, economic interest, defense, foreign policy, "British" constitutions, and common political ideals—is to list points of increasing divergence. The Commonwealth countries still have many important interests in common, among them the strengthening of the U.N., and the success of world co-operation in economic development, and they still share a desire to remain together, but it becomes increasingly difficult confidently to assert that this desire will continue in all members. In 1949 Field-Marshall Smuts, in the South African House of Assembly, voiced a fear that the Commonwealth would become like the medieval Holy Roman Empire: "something which is unreal and which has no meaning, no substance of unity in it and to which it is not worth while to belong any more." This fear cannot easily be dismissed in the light of such events as the admission of republics; the different qualities which the crown symbolizes to different members; the lengthy dispute between India and Pakistan over Kashmir (although the significant point here may be the length of time the dispute continued without war); the increasing divergence between the British model and the constitutional evolution of, for example, Pakistan and Ghana; the pressures upon the United Kingdom to enter into closer relations with Western Europe; the different "cold war" postures of the older European members and the newer ones in Asia and Africa; and the racial tensions tragically dramatized in, but not confined to, South Africa.

In 1960 it seemed that the Commonwealth must either become an increasingly meaningless association, or lose some of its members before, possibly, developing a new harmony and cohesion. The withdrawal of South Africa in 1961, accompanied by clear declarations of the Commonwealth's abhorrence of apartheid, suggests that the association sets some limits to the behavior of its members and is resolved not to become an empty vessel. The joint disarmament proposals endorsed by the Prime Ministers' Conference of the same year point in the same direction. It is nevertheless clear that there are few areas in which agreement on policy can reasonably be expected so long as the Commonwealth seeks to include a large and diverse membership. Equally clearly, a Commonwealth which cannot contain a diverse membership is of little value. The future therefore continues to be uncertain. The Commonwealth's history of adaptability and flexibility alone, perhaps, provides ground for optimism.

11 - The British Political System: An Overview

The concentration of constitutional authority and power in the cabinet means that there can be no doubt as to who or what composes the government in Britain. For anything within its jurisdiction which goes wrong, or right, the cabinet usually, and justifiably, receives the blame, or praise. The very fact that the cabinet must accept or endorse any proposal for it to become effective policy not only makes the cabinet the focal point for all important political pressures and influences. It also confers upon the cabinet the ability significantly to resist or shape the influences which bear upon it and thus uphold the policies or principles to which it may be committed. Any surrender to blatant sectional pressure is taken to be a manifestation of weakness on the part of the government. Such a concentration of power and responsibility is not to be found in all democratic countries, however conducive it may be to strong and healthy government.

This system is democratic and not simply another example

of autocracy because it is possible constitutionally to reward and punish as well as to praise or blame, and because this power ultimately belongs to the electorate. The electoral system may not be entirely "just," the parties may deprive their ordinary members of full freedom of political maneuver, and the House of Commons may be a less important body than once it was, but the system has the corresponding merit that it is the electorate which directly *decides* who shall form the government and, to a significant if debatable extent, what policies shall be followed. It is, indeed, sometimes suggested that the resulting government obtains a "mandate" from the people to do certain things which it may neither ignore nor exceed in any important respect.[1]

The notion of a mandate from the electors is open to objection: no government faced with changing circumstances can be expected to act entirely in terms of its previous election program; it is not possible to decide which issues were the important ones and, even if it were, which were reasons why a party won and which were proposals despite which it won; and the electorate, in any event, appears to attach much less importance to programs and issues than do politicians or publicists. On these grounds alone it is clear that a government's electoral program is and should be neither a strait-jacket nor even a complete blueprint, and that the idea of a mandate is vague at best and must be handled with extreme caution. It is nonetheless significant. The doctrine reflects a widespread belief that a party program should be reasonably full and that for the successful party subsequently to depart radically from its spirit and intentions is dishonorable. The mere existence of the doctrine, moreover, suggests that, for much of the time, these expectations are satisfied, and emphasizes that the parties normally possess distinctive general approaches of which the parties' programs and behavior are interconnected manifestations. The doctrine of the mandate does not mean that governments do the things they do simply *because* they committed themselves in their programs any more than it means their programs will stop them from doing things which appear to them, as Conservative or Labour leaders, to be necessitated by the demands of office. But it reflects the fact and expectation that, to an important degree, the general policies

---

[1] See Chapter 5 above, and the discussions in, for example, the Appendices to W. Harrison, *The Government of Britain*, 6th ed. (London: Hutchinson, 1960); and Sir Ivor Jennings, *Cabinet Government*, 3d ed. (Cambridge: University Press, 1959), pp. 503–9.

and approach of a government may be predicted solely on the basis of the election results and of the party programs offered at the previous election. Significantly, neither in France nor in the United States, for example, does the concept of the mandate play the same part in constitutional or political debate.

The power, stability, and accountability of governments clearly are vitally dependent upon the existence and nature of the predominantly two-party system. So, too, is the power of the electorate to decide the general composition and approach of governments. On the other hand, a critic might say, the character of the two-party system, without even primary elections to supplement the interparty contest, severely restricts the voters' choice. A system wherein the voter is free only to choose between disciplined parties, in the selection of whose leaders and representatives he has no direct control—the critic might continue—hardly deserves to be called government by consent.[2] That the effective choice of the electorate is limited in this way must be granted. But it does not necessarily follow that the resulting system is not one of government by assent. (*Assent* preferably, since government by *consent,* strictly speaking, would involve something like government by continuous referendum and would probably be unworkable. In any case, it has never been tried.)

The introduction either of a multiparty system, as in the French Third and Fourth Republics, or of a more flexible and loosely knit two-party system, as in the United States, would perhaps extend the range of choice open to voters and to ordinary M.P.'s—but at a price.[3] Such a change would inevitably lessen the direct control of the electorate over the personnel and policies of government: the electors would directly decide who should represent them, and might make their decision in the light of a wider selection of individuals and viewpoints, but their decision would less directly determine the behavior of government. And the resulting greater diffusion of power (among members of the legislature, or between them and the executive) would almost certainly blur the lines of accountability. This alternative is not clearly more democratic than the existing British system. The latter, moreover, has the advantage that the two-party

[2] Rousseau and Marx made somewhat similar criticisms in previous centuries.

[3] In practice it is not obvious that important minority viewpoints have been ignored any less frequently in these countries than in Britain.

system on the whole makes it more likely that the electorate, and their representatives, will be confronted with real and not utopian alternatives, and that there will be some genuine difference of approach between the contenders for office. Both are conducive to stable and mature government.

The critic's case would be more acceptable if the party struggle existed in a political vacuum. Through Parliament, the press, books, radio, TV, public meetings, and demonstrations the political debate in Britain is continuous. By-elections are liable to take place at any time. Pressure groups of all kinds do not hibernate between elections. By all these means governments and parties are made aware of public reactions to their policies and actions. The process of selecting party leaders and formulating party policies reflects these influences at all times. Indeed, the parties are themselves the battlegrounds for a continuous conflict between all manner of ideological, tactical, group, and personal conflicts. General elections are thus the occasion for a choice between alternatives which have already been shaped by the complicated interaction which helps to make up "public opinion."

Elections are, probably, the most important components of the democratic process, in that the possibility of losing an election is the most effective constitutional sanction upon governments and the main spur to opposition parties to heed public opinion. But in Britain account must also be taken of the continuous and direct confrontation of the two major parties which ensures that governments shall receive both organized support and organized opposition, and that Parliament and the electorate shall be presented with the continuous choice between *this* existing government and *that* alternative government. Such a system is democratic both in the sense that it reserves to the electors the ultimate power to accept and reject governments and in the sense that each party is forced by the competing attractions of the other party to heed the wishes of the governed.

There are dangers inherent in the British system, but the possibility that freedom and choice will be obliterated or emasculated by a two-party "dictatorship" is not among the more serious ones: or, at least, not in the sense that the parties will ignore any important stream of public opinion. A more serious danger is that both may fail to raise awkward problems for fear that the other will make electoral capital therefrom— as, it may be argued, both major parties have failed to grasp the nettle of Britain's relations with the rest of Europe or to insist that consumption rather than investment bear the brunt of temporary economic sacrifice. It may be that the great weakness, as well as the great strength, of the system resides in the fact that the quality of government and its responsiveness to public attitudes depends upon the nature and existence of an alternative government at any given time. The weakness of the Labour party after 1931 (qualitatively as well as quantitatively) and, indeed, the divisions and weaknesses among the parties opposed to Conservative rule throughout the interwar period, must bear much of the responsibility for the failings of British governments in those years. For this reason, too, the steady loss of ground by the Labour party since 1951 should alarm many other than Labour supporters.

As far as any purely institutional arrangements can ensure it, the British system, broadly speaking, provides the country with strong, stable, and responsive government. It is, moreover, an adaptable system, as was demonstrated by its capacity to meet the different but equally testing requirements both of waging World War II and, after 1945, of simultaneously reconverting the economy to more peaceful purposes and carrying through Labour's extensive program of social reform. Many particular features of the system, as we have seen in earlier chapters, are the subject of detailed criticism. So far as the constitution as a whole is concerned, however, the British people are apparently content, even complacent. Indeed, an outstanding feature of the postwar political scene has been the absence of any sizable group consistently opposed to the basic principles of the constitution or to any of the most important institutions of government. Not since the violent feelings engendered by the debate over the powers of the House of Lords in 1910–11 and by the contemporaneous problems of Irish Home Rule, women's suffrage, and the growing power of trade unions—not even (in restrospect at least) during the general strike of 1926—has there been any serious threat to constitutional order. This is perhaps sufficient testimony to the fundamental stability and acceptability of the British political system.

A very important element making for this stability is, of course, the existence of the numerous formal, semiformal, and informal links between government and the principal established groups within the economy and society as a whole. The importance of these links is widely appreciated, or possibly exaggerated, in popular references to "The Establishment," or in questions about who really governs the country,[4] neither of which are the monopoly of any particular political viewpoint. In a relatively compact and integrated society like the British, it is comparatively easy for people in the world of government, or education, or trade unions, or any other particular "world," to know about each other and even to become acquainted. It is also comparatively easy for the "top people" in all the worlds important for politics to become similarly related, assisted in many cases by a common background and education, but often brought together merely by their concern with government and administration.

Even where the common background is lacking, moreover, the weight of tradition and contact with others (particularly with the civil service, it may be surmised) appears to educate newcomers to ruling circles in established ways of doing business. Through the existence of these ruling circles—and this is what matters in our present context—the opinions and desires of government and of the major social interests become known to each other naturally, as it were, with obvious gains both to the government and to the interests and with a consequent strengthening of the whole political system. Moreover, for the most part this aspect of the system seems to be acceptable to the British people today. As one percipient American observer has put it: "by long tradition, England (*sic*) is a country that is '*run*' and expects to be run, unlike America which 'goes.'" [5]

It is tempting, and not uncommon, to conclude that Britain is ruled by an oligarchy of powerful men. It is certainly true that the doors into the corridors of power open most readily to those with wealth, or with the proper social and educational backgrounds, and that many of the adjacent rooms communicate with one another. But to change the metaphor, the ruling circles are by no means closed to all but rich public-school boys of middle- or upper-class origin. For this and other reasons it is misleading nowadays to talk of a "ruling class," which may imply that all rulers are drawn from the one social class.

As we have seen, there is a marked correlation between social class and the possession of power. But it is not always clear which is the cart and which the horse, particularly because the

[4] See the very interesting special number of *The Twentieth Century* (October, 1957), entitled "Who Governs Britain?" for a series of different answers to this question.

[5] Marjorie Bremner, "Noblesse Oblige," in the special number of *The Twentieth Century* cited above, pp. 391–400. The emphasis is in the original.

higher levels of government, administration, and industry are increasingly open and flexible. It is also a marked feature of British politics that almost every protest movement includes upper-class members and spokesmen, just as most established leaders have devoted lower-class followers. It is equally misleading to refer, without qualification, to rule by an oligarchy. Power and influence are, and probably must be, unequally divided. The essential point in Britain is that it is divided, and not monopolized. Government, moreover, is never simply a question of *who* has power: it also involves such questions as what the rulers have to do, how they have to do it, and what others they must appease in order to retain their positions.

That there are important elements of oligarchy in Britain cannot be gainsaid—but the "oligarchy" is not composed merely of one ruling class, it is not united on policy, and its power is not undisputed. It is probably more accurate, therefore, to say that there exists something like an oligarchy of interests as well as something like a democracy of numbers, to adapt the vocabulary of traditional American debate. If it is true that the oligarchy of interests limits the operations of the democracy of numbers, the reverse is also true. What is important is that tension continues, that debate remains legally and politically free, and that the governmental system itself is not irrevocably and exclusively the creature of either numbers or interests. From this, as we have suggested before, comes much of the flavor of British politics.

In recent years the debate has been conducted in a remarkably orderly fashion, reflecting the generally peaceful way in which disputes have come to be settled for the past several decades. Not since before World War I has armed force been used against strikers or even threatened against any section of the community.[6] The general strike of 1926 today seems notable not so much for its apparent threat to the normal constitutional means of fighting for political change as for the good temper and restraint shown alike by strikers, police, and volunteer strikebreakers.[7] The Campaign for Nuclear Disarmament marches in orderly fashion each year, and even its more militant "direct-

---

[6] At home, that is to say. It may be, as has sometimes been suggested, that Britain has benefited from the export of its more violent and ruthless citizens to other parts of the world. Certainly the British record in some of its past or present colonial territories is less enviable than its record at home (*home* here does not include Ireland).

[7] See J. Symons, *General Strike* (London: Cresset, 1957).

action" colleagues are committed only to staging passive and nonviolent protests. Crimes of violence and senseless destruction have apparently increased sufficiently to alarm some people, it is true, and racial tensions have occasionally spilled over into bloodshed. But these are generally, and rightly, regarded as atypical phenomena which serve only to emphasize the prevailingly peaceful and even "civilized" way in which disputes are conducted. This has not always been so in Britain but, for the past century, the repression of social and individual aggression seems to have become part, at least, of the English character.[8] Constitutional stability would seem to have deep roots.

Since the eighteenth century the British constitution has been an object of particular interest both to students and practitioners of government. One reason has been simply that during this time the policies of British governments have been of great importance to the world. More important, probably, has been the fact that to many people abroad the institutional arrangements of British government seemed to contain some special recipe for combining freedom and order, either or both of which had too often been absent in their own countries. To this day it is not impossible to find overseas students of the constitution whose writings betray envy as well as intellectual curiosity.[9] At the same time British writers have not allowed undue national modesty to inhibit their own expressions of praise and approval. But is there any reason that a modern student of politics should pay particular heed to the British system?[10]

Government in Britain, it may be argued, has certain points of inherent interest to any student of politics. They have already been described and discussed in this and earlier chapters, but some of the main ones may be listed again. They include: the particularly vital relationship between constitutional law and the conventions, and their continuing mutual influence as the constitutional structure is adapted to changing circumstances;[11]

[8] See Geoffrey Gorer, *Exploring English Character* (London: Cresset, 1955), especially pp. 12–18, and 278–312.

[9] As two examples from many, ancient and modern, one might cite two books by French authors: Montesquieu's classic *Esprit des Lois,* first published in 1748, and a recent laudatory account, A. Mathiot, *The British Political System* (Stanford, Calif.: Stanford University Press, 1958).

[10] Someone who has just devoted a good deal of time to writing about the system, particularly if he is British, is perhaps the last person to give a disinterested answer to this question. Nevertheless, one must be suggested.

[11] For a fuller discussion of this point see G. Marshall and G. C. Moodie, *Some Problems of the Constitution* (London: Hutchinson, 1959), Chapter 2, and the references cited there.

the essential role of the party system in determining the evolution and working of the constitution; the development, closely related to the party system, of the concept of a governmental dialogue between the government and the loyal opposition; the combination of a concentration of governing authority with a wide diffusion of political freedom and the right to participate; the combination of stable government with the right of a mass electorate to pass effective judgment upon the government; the association of strong party government with a permanent professional administration and an independent judiciary; the comparative security of individual liberties despite the absence of any "bill of rights"; and the way in which all these have reflected and sustained the continuing tensions between political democracy and social oligarchy (or at least hierarchy). These characteristics of the system all represent distinctive answers to perennial problems. They may not be the only answers, nor ones acceptable to all people, nor are they necessarily unique— but they are answers which have demonstrated a notable capacity to survive and to satisfy.

The other major point of interest about the British system is that many of these answers have been exported or copied, and therefore have been tested or are in process of being tested in widely differing conditions. In some degree the British system of government has inspired many constitutions in Europe throughout the nineteenth (particularly) and twentieth centuries —many of which have long since perished; it has been transplanted to the older, European-ruled, independent members of the Commonwealth, to unitary states like New Zealand as well as to federations in Australia and Canada; and it has provided at least the initial constitutional means whereby independent power has been wielded in India, Pakistan, Ceylon, Ghana, Nigeria, and the many other formerly dependent territories of Britain's colonial empire. Given this plethora of "British constitutions," it is remarkable that so few comparative studies have been made. For here, one would suppose, may be found the closest approximation there has ever been to a controlled experiment in the relationship between a democratic system of government and the social, economic, and cultural conditions in which it must operate. The "results" of this experiment, moreover, must be highly significant in relation to more general questions about the exportability and the autonomy of particular institutions. No final answers are likely to be obtained, but at the very least it should be possible to obtain more refined hypotheses and more probable generalizations from this unrivaled source of comparative material. Even if this is too optimistic a view, it is safe to say that some of the most interesting chapters in the history of the British constitution will probably be written in these countries, and that those chapters will be largely incomprehensible except against the background of some knowledge of the original product. This is not the place even to speculate upon the political and constitutional future of the Commonwealth countries. But something must be said about the immediate prospects and problems of the political system in Britain itself.

Two things seem likely to be of paramount importance in the development of British politics in the immediate and foreseeable future. They are the international situation and the ability of the Labour party (or its successor) swiftly to regain electoral momentum and a sense of direction. Upon the first depends not only whether Britain will be annihilated in a nuclear war but, assuming as we must that the country will survive physically, how much freedom it will have to shape its own destiny. The key question, again leaving aside the catastrophic and (one hopes) remote possibility of foreign occupation, is that of Britain's relations with the rest of Western Europe. Specifically, it is whether, and on what terms, Britain becomes associated with the European Economic Community and the political union which will probably emerge therefrom. The immediate political result of admission as a member would be to strengthen the British right wing, in part because the resulting greater prosperity would bolster the present popular reluctance to raise awkward questions or face fundamental issues about the nature of the economy and society, and in part because the union itself seems likely to remain predominantly conservative in color. (If, as seems likely, the alternative is a slow economic decline rather than a dramatic and apparently avoidable crisis, then the left could draw no more comfort from a continuance of Britain's policy of European semi-isolation.)

At least until the union became federal, the governmental result for Britain would be to multiply the relations between the government and industry as the former becomes an important intermediary between national industry and international policy and possibly the most important spokesman for industry in the management of the new economic unit. Any explanations of British policies thereafter would also have to take account of other European governments and interests. It is, however, increasingly clear that the actions of these governments and interests are, in any event, assuming more and more importance for Britain, and it may well be that only by closer association with Europe may Britain hope effectively to influence them. Becoming a member of a federal union would obviously involve a radical realignment of political forces, the constitutional results of which are unpredictable. A lesser union, on the other hand, would leave the essential fabric largely undisturbed, but could not avoid tending to strengthen still further the power of the administration as against that of Parliament, and to make the electorate feel that issues are yet more complex and decisions still more remote from the ordinary individual.

At the general election of October, 1959, for the first time ever, one of the two major parties lost seats for the fourth successive election, and votes for the third.[12] The studies and explanations which have been published since that time all suggest that the loss of support by the Labour party reflects more than purely temporary shifts of allegiance. Manual workers, from whose ranks Labour has traditionally derived the bulk of its support, form a declining proportion of the population as administration and distribution become increasingly important. It also seems that an increasing proportion of skilled manual workers are coming to think of themselves as middle class rather than working class as their standard of living rises, as they acquire such former "luxuries" as leisure, household appliances, and motorcars, and as many more of them come to own their own houses. Furthermore, and at least equally ominous for the future, it appears that the number of young people prepared to vote Labour has declined seriously—a phenomenon which was readily apparent at Labour meetings for some years previously and has now been confirmed by election studies.[13] Simultaneously, the public had become increasingly uncertain what the

[12] By the time the Liberal party had experienced a similar record of defeat it had ceased to be one of *two* major parties and had become a third party.

[13] For the explanations, see D. E. Butler and R. Rose, *The British General Election of 1959* (London: Macmillan, 1960); Mark Abrams, "Why Labour Has Lost Elections," *Socialist Commentary* (May–August, 1960); and H. A. Turner, "Labour's Diminishing Vote," *The Guardian* (October 20, 1959). Discussion has taken place in all serious journals and newspapers in the months following the election, but particular reference may be made to a series of articles and notes in *Encounter* (March–October, 1960), and to two Fabian Society pamphlets by two Labour M.P.'s: C. A. R. Crosland, *Can Labour Win?* (May, 1960), and R. H. S. Crossman, *Labour in the Affluent Society* (June, 1960).

party stands for, an uncertainty which can only have been intensified by the policy disputes within the party that broke out in the years immediately following the election.

Labour's defeat in 1959 did not create the deep divisions over public ownership and defense which dominated the succeeding party conferences, but by removing the immediate prospect of power it destroyed one principal incentive to unity. Coincidentally, the trade-union ballast has become a less effective cohesive force than hitherto. The parliamentary leadership can no longer rely upon the trade unions to maintain control over conference—the battles are being fought within and between the unions to a greater extent than ever. Moreover, the unions are no longer so great an electoral asset as they once were: the expanding white-collar trades are resistant to organization and, when organized, white-collar workers are less likely than industrial ones to affiliate with the T.U.C., let alone the Labour party; and within industry the unions appear increasingly to be rigid and inefficient, out of touch with their rank-and-file members, attracting progressively less enthusiasm and loyalty (particularly among the younger workers), but yet hostile to criticism and reluctant to reform. This summary may exaggerate the situation, but not the outside impression thereof—an impression only partly ascribable to an unsympathetic press. As a result, the unions no longer appear as underdogs whose rights must be safeguarded by governments. Instead, public-opinion polls reflect increasing hostility, even among the families of trade unionists.[14] However much the trade unions may thus embarrass the Labour party, the fact remains that without their organization and money the Labour party could hardly survive. The widespread knowledge of this dependence, moreover, is probably one reason why the numerous elements within the party stay together: none could succeed without the unions, and none know whom the unions would support were the party to split.

The prospect before the Labour party in the early 1960's is of another long period in opposition. Whether the cause lies with its policies and propaganda, its organization, its disunity, or only with its failure to educate the electorate, the gap between the party and the voters is too great speedily to be bridged. Meantime, the Liberal party, for all its increased popular vote, is still far from strong enough to become once more the alternative

[14] See, for example, the results cited in A. Wedgwood Benn and others, *Where?* (London: Fabian Society, 1959), p. 14; and D. E. Butler and R. Rose, *op. cit.*, pp. 28–29.

government. Even were Labour to disintegrate, it is unlikely that the Liberals would be the only gainers: non-voters, a new and more left-wing party, and the Conservatives would each probably absorb some of the former Labour vote. Except in the unlikely event of a new Liberal-Labour union, therefore, Britain faces a lengthy period of unbroken Conservative rule for lack of an effective alternative government. Until and unless a new radical reform consensus develops, even a sharp economic crisis is more likely to lead to stronger and tougher measures from a Conservative government, directed particularly at the welfare services and the power of the trade unions, than to a change of majority.[15] It may be surmised that only when the left as a whole has become clearer about the defects of modern British society as they are experienced in everyday life, and about the appropriate remedies, will it regain momentum. Only then, too, will it be in a position seriously to combat the prevailing attitude of the public which, with the exception of a small but articulate minority,[16] apparently prefers to cultivate its own garden and pursue its own private ambitions than to concern itself with public political action.

It is important to remember that in 1959 the Conservatives won a fractionally smaller proportion of votes cast than did the Labour and Liberal parties combined (49.4 per cent as against 49.7 per cent).[17] One might have envisaged, incorrectly as it turned out, a similar lack of effective opposition after the Liberal defeat of 1895 and the Conservative defeat of 1945. Nevertheless, the factors mentioned above indicate a continuation rather than a speedy end of a Conservative monopoly of power.

Division or weakness on the part of the opposition, as we have already suggested, undermines one of the essential checks in the British system. The check is not abolished, of course, nor

[15] Even assuming that an election were held during the crisis, which is unlikely unless the crisis developed unexpectedly toward the end of a parliament's life.

[16] For examples of dissent, see the files of the *Universities and Left Review* and its successor, the *New Left Review* (produced by fusion with the *New Reasoner* in 1959); N. Mackenzie, ed., *Conviction* (London: McGibbon and Kee, 1958); E. Thompson, ed., *Out of Apathy*, 1960; Michael Young's pamphlet *The Chipped White Cups of Dover*, 1960; and R. M. Titmuss, *The Irresponsible Society* (London: Fabian Society, 1960), and his B.B.C. talk of the same title, reprinted in *The Listener* (August 11, 1960), pp. 207–9. For examples of Conservative reform thinking, see the files of *Crossbow*, the periodical issued by the Bow group of Conservatives, and some of the other publications of this group.

[17] Butler and Rose, *op. cit.*, p. 204.

is free government destroyed, so long as elections and other parties continue. But the quality and general responsiveness of government is likely adversely to be affected as the government is less urgently concerned with the possibility of electoral defeat and therefore becomes more vulnerable to its own backbenchers, especially on the right, and to those pressure groups traditionally closest to the Conservative party. The formal structure of government is unlikely to change at all radically, but within the constitutional framework the oligarchy of interests (as we have called it) is almost certain to gain ground at the expense of the democracy of numbers.[18]

This may be a gloomy prognosis, but it is not a forecast of disaster. At its very worst, the prospect is one of relatively polite government at the behest of an extensive, if irresponsible, oligarchy. Its sins would be those of apathy, rigidity, and extreme complacency rather than those associated with modern authoritarianism. There is not in Britain the tradition, nor yet the intensity of social conflict, to sustain even a moderate dictatorship comparable to that of Charles de Gaulle in the Fifth Republic. In Britain the mask of privilege has customarily been relatively civilized and the behavior of its wearers tempered by the belief in *noblesse oblige*. Moderation and the cult of reasonableness, moreover, have been almost essential prerequisites for public and governmental recognition.[19] There is little or no ground for believing that this tradition has been eroded, or will be in the near future.

If there is any danger to constitutional order in Britain, it is most likely to materialize if and when a strong radical party once again threatens to win power. After a long period without radical social and economic reform, it is not impossible that the right might resort to an unconstitutional defense of its position or an impatient left be driven prematurely to despair of achieving its objectives by constitutional means. In this century we have witnessed too many examples of political coercion and intolerance to assert with complete confidence that any society will surmount stress without degenerating in its public life and behavior. Moreover, to judge by the frequent advocacy of violent resistance to the Liberal plans for Ireland in 1913, and by the passionate opposition to Labour in some middle-class circles

---

[18] Not that the Labour party should be identified with the latter.

[19] See, for example, the comments upon criteria for membership of official advisory bodies in P. E. P., *Advisory Committees in British Government* (London: Allen and Unwin, 1960), pp. 112–13.

after 1945, the attachment to the constitution of some Conservatives is less profound than Conservative rhetoric normally suggests, just as left-wing attachment, on the whole, has been deeper
than its rhetoric sometimes indicated. To forestall this danger
is the responsibility of the leaders of all political parties, and
especially of those in power.

Even as late as 1950 many people looked to Britain for inspiration, in the hope that in its peculiar blend of social regulation and respect for the individual human they might find a
model for economic and social development which would escape
the perils of private irresponsibility and public regimentation.
It calls for a slightly more sanguine temperament to sustain
this hope in the 1960's. But a Briton may be pardoned for believing that not only by way of awful example will his country
continue to interest seekers after social and political sanity.

Bibliographical Guide

This guide is intended to serve mainly as an indication of other secondary sources from which further information may be obtained about the
principal topics which have been discussed in this book. Upon all of them,
and upon other items mentioned in footnotes to the text, the author has
drawn in greater or lesser degree; this list is therefore also a record of indebtedness to the authors included. (It is a complete record neither of
additional sources nor of indebtedness.)

I would like particularly to record my gratitude to the authors and
publishers concerned for permission to adapt material from D. E. Butler,
The British General Election of 1955 (London: Macmillan, 1955), pp. 38–46,
for the tables on pp. 120–22 above; and R. K. Kelsall, *Report on an
Inquiry into Applications for Admission to Universities* (London: Association
of Universities of the British Commonwealth, for the Committee of Vice-
Chancellors and Principals of the Universities of the United Kingdom, 1957),
p. 10, for the table on p. 42 above.

Note that H.M.S.O. is used throughout as the standard abbreviation for
Her Majesty's Stationery Office.

History
Campion, Lord, and others, *British Government since 1918* (London: Allen
and Unwin, 1950).

Chrimes, S. B., *British Constitutional History* (London: Oxford University Press, 1947).

Emden, C. S., *The People and the Constitution*, 2d ed. (London: Oxford, 1956).

Keir, Sir David L., *The Constitutional History of Modern Britain since 1485*, 6th ed. (London: A. & C. Black, 1960).

Kemp, Betty, *King and Commons, 1660–1832* (London: Macmillan, 1957).

Le May, G. H., *British Government 1914–53: Select Documents* (London: Methuen, 1954).

Namier, Sir Lewis B., *Monarchy and the Party System* (London: Oxford, 1952).

Pares, R., *King George III and the Politicians* (London: Oxford, 1953).

Somervell, D. C., *Modern Britain, 1870–1950* (London: Methuen, 1952).

Constitutional Law

Dicey, A. V., *Introduction to the Study of the Law of the Constitution* (London: Macmillan, 10th ed. by E. C. S. Wade, 1960).

Griffith, J. H. G., and Street, H., *Principles of Administrative Law*, 2d ed. (London: Pitman, 1958).

Keir, Sir David L., and Lawson, F. H., *Cases in Constitutional Law*, 4th ed. (Oxford: Clarendon Press, 1954).

Wade, E. C. S., and Phillips, G. G., *Constitutional Law*, 4th ed. (London: Longmans, 1952).

The Constitution: General

Amery, L. S., *Thoughts on the Constitution* (London: Oxford, 1947).

Bagehot, W., *The English Constitution* (London: Oxford University Press, first published in 1867).

Finer, S. E., *A Primer of Public Administration* (London: Muller, 1950).

Greaves, H. R. G., *The British Constitution*, 3d ed. (London: Allen and Unwin, 1955).

Harrison, W., *The Government of Britain*, 6th ed. (London: Hutchinson, 1960).

Laski, H. J., *Parliamentary Government in Britain* (London: Allen and Unwin, 1939).

———, *Reflections on the Constitution* (Manchester: The University Press, 1951).

Marshall, G., and Moodie, G. C., *Some Problems of the Constitution* (London: Hutchinson, 1959).

Morrison, H., *Government and Parliament*, 2d ed. (London: Oxford, 1960).

Wheare, K. C., *Government by Committee* (Oxford: Clarendon Press, 1955).

Monarchy, Cabinet, and Prime Minister

Carter, B. E., *The Office of Prime Minister* (London: Faber, 1956).

(Haldane) Committee on the Machinery of Government, *Report* (London: H.M.S.O., Cnd. 9230 of 1919).

Jennings, Sir Ivor, *Cabinet Government*, 3d ed. (Cambridge: University Press, 1959).

Mackintosh, J. P., *The Cabinet in Britain* (London: Stevens, to be published in 1961).

Nicolson, Sir Harold, *George V: His Life and Reign* (London: Constable, 1953).

Wheeler-Bennett, Sir John, *George VI: His Life and Reign* (London: Macmillan, 1958).

Parliament

Boardman, H., *The Glory of Parliament* (London: Allen and Unwin, 1960).
Bromhead, P. A., *The House of Lords in Contemporary Politics* (London: Routledge and Kegan Paul, 1958).
Campion, Lord, *Introduction to the Procedure of the House of Commons,* 3d ed. (London: Macmillan, 1958).
————, ed., *Parliament: A Survey* (London: Allen and Unwin, 1952).
Chubb, B., *The Control of Public Expenditure* (Oxford: Clarendon Press, 1952).
Crick, B., *Reform of the Commons* (London: Fabian Society, 1959).
Eaves, J., Jr., *Emergency Powers and the Parliamentary Watchdog: Parliament and the Executive in Great Britain, 1939–1951* (London: Hansard Society for Parliamentary Government, 1957).
Gordon, S., *Our Parliament,* 5th ed. (London: Hansard Society, 1958).
Herbert, A. P., *The Ayes Have It* (London: Methuen, 1937).
Hughes, C., *The British Statute Book* (London: Hutchinson, 1957).
Jennings, Sir Ivor, *Parliament,* 2d ed. (Cambridge: University Press, 1957).
May, Sir Thomas Erskine, *Treatise on the Law, Privileges, Proceedings and Usage of Parliament* (London: Butterworth, 16th ed., by Fellows and Cocks, 1957).
Nicolson, N., *The People and Parliament* (London: Wiedenfeld and Nicolson, 1959).
Parliamentary Reform 1933–1958 (London: Hansard Society, 1959).
Richards, P. G., *Honourable Members* (London: Faber, 1959).

Administration and Civil Service

Chapman, B., *The Profession of Government* (London: Allen and Unwin, 1959).
Chester, D. N., and Willson, F. M. G., *The Organisation of British Central Government 1914–1956* (London: Allen and Unwin, 1957).
Dale, H. E., *The Higher Civil Service* (London: Oxford, 1941).
Greaves, H. R. G., *The Civil Service in the Changing State* (London: Harrap, 1947).
Kelsall, R. K., *Higher Civil Servants in Britain* (London: Routledge and Kegan Paul, 1955).
Mackenzie, W. J. M., and Grove, J. M., *Central Administration in Britain* (London: Longmans, 1957).
Monck, B., *How the Civil Service Works* (London: Phoenix House, 1952).
Munro, C. K., *The Fountains in Trafalgar Square* (London: Heinemann, 1952).
Robson, W. A., ed., *The Civil Service in Britain and France* (London: Hogarth, 1956).
————, ed., *Problems of Nationalised Industries* (London: Allen and Unwin, 1952).
————, *Nationalised Industry and Public Ownership* (London: Allen and Unwin, 1960).
Wilson, H. H., and Glickman, H., *The Problems of Internal Security in Great Britain, 1948–53* (Garden City, N.Y.: Doubleday, 1954).

Judicial System

Allen, C. K., *Law and Orders*, 2d ed. (London: Stevens, 1957).

Archer, P., *The Queen's Courts* (Harmondsworth: Penguin Books, 1956).

Hanbury, H. G., *English Courts of Law* (London: Oxford, 1944).

Hart, J. M., *The British Police* (London: Allen and Unwin, 1951).

Jackson, R. M., *The Machinery of Justice in England*, 2d ed. (Cambridge: University Press, 1953).

Keeton, G. W., *The Passing of Parliament*, 2d ed. (London: Benn, 1954).

Report of the (Donoughmore) Committee on Ministers' Powers (London: H.M.S.O., Cmd. 4060 of 1932).

Report of the (Franks) Committee on Administrative Tribunals and Enquiries (London: H.M.S.O., Cmd. 218 of 1957).

Robson, W. A., *Justice and Administrative Law*, 3d ed. (London: Stevens, 1951).

Smith, S. A. de, *Judicial Review of Administrative Action* (London: Stevens, 1960).

Local Government

Birch, A. H., *Small Town Politics* (London: Oxford, 1959).

Chester, D. N., *Central and Local Government* (London: Macmillan, 1951).

Drummond, J. M., *The Finance of Local Government* (London: Allen and Unwin, 1952).

Jackson, R. M., *The Machinery of Local Government* (London: Macmillan, 1958).

Local Government in Scotland (Edinburgh: H.M.S.O., 1958).

Robson, W. A., *The Development of Local Government*, 3d ed. (London: Allen and Unwin, 1954).

———, *The Government and Misgovernment of London*, 2d ed. (London: Allen and Unwin, 1948).

Warren, J. H., *The English Local Government System*, 5th ed. (London: Allen and Unwin, 1957).

A West Midland Study Group, *Local Government and Central Control* (London: Routledge and Kegan Paul, 1956).

Political Parties

Bailey, S. D., ed., *The British Party System* (London: Hansard Society, 1952).

Bulmer-Thomas, L., *The Party System in Great Britain* (London: Phoenix House, 1954).

Cole, G. D. H., *British Working Class Politics, 1832–1914* (London: Routledge and Kegan Paul, 1941).

———, *A History of the Labour Party from 1914* (London: Routledge and Kegan Paul, 1948).

Duverger, M., *Political Parties* (London: Methuen, 1954).

Fulford, R., *The Liberal Case* (Harmondsworth: Penguin Books, 1960).

Hailsham, Lord, *The Conservative Case* (Harmondsworth: Penguin Books, 1960).

Harrison, Martin, *Trade Unions and the Labour Party since 1945* (London: Allen and Unwin, 1960).

Jenkins, R., *The Labour Case* (Harmondsworth: Penguin Books, 1960).

McKenzie, R. T., *British Political Parties* (London: Heinemann, 1955).

Pelling, H., ed., *The Challenge of Socialism* (London: A. & C. Black, 1954).

White, R. J., ed., *The Conservative Tradition* (London: A. & C. Black, 1950).

Elections

Benney, M., and others, *How People Vote* (London: Routledge and Kegan Paul, 1956).

Birch, A. H., *Small Town Politics* (London: Oxford, 1959).

Bonham, J., *The Middle Class Vote* (London: Faber, 1954).

Butler, D. E., *The British General Election of 1951* (London: Macmillan, 1952).

———, *The British General Election of 1955* (London: Macmillan, 1955).

———, *The Electoral System in Britain 1918–51* (London: Oxford, 1953).

———, and Rose, R., *The British General Election of 1959* (London: Macmillan, 1960).

Lakeman, E., and Lambert, J. S., *Voting in Democracies*, 2d ed. (London: Faber, 1955).

Milne, R. S., and Mackenzie, H. C., *Straight Fight* (London: Hansard Society, 1955).

———, *Marginal Seat* (London: Hansard Society, 1958).

Nicholas, H. G., *The British General Election of 1950* (London: Macmillan, 1951).

Ross, J. F. S., *Elections and Electors* (London: Eyre and Spottiswoode, 1955).

———, *Parliamentary Representation*, 2d ed. (London: Eyre and Spottiswoode, 1948).

Pressure Groups

Eckstein, H., *Pressure Group Politics: The Case of the British Medical Association* (London: Allen and Unwin, 1960).

Finer, S. E., *Anonymous Empire* (London: Pall Mall Press, 1958).

———, *Private Industry and Political Power* (London: Pall Mall Press, 1958).

P. E. P. (Political and Economic Planning), *Advisory Committees in British Government* (London: Allen and Unwin, 1960).

Potter, A., *Organized Groups in British National Politics* (London: Faber, 1961).

Report of the Committee on Intermediaries (London: H.M.S.O., Cmd. 7904 of 1950).

Stewart, J. P. D., *British Pressure Groups* (London: Oxford, 1958).

Wilson, H. H., *Pressure Group: Commercial Television* (London: Secker and Warburg, 1961).

The Press

Hoggart, R., *The Uses of Literacy* (London: Chatto and Windus, 1957).

Martin, K., *The Press the People Want* (London: Hogarth, 1947).

Report of the Royal Commission on the Press (London: H.M.S.O., Cmd. 7700 of 1949).

Williams, F., *Press, Parliament, and People* (London: Heinemann, 1946).

———, *Dangerous Estate: The Anatomy of Newspapers* (London: Longmans, 1957).

Economy and Society

Allen, V. L., *Power in Trade Unions* (London: Longmans, 1954).

Birnie, A., *Economic History of the British Isles*, 8th ed. (London: Methuen, 1955).

Carr-Saunders, A. M., and others, *Social Conditions in England and Wales* (Oxford: Clarendon Press, 1958).

Cole, G. D. H., *An Introduction to Trade Unionism* (London: Allen and Unwin, 1954).

———, *The Post-War Condition of Britain* (London: Routledge and Kegan Paul, 1956).

———, *Studies in Class Structure* (London: Routledge and Kegan Paul, 1955).

Dunning, J. H., and Thomas, C. J., *British Industry* (London: Hutchinson, 1960).

Flanders, A., and Clegg, H. A., *The System of Industrial Relations in Britain* (Oxford: Blackwell, 1954).

Florence, P. S., *Industry and the State* (London: Hutchinson, 1957).

———, *The Logic of British and American Industry* (London: Routledge and Kegan Paul, 1953).

Glass, D. V., ed., *Social Mobility in Britain* (London: Routledge and Kegan Paul, 1954).

Gorer, G., *Exploring English Character* (London: Cresset, 1955).

Guénalt, Paul H., and Jackson, J. M., *The Control of Monopoly in the United Kingdom* (London: Longmans, 1960).

Lipset, S. M., and Bendix, R., *Social Mobility in Industrial Society* (Berkeley, Calif.: University of California Press, 1959).

Marsh, D. C., *The Changing Social Structure of England and Wales 1871–1951* (London: Routledge and Kegan Paul, 1958).

P. E. P., *Government and Industry* (London: Allen and Unwin, 1952).

Roberts, B. C., *Trade Union Government and Administration in Great Britain* (London: Bell, 1956).

Rogow, A. A., *The Labour Government and British Industry 1945–1951* (Oxford: Blackwell, 1955).

Shonfield, A., *British Economic Policy* (Harmondsworth: Penguin Books, 1958).

Shore, P., "In the Room at the Top," in N. Mackenzie, ed., *Conviction* (London: McGibbon and Kee, 1958), pp. 23–54.

Williams, F., *Magnificent Journey: The Rise of the Trade Unions* (London: Odham's Press, 1954).

Wootton, B., *The Social Foundations of Wages Policy* (London: Allen and Unwin, 1954).

Worswick, G. D. N., and Ady, P. H., eds., *The British Economy 1945–50* (London: Oxford, 1952).

Social Services

Brockington, F., *The People's Health* (London: Phoenix House, 1955).

Central Office of Information, *Social Services in Britain*, 3d ed. (London: H.M.S.O., 1957).

Gardiner, R. K., and Judd, H. O., *The Development of Social Administration*, 2d ed. (London: Oxford, 1959).

Harvey, A., *Casualties of the Welfare State* (London: Fabian Society, 1960).

Peacock, A. T., *The Economics of National Insurance* (Edinburgh: Hodges, 1952).

Raynes, H. E., *Social Security in Britain* (London: Pitman, 1957).

Titmuss, R. M., *Essays on the "Welfare State"* (London: Allen and Unwin, 1958).

———, *The Irresponsible Society* (London: Fabian Society, 1960).

Education

Central Office of Information, *Education in Britain* (London: H.M.S.O., 1955).

Curtis, S. J., *History of Education in Great Britain*, 3d ed. (London: University Tutorial Press, 1953).

Dent, H. C., *Growth in English Education 1946–52* (London: Routledge and Kegan Paul, 1954).

Dongerkery, S. R., *Universities in Britain* (London: Oxford, 1953).

Moodie, G. C., *The Universities: A Royal Commission?* (London: Fabian Society, 1959).

Foreign Policy

Acland, Sir Richard, *Waging Peace* (London: Muller, 1958).

Allen, H. C., *Anglo-American Relationship since 1783* (London: A. & C. Black, 1960).

Angell, Sir Norman, *Defence and the English-Speaking Role* (London: Pall Mall Press, 1958).

Beloff, M., *The Great Powers: Essays in Twentieth Century Politics* (London: Allen and Unwin, 1959).

Connell, J., *The "Office": A Study of British Foreign Policy and Its Makers, 1919–51* (London: Wingate, 1958).

Eden, Sir Anthony, *Full Circle* (London: Cassell, 1960).

Epstein, L. D., *Britain—Uneasy Ally* (Chicago: University of Chicago Press, 1954).

Foot, M. R. D., *British Foreign Policy since 1898* (London: Hutchinson, 1956).

Goodwin, G. L., *Britain and the United Nations* (London: Oxford, 1957).

King-Hall, Sir Stephen, *Defence and the Nuclear Age* (London: Gollancz, 1958).

McKitterick, T. E., and Younger, K. G., *Fabian International Essays* (London: Hogarth, 1957).

Nutting, A., *Europe Will Not Wait* (London: Hollis and Carter, 1960).

Royal Institute for International Affairs, *Britain in Western Europe* (London: Oxford, 1956).

Schuman, F. L., *International Politics*, 6th ed. (N.Y.: McGraw-Hill, 1958).

Strang, Lord, *The Foreign Office* (London: Allen and Unwin, 1955).

Voigt, F. A., *Pax Brittannica* (London: Constable, 1949).

White, T. H., *Fire in the Ashes* (N.Y.: Sloane, 1953).

Young, W., *Strategy for Survival* (Harmondsworth: Penguin Books, 1959).

The Commonwealth

Hancock, W. K., *Survey of British Commonwealth Affairs: Problems of Nationality 1918–1936* (London: Oxford, 1937).

Harvey, H. J., *Consultation and Cooperation in the Commonwealth* (London: Oxford, 1952).

Jennings, Sir Ivor, *The Commonwealth in Asia* (London: Oxford, 1951).

Keith, A. B., *Speeches and Documents on the British Dominions 1918–1931* (London: Oxford, 1932).

Macmillan, W. H., *The Road to Self-Rule* (London: Faber, 1959).

Mansergh, N., *Survey of British Commonwealth Affairs: Problems of External Policy 1931–1939* (London: Oxford, 1952).

————, *Problems of Wartime Cooperation and Post-War Change 1939–1952* (London: Oxford, 1959).

————, *Documents and Speeches on British Commonwealth Affairs 1931–1952* (London: Oxford, 1953).

Miller, J. D. B., *The Commonwealth in the World* (London: Duckworth, 1959).

Wheare, K. C., *The Constitutional Structure of the Commonwealth* (Oxford: The Clarendon Press, 1960).

Periodicals, etc.

The principal British periodicals dealing with government are:

Parliamentary Affairs
Political Studies
The Political Quarterly (especially useful are its occasional special numbers devoted to such single topics as trade unions, defense, or pressure groups)
Public Administration
The British Journal of Sociology
Public Law

American periodicals also print articles on British subjects. Notable are:

The American Political Science Review
Political Science Quarterly

The more serious British monthly and weekly journals and national newspapers also carry much relevant descriptive and analytical material.

Government publications issued by H.M.S.O. are indispensable. Among those of particular value may be mentioned:

Central Office of Information reference pamphlets
Annual Abstract of Statistics
Census 1951 Great Britain: One Per Cent Sample Tables
The Registrar-General's Statistical Review of England and Wales (annual)
The Annual *Reports* to Parliament of such departments as the Ministry of Health and the Ministry of Education.

Almost all the books listed include further bibliographical references.

A useful, if incomplete, supplement to this guide is J. Palmer, *Government and Parliament in Britain: A Bibliography* (London: Hansard Society, 1960).